Multilingualism and Creativity

MIX
Paper from
responsible sources
FSC® C018575
FSC
www.fsc.org

BILINGUAL EDUCATION AND BILINGUALISM
Series Editor: Nancy H. Hornberger, *University of Pennsylvania, USA* and Colin Baker, *Bangor University, Wales, UK*

Bilingual Education and Bilingualism is an international, multidisciplinary series publishing research on the philosophy, politics, policy, provision and practice of language planning, global English, indigenous and minority language education, multilingualism, multiculturalism, biliteracy, bilingualism and bilingual education. The series aims to mirror current debates and discussions.

Full details of all the books in this series and of all our other publications can be found on http://www.multilingual-matters.com, or by writing to Multilingual Matters, St Nicholas House, 31–34 High Street, Bristol BS1 2AW, UK.

Multilingualism and Creativity

Anatoliy V. Kharkhurin

MULTILINGUAL MATTERS
Bristol • Buffalo • Toronto

Library of Congress Cataloging in Publication Data
A catalog record for this book is available from the Library of Congress.
Kharkhurin, Anatoliy V.
Multilingualism and Creativity/Anatoliy V. Kharkhurin.
Bilingual Education and Bilingualism: 88
Includes bibliographical references and index.
1. Multilingualism—Psychological aspects. 2. Creativity (Linguistics) 3. Psycholinguistics.
I. Title.
P115.4.K43 2012
404'.2019–dc23 2012022006

British Library Cataloguing in Publication Data
A catalogue entry for this book is available from the British Library.

ISBN-13: 978-1-84769-795-0 (hbk)
ISBN-13: 978-1-84769-794-3 (pbk)

Multilingual Matters
UK: St Nicholas House, 31–34 High Street, Bristol BS1 2AW, UK.
USA: UTP, 2250 Military Road, Tonawanda, NY 14150, USA.
Canada: UTP, 5201 Dufferin Street, North York, Ontario M3H 5T8, Canada.

The policy of Multilingual Matters/Channel View Publications is to use papers that are natural, renewable and recyclable products, made from wood grown in sustainable forests. In the manufacturing process of our books, and to further support our policy, preference is given to printers that have FSC and PEFC Chain of Custody certification. The FSC and/or PEFC logos will appear on those books where full certification has been granted to the printer concerned.

Typeset by DiTech.
Printed and bound in Great Britain by the MPG Books Group.

To my son Ariel

Contents

Preface

In 1992, I left Russia and started a long journey of higher education. During this journey, I resided in several countries through which I acquired several languages and multicultural experiences. Moreover, all these years, I have been actively involved in creative writing. Therefore, when the time was ripe to select a topic for my dissertation in experimental psychology, it seemed clear that I should focus on the one that directly grew out of my personal experience: multilingualism and creativity. This work initiated a longitudinal project, which constitutes the core of this monograph.

To my surprise, I soon found out that the relationship between multilingualism and creativity received little attention in the scientific community. In about 40 years, this theme had been explored in only 40 studies. Ricciardelli (1992b) presented an overview of the empirical investigations on this topic that had been conducted in the 1970s and 1980s. Although these studies were all more than 20 years old, there had been virtually no scientific investigation conducted thereafter. In his chapter on bilingualism and creativity published in 2008, Simonton (2008: 150) rightly put it: 'Almost no research directly relevant to this topic has been published since then, making its results still pertinent to the present discussion.' This book makes an attempt to resuscitate this theme and provides a solid theoretical framework supported by contemporary empirical investigations of the relationship between multilingualism and creativity.

Changing realities in the modern world have an impact, especially on the human sciences. Vastly increased human mobility, communication technologies, and the accelerating integration of the global economy have increasingly abolished geographic boundaries and brought together people from different cultural and linguistic backgrounds. The close interaction of people speaking different languages emphasizes the phenomenon of multilingualism as never before. New scientific research reflects on these tendencies and provides a rapidly growing body of empirical investigation into the phenomenon of multilingualism. During the past few decades, research in the area of the cognitive development of bilinguals has made tremendous progress. There is convincing evidence that speaking more than one language extends rather than diminishes individuals' cognitive capacities (see Bialystok, 2005, for an overview). This book extends this view and presents evidence that multilingualism also contributes to individuals' creative potential.

Although multilingualism is well elaborated in scientific investigation, researchers still debate about the definition of this phenomenon. Multilinguals rarely have equal fluency in their languages. They usually acquire and use these languages for different purposes, in different domains in life, and with different people (Grosjean, 1998). There was a long lasting discussion in the literature about limiting multilingual study to the so-called true multilinguals – those equally skilled in all their languages (cf. Peal & Lambert, 1962). However, there are indications that such individuals are extremely rare. For example, by this strict definition, out of 238 participants in my dissertation study (Kharkhurin, 2005) who indicated that they spoke both English and Russian, only seven could be considered 'perfectly balanced' or 'true' bilinguals. What about the rest of the sample? They were not 'perfectly balanced' for their command of both languages was not identical. At the same time, they were representative of the majority of multilingual population for individuals speaking several languages rarely display equal command of these languages. Thus, while it might be conceivable to limit one's experimental sample to perfectly balanced multilinguals, this would greatly sacrifice the generalization to the multilingual population at large. Therefore, it is prudent to consider multilingualism in a broader sense including not only individuals who are fluent in all their languages but also individuals who actively use, or attempt to use, more than one language, even if they have not achieved fluency in all of them (Kroll & de Groot, 1997).

As a reader might have already noticed, I have brought into play two terms to refer to the phenomenon of speaking several languages: bilingualism and multilingualism. Throughout this book, these terms are used interchangeably, the former generally refers to an ability to speak two languages, whereas the latter refers to the ability to speak more than two languages. As literature indicates, most research in the field has been conducted with bilinguals. This could be due to the fact that a large majority of the studies have been carried out in North America. Historically, the overwhelming part of the population in the United States speaks only one language, English, and has little incentive to acquire any foreign language. The rest – primarily the migrants of Latino or Asian origins – had to acquire English in addition to their native tongue in order to integrate into mainstream society. Once they reached mastery in English, they had weak inducement to learn any other foreign language. Therefore, this country presents a clear pattern of monolingual/bilingual dichotomy. To the North, Canada is divided into English and French speaking provinces, and the population either speaks only the language of the province or both English and French. Therefore, this country replicates the pattern of monolingual/bilingual distinction. Thus, the studies conducted at the dawn of multilingual research in North America were focused primarily on the bilingual population.

In contrast, Europe presents a different pattern of language distribution. For example, a survey *Europeans and their Languages* (2006: 8) reports that '56% of EU citizens are able to hold a conversation in a language other than their mother tongue and 28% state that they master two languages along with their native language.' Moreover, European migrants to North America also changed the pattern of language distribution on this continent. For example, 53.70% (58 out of 108) of the immigrants from the former Soviet Union who participated in my dissertation study mentioned above indicated that they were exposed to languages other than Russian and English. I have revealed a similar tendency with language distribution in the Middle East. That is, 31.76% (303 out of 954) of participants who participated in various studies that I have conducted between the fall 2008 and the spring 2010 indicated that they speak more than two languages. These figures suggest that multilingual practice is prevailing around the globe. Similar observations encouraged researchers to initiate scientific investigations of multilingual individuals – those speaking more than two languages. These studies, however, are thin on the ground and are still outnumbered by bilingual research. Thus, although this monograph uses the terms bilingualism and multilingualism interchangeably, it acknowledges the potentially critical differences. The past research conducted with participants speaking only two languages is referred to with the term bilingualism, whereas, if I believe that processes observed in the bilingual mind could also be expected to occur in the multilingual mind, I use the term multilingualism.

Once the first term in the title of this book has been brought to the stage, I move on to introduce the second one. Creativity is a broad and versatile construct that encompasses a variety of theories, models, and definitions. There are dozens of monographs, edited volumes, and handbooks presenting creativity from a perspective of a product, an individual or a process. This monograph refrains from any attempt to provide an overview of the creativity research. Rather, it constructs a particular theoretical framework in which multilingualism is claimed to have impact on creative endeavors. In this framework, individuals' practice with multiple languages is argued to influence specific cognitive processes that in turn may lead to an increase in their creative performance. Creative capacity, therefore, is perceived as a continuation of human cognition; that is, cognitive processes that are involved in everyday human activity may also lead to activity that is considered as creative thinking. This approach is termed creative cognition; it stipulates that variations in the use of specifiable cognitive processes may result in production of creative outcomes and even achievement of extreme levels of accomplishment. Thus, in this book I focus on those cognitive mechanisms that on one side might benefit from multilingual practice and on the other side could facilitate creative thinking.

The monograph opens with Chapter 1 introducing the reader to a cognitive perspective in creativity research – creative cognition. It proceeds with a discussion of major cognitive models of creativity and pays particular attention to two processes that are generally accepted as the key components of creative thinking: divergent and convergent thinking. The purpose of Chapter 2 is to sketch those aspects of multilingual cognitive functioning that in my opinion play a crucial role in creative functioning of multilingual individuals. It reviews the research focusing on the relationship between bilingualism and the cognitive and linguistic performance of children and adults, and specifies possible reasons for bilingual cognitive advantages. Furthermore, it elaborates on an individual's experiences with different linguistic systems and cultural settings. These factors are presented as key components in multilingual development, which presumably play a crucial role in multilingual cognition. Finally, the chapter presents a model of bilingual memory, and discusses the effect of multilingual developmental factors on an individual's cognitive performance in terms of this model. Chapter 3 introduces the core topic of the monograph, namely, the relationship between multilingualism and creativity. It reviews the historiometric and psychometric research of this relationship, and presents a theoretical framework for multilingual creative advantages. After reviewing the existing empirical studies in the field, it provides a critical analysis of the methodological issues that impose serious limitations to the reliability of this research. I made an attempt to overcome these limitations and initiated a project that investigated a relationship between multilingualism and creativity using improved scientific strategies. In contrast to most studies in the field, I have compared the creative performance not only of bilinguals and monolinguals but also of bilinguals with different histories of linguistic and cultural experiences. Moreover, I attempted to empirically identify cognitive mechanisms underlying creative thinking that could benefit from multilingual and multicultural practices. Chapters 4 and 5 present a brief description of the studies in this project, and discuss the results of these studies in the context of multilingual creative development. The last two chapters tap into potential implications of the findings in multilingual creativity for creativity research and education, respectively. Chapter 6 elaborates on two distinct creative capacities – generative and innovative – identified in my research, and discusses them in light of another dichotomy accepted in creativity research, divergent/convergent thinking. Furthermore, it makes an argument that a widely utilized definition of creativity emphasizing the novelty and appropriateness of a creative product reduces the scope of this complex and versatile phenomenon. In this chapter, I provide an alternative four-dimensional construct that in addition to novelty and utility includes aesthetic and authentic functions. Based on this extended construct, I propose an alternative model that claims to encompass different approaches to creative thinking. Chapter 7 picks up on one of the widely discussed topics in both multilingualism and creativity research that comes from pedagogical considerations. After discussing evidence supporting and criticizing existing multilingual and creative educational endeavors, it proposes a new program that combines strategies from both fields. The purpose of the program is to enrich traditional school curriculum with methods and techniques enhancing foreign language learning and fostering creativity. To accomplish this goal, the program utilizes the holistic approach, which combines cognitive, personal, and environmental factors in education. The chapter sketches the essential attributes of a bilingual creative education program. The concluding chapter specifies the future directions for the research in multilingual creativity.

Having thus introduced the aims and the organization of the book, I would like to end with a few words of thanks. I am deeply indebted to James Sater for his faithful friendship and numerous illuminating discussions on scientific and other matters, which facilitated completion of this book. I am grateful to Jeanette Altarriba, Viorica Marian, Richard Gassan and Angela Maitner for having reviewed parts of the manuscript at various stages. I also thank the editors at Multilingual Matters as well as the anonymous reviewers for their very helpful comments on earlier drafts. Special thanks go to my colleagues and students at Brooklyn College, Moscow State University and Azadi Psychiatric Hospital who provided invaluable help with data collection. Finally, I would like to thank Amir Berbic for designing the cover image for this book.

1 Creative Cognition

Overview

Throughout the history of human civilization, numerous attempts to understand human creativity have been made. The interest in human creative capacity never ceased, and contemporary creativity researchers are still arguing about the definition of creativity. There is a long-standing debate in the creativity literature whether the capacity for creative thought is limited to a certain class of gifted or 'especially' talented people or is available to the general population. The former view considers creative people as a minority who are capable of genuine creative thinking, and thus creativity has little bearing on the everyday cognitive activities of the general population. In this view, geniuses use cognitive processes that are radically different from those employed by most individuals in everyday problem solving. In contrast, the latter, creative cognition approach argues against the notion that extraordinary forms of creativity are the products of mysterious and unobservable processing. It advocates belief in the continuity of cognitive functioning between mundane and creative performance.

This chapter introduces creative cognition approach as a research paradigm of the relationship between multilingualism and creativity. The focus of creative cognition is not on personality traits that characterize a creative individual, not on characteristics of a product that indentify it as creative; the focus is on the cognitive processes and functions that underlie creative thinking. The creative cognition assumes that both eminent creative accomplishments such as Kasimir Malevich's *Black Square* or Albert Einstein's *Theory of Relativity* and mundane creative performances such as a new cooking recipe or a new decoration for the Christmas tree draw on the same thinking processes. The difference constitutes the variations in the use of specifiable processes or combinations of processes. According to this paradigm, if creative thinking constitutes specific processes, it can be studied by analyzing these processes.

Following one of the earliest models in creativity research, creative thinking is assumed as a stage process. A creative thought undergoes certain stages during which a problem is identified, elaborated on and evaluated to produce a creative outcome. For example, a writer conceives a literary work. He defines a problem in terms of a genre such as an essay, a romance or a novel, a topic such as historical, philosophical or detective story, a time period, main characters and so on. Furthermore, the author elaborates on the problem. He develops a plot line, personalities of his characters, dialogues and so on. During this phase, the author may stumble and even experience the writer's block, which would require hanging up the problem for a while and occupying oneself with other problems and thoughts. Eventually, a solution to the problem emerges without any conscious effort and the author successfully completes his work. Then, the solution to the problem needs to be evaluated and refined, so the author goes over several drafts to produce a final draft.

What are the underlying mechanisms triggering creative thought? The information processing models of creative thinking perceive this process as information flow that carries creative idea from one stage to the next. Various ideas are represented in the form of mental or conceptual representations that are organized in the conceptual networks. For example, if one thinks about a bird signing perched on a tree branch, the conceptual representations of a bird, a tree branch and signing are activated simultaneously along with other representations, which are associated with the singing bird such as sky and melody. Thus, thinking process involves simultaneous activation of various conceptual representations thereby establishing connections between different concepts. Creative thinking process is characterized by ability to establish distant associations that link concepts from distant categories, more distant than the ones activated during noncreative thinking. In the example of the singing bird, creative thought may trigger activation of remote associations such as freedom and loneliness. That is, an image of the signing bird may signify a free spirit or symbolize a lonely soul.

The ability to establish distant associations constitutes a key mechanism of divergent thinking, which is perceived by many researchers as one of the major components of creativity. The ideas in creative mind diverge to activate a multitude of creative solutions to a problem. One may think of a plowman scattering seeds in the soil. Some of these seeds will dry up, but the other will sprout up. Similarly, not all solutions generated during divergent thinking may lead to a creative solution, but a larger pool of ideas generated during this process may result in a better creative problem solving. The solutions generated during divergent thinking are subsequently evaluated during convergent thinking, which narrows all possible alternatives down to a single creative solution. Continuing the plowman metaphor, when the seeds sprout up one gathers the best harvest. Therefore, creative cognition tradition assumes creative thinking as an ability to initiate multiple cycles of divergent and convergent thinking, which result in creative outcome.

This chapter discusses creative cognition and models of creativity constructed within this paradigm.

Cognitive Paradigm in Creativity Research: Creative Cognition

The conceptual framework of creative cognition rests on two major assumptions. First, it adopts a common view (e.g. Martindale, 1989; Sternberg & Lubart, 1995) that characterizes creative products as novel (i.e. original or unexpected) and appropriate (i.e. useful or meeting task constraints). Second, 'ideas and tangible products that are novel and useful are assumed to emerge from the application of ordinary, fundamental cognitive processes to existing knowledge structures' (Ward, 2007: 28). Creative capacity, therefore, is assumed as an essential property of normative human cognition (Ward *et al.*, 1999).

This perspective can be illustrated with examples of creative involvement in ordinary human activity. Beyond the obvious examples of artistic, scientific, and technological advancement that are usually listed as instances of creativity, there is the subtler, but equally compelling generativity associated with everyday thought. One of the most striking examples of generativity is the productivity of language: we are able to construct an infinite number of grammatical sentences using a limited number of words and a small set of rules (Chomsky, 1972). The generated sentences can be unique both to an individual's linguistic practice and to the common practice of a given language. In line with creative cognition premises, the generativity goes beyond everyday human cognition and satisfies the criteria of creative products: novelty and utility. This example illustrates that everyday human activity may rely on processes that can be considered as those underlying creative thinking. However, there is no doubt about the existence of individual differences in creativity. Some individuals produce more creative outcomes than others, and a limited few achieve extreme levels of accomplishment (Eysenck, 1995). Although the creative cognition approach admits these differences, they can be understood in terms of variations in the use of specifiable processes or combinations of processes, the intensity of application of such processes and the richness and flexibility of stored cognitive structures to which the processes are applied (Ward *et al.*, 1997). In other words, an individual's creative involvement can be stipulated by known and observable fundamental cognitive principles such as the capacity of one's memory systems (e.g. working memory), memory retrieval, mapping of old knowledge onto novel situations, conceptual structures, and knowledge combination and manipulation. This suggests that different individuals would demonstrate different creative abilities due to variation in their cognition. This variation though seems to be of quantitative rather than of qualitative nature. That is, the difference between creative endeavors of Albert Einstein and a housewife is determined not by the distinct nature of employed processes, but by the quantity of the same processes.

The methodological application of creative cognition paradigm constitutes a psychometric approach in which creativity can be investigated using conventional tools of experimental psychology. If creative thinking relies on the same processes as mundane thinking, we can study the former using the same methods as we employ in studying the latter. In this framework, creative thinking is perceived as a complex and versatile construct that may be effectively studied by examining the variety of processes and functions involved in a creative work (Guilford, 1950). They include but are not limited to problem definition and redefinition, divergent and convergent thinking, synthesis, reorganization, analysis and evaluation.

Cognitive Models of Creativity

One of the most influential models that identified different levels of creative processing was Wallas's (1926) four-stage model formulated on the ground of introspective reports provided by eminent people (see Lubart, 2000, for an overview). As Torrance (1988: 45) noted, 'One can detect the "Wallas process" as the basis for almost all of the systematic, disciplined methods of training in existence throughout the world today.' In his presidential address to the American Psychological Association, Guilford (1950: 451) also emphasized that 'there is considerable agreement that the complete creative act involves four important steps.' These steps are preparation, incubation, illumination and verification. In preparation stage, the creative problem is consciously represented. A creative thinker has to identify the problem, define it in the appropriate terms and make necessary observations and studies. During incubation, the thinker hangs up the problem for a while and occupies him- or herself with other problems and thoughts. In this stage, conscious attention turns away from the problem and gives way to unconscious processing. The incubation is followed by illumination, which corresponds to an 'Aha!' effect when a solution to the problem finally emerges without any conscious effort. The transformation of the unconsciously formulated creative solution into the consciousness takes place during verification, when this solution needs to be tested and refined.

Some relatively recent empirical work draws clearly on the four-stage model and some contemporary models of creative thinking incorporate some aspects of the basic four-stage model. However, there is a growing body of evidence suggesting that this model oversimplifies the multifaceted construct of creativity. For example, Eindhoven and Vinacke (1952) asked artists and nonartists to produce a picture that illustrated a poem presented at the beginning of the study. Indices such as the amount of time spent reading the poem, time spent formulating the initial picture and the number of different sketches made were noted. This study reported no evidence supporting four discrete stages in the creative process; rather the creative performance was described as an integrated work of different processes that cooccur in a recursive way throughout the course of creative thinking.

This more complex integrated view of creativity has been discussed in a number of other studies. Based on an analysis of interviews of fiction writers, Doyle (1998) described the creative process of writing fiction as beginning with a 'seed incident' that interests or provokes an author, which is followed by 'navigating' between different 'spheres of experience' to develop a story (e.g. moving between a fictional sphere, the written work and a revising mode). The interviews with artists conducted by Calwelti *et al.* (1992) revealed evidence for the combination of different processes such as centering on a topic, working on new ideas, expanding ideas, evaluating, and taking distance from one's work. Israeli (1962, 1981) studied creative process in art through introspection, interviews, observations and examinations of sketchbooks and finished works. He found that the creative process involves a series of high-speed short interactions between productive and critical modes of thinking, as well as planning and compensatory actions. In Getzels and Csikszentmihályi's (1976) seminal study of art students making a still-life drawing, activities involved in formulating or defining the artistic problem were observed both in the predrawing phase and the drawing production phase. The researchers noted, 'In a creative process, stages of problem definition and problem solution need not be compartmentalized' (Getzels & Csikszentmihályi: 90). Finally, Goldschmidt (1991) formulated an overall conceptual framework of an architectural design as a result of protocol analysis of the sketching process in architectural designers. In this framework, new designs were formed in parts with deletions, transformations, a dialectic movement between general design qualities and issues in the specific task and moments of active sketching mixed with moments of contemplation.

Thus, the analysis of creative thought in terms of four distinct stages has been criticized for a lack of detailed description of the underlying processes. As Guilford (1950: 451) pointed out in his presidential address, 'Such an analysis is very superficial from the psychological point of view. It is more dramatic than it is suggestive of testable hypotheses. It tells us almost nothing about the mental operations that actually occur.' He has encouraged psychologists to conduct a systematic empirical study of the processes involved in creative thinking.

During the past 60 years since his speech, a large number of studies explored the nature of the processes involved in creativity, and a substantial class of models was proposed to describe them. However, in spite of quantitative diversity most of these models seem to focus on similar kinds of processing. For example, Rothenberg (1996: 207) describes Janusian thinking as ability for 'actively conceiving multiple opposites or antitheses simultaneously.' This concept is similar to another Rothenberg's (1979: 7) idea of homospatial thinking that 'consists of actively conceiving two or more discrete entities occupying the same space, a conception leading to the articulation of new identities.' At the same time, Koestler (1968: 183) introduced the concept of bisociation, which he defined as ability for 'combining two hitherto unrelated cognitive matrices in such a way that a new level is added to the hierarchy, which contains the previously separate structures as its members.' Another model talked about remote associations – an ability of creative individuals to build connections between unrelated ideas or objects (Mednick, 1962). The primary concern of these models is with information synthesis or combination. They all converge on the idea of the simultaneous activation and manipulation of different, often unrelated concepts and categories. These activated instances create a new conceptual plane on which the original and novel ideas might be established. In other words, an important property of creative thinking constitutes working with mental elements that would not be engaged during noncreative thinking. An instance of noncreative thinking describes a rose as thorn plant with short life cycle. Another instance of noncreative thinking presents an individual with sorrowful life as the one whose aggressive behavior intends to protect against intrusion from the outer world. Now, these two instances produced by let's say, a gardener and a psychologist, respectively, can be combined by a poet in a line of creative thought. This line considers the thorns of a rose as a protective personality trait and makes a link between two unrelated instances: a rose and a sorrowful life. The result is a poetic line about a life of a rose that is short and full of sorrow.

The weakness of the reviewed models constitutes inability to specify a mechanism, which engages multiple concepts or categories in a simultaneous information processing. Another set of models makes an attempt to describe this mechanism. These studies emphasize a central role of analogy and metaphor in creative engagement (Ward et al., 1997). A metaphor is an analogy between two instances, conveyed by the use of one instead of another. Assigning personality traits to an inanimate object as in the rose example in the previous paragraph illustrates a poetic metaphor formation. The analogy was built between two instances, a person and a rose, by means of assigning properties of the former to the latter. The effect of a metaphor is achieved via association, comparison, and resemblance of these instances. A number of researchers see a metaphor as a source of selective comparisons that can offer new perspectives on a problem, highlight or create similarities to other domains and yield insights for problem redefinition. For example, Kuhn (1993) suggests that in science, metaphors play the role of the building blocks of paradigms. These studies indicate that metaphor formation seems to be beneficial for creativity. The question is how metaphors are generated. MacCormac (1986) argues that emotion provides the motivation for the production of creative metaphors. This idea has been tested in a number of experimental studies on metaphor formation (Fainsilber & Ortony, 1987; Williams-Whitney et al., 1992). These studies showed that participants generate more novel metaphors when they are emotionally involved in the task. Furthermore, Miall (1987) demonstrated that patients with frontal lobe lesions reveal emotional problems and difficulties forming metaphors. Summarizing the existing data on metaphor generation, Lubart and Getz (1997) proposed an emotional resonance mechanism by which the metaphor can be generated. According to this model, emotion-based endocepts that are attached to the specific concepts or images in memory communicate with each other by means of an automatic resonance mechanism that propagates an active emotional pattern through memory. A resonance detection threshold controls whether a resonance-activated endocept/concept enters consciousness. Altogether, this class of models suggests that emotions link distant concepts in the process of metaphor formation, and this process may stimulate generation of novel and original ideas.

All reviewed cognitive models of creativity converge on at least one important property of creative thought – ability to establish distant associations that link concepts from distant categories. The communication between concepts is assumed to be an unconscious process during which the activation is propagated throughout the conceptual network. This property constitutes a key mechanism of divergent thinking, which is perceived by many researchers as one of the major components of creativity.

More specific, in psychometric tradition, creative capacity is perceived as an ability to initiate multiple cycles of divergent and convergent thinking (Guilford, 1967). A combined effort of these two types of thinking creates an active, attention-demanding process that allows generation of new, alternative solutions (Mumford et al., 1991). The fundamental difference between these two processes is that convergent thinking is a conscious attention-demanding process, whereas divergent thinking occurs in an unconscious mind where attention is defocused and thought is associative. Convergent thinking seeks one correct answer to the question or solution to a problem, which must have a single answer or solution (Runco et al., 2006). Divergent thinking on the other hand, involves a broad search for information and generation of numerous novel alternative answers or solutions to a problem, which has no single solution (Guilford, 1967). The solutions generated during divergent thinking are subsequently evaluated during convergent thinking, which narrows all possible alternatives down to a single solution. The following sections provide a detailed discussion of the processes underlying divergent and convergent thinking to the extent pertinent to the content of this book.

Divergent Thinking

The unconscious functioning of divergent thinking can be explained by an automatic spreading activation mechanism that simultaneously triggers a large number of mental representations. This mechanism establishes associations that link concepts from distant categories. This section details how the distributed representation in conceptual memory may facilitate divergent thinking.

Knowledge representations are stored in conceptual memory. Everything we know, everything we have learnt is assumed to form a network, in which concepts represent units of meaning. When we address one concept or another, the corresponding unit of meaning becomes activated and shares this activation with other units related to the given one. Therefore, conceptual memory is assumed as a pattern of spreading activation (McClelland & Rumelhart, 1985) over a large set of mutually linked units of meaning (or conceptual features) organized in the conceptual networks (Lamb, 1999). In this view, mental representations are seen as an emergent property of neural activity in the conceptual system (Bunge, 1980). Any sensory experience, as well as any product of our thought process, is stored as a pattern of neural activity and leaves a trace in our memory. The spreading activation mechanism transfers activation between conceptual features providing facilitation for related concepts and inhibition for unrelated ones. This property of the conceptual system was illustrated in priming studies (e.g. Meyer & Schvaneveldt, 1971) that show that semantically related words tend to influence each other. The activation of the conceptual features is assumed to be an unconscious process, and only those features that receive enough activation are selected for conscious processing.

The associations between distant mental representations can be established due to the distributed nature of the conceptual system. The same conceptual features may be part of the representation of different concepts. For example, the concept CAT shares a set of conceptual features with the concept DOG (e.g. 'four paws', 'tail', 'animal', etc.). The activation of the conceptual representation of a dog may result in a partial activation of the conceptual representation of a cat as has been shown in semantic priming studies. These two concepts however, differ in some essential features that are unique for each of them (e.g. the 'barking' feature for the DOG and the 'meowing' feature for the CAT). Owing to the distributed nature of conceptual system, these features can activate other conceptual representations (e.g. the 'bark' feature can send partial activation to the conceptual representation of a fox) and, therefore, additional associations can be formed. However, the activated concepts are likely to be members of the same or similar categories (as the concepts CAT and FOX in the previous example are the members of a category *animal*). Only people with exceptional associative thinking abilities may relate concepts that are stored beyond the category boundaries. Various factors in an individual's development such as intelligence, education, personal experience, and multilingual practice (as the following chapters demonstrate) may stimulate relating concepts beyond category boundaries.

In light of this discussion, divergent thinking refers to the ability to access simultaneously a large number of unrelated conceptual representations. This property of divergent thinking may benefit from a greater diversity of associations to the same concept (Lubart, 1999). Spreading activation among distributed conceptual representations may build the links between distant, often unrelated concepts. As previously discussed cognitive models of creative problem solving indicate, a large number of simultaneously activated solutions may establish a rich plane of thought from which original and novel solutions might be extracted. In other words, some individuals have exceptional ability to simultaneously engage seemingly unrelated ideas during creative problem solving. These ideas establish a thought platform on which creative solutions can be generated. This aptitude is referred to with divergent thinking capacity.

The ability to keep active multiple unrelated conceptual representations simultaneously has an apparent benefit for creative production – a capacity to concurrently process a large number of properties of different conceptual categories. When people try to come up with a novel idea, their imagination is generally limited by a particular set of properties characterizing a category to which this innovation should belong (Ward, 1994). They tend to select the most common set of properties of a category as a starting point for their creations (Ward et al., 1997). A number of studies in various domains of creative production show that the semantic structure of a category has a substantial influence on what people produce (Ward et al., 2002). 'Structured imagination' (cf. Ward, 1994) limits individuals' 'thinking outside the box'; that is, people have difficulties violating the conceptual boundaries of a standard category when creating a new exemplar of that category. For example, when participants were asked to create an alien creature in the task described in the following paragraph, they could not help but producing the one that greatly resembled a humanoid creature (see example in Figure 4.2a on p. 75). This creature is comprised of surface properties of a human; that is, it is bilaterally symmetrical and has four limbs and two eyes. This example illustrates that we tend to preserve the standard category boundaries, to think inside the box even when asked to be creative. In this respect, creative thinking may benefit from actively employing a spreading activation mechanism of divergent thinking, which engages conceptual representations from multiple categories (Kharkhurin, 2009). This multifaceted processing in turn may render a mental state in which at least several sets of category properties become available for the thought process. The activation of properties of different categories may potentially help to overcome the limitations of structured imagination and therefore facilitate nonstandard creative thinking.

The alien creature invention paradigm (cf. Ward, 1994) is used to assess structured imagination. In the studies utilizing this paradigm, participants are asked to imagine, draw and describe a creature living on a planet very different from Earth. The alien creature invention studies provide evidence that the instructions to violate category boundaries boosted creative thinking (Ward et al., 2002). Moreover, the drawings of the creatures that revealed more violations of a standard set of properties characterizing a category were rated as more creative by other people. Kozbelt and Durmysheva (2007) coded the drawings of invented alien creatures produced by participants on three *invariants*, the features that commonly appear in most participants' responses. They found that violation of the standard invariants positively correlated with judges' creativity rating of the product, although the effect was rather small. They concluded that the drawings in which the standard characteristics of an alien creature category were violated obtained higher creativity rating by the independent judges. Kharkhurin (2009) utilized similar approach and found that the capacity for invariant violation predicted the creativity rating by independent judges. Thus, divergent thinking may facilitate simultaneous access to conceptual representations from different categories and thereby may overcome the limitations of structured imagination.

Mumford and his colleagues (1991) indicated several ways in which the creative problem solving process differs from the standard, noncreative process. The major difference is rooted in the ability to initiate multiple cycles of divergent and convergent thinking, which creates a conceptual plane on which new, alternative solutions might be generated. In contrast, in routine problem solving, people apply previously acquired procedures and search for ready-made solutions, all of which mainly involve convergent thinking (see also Hudson, 1969; Mayer, 1999b). Traditionally, therefore, creative ability is associated with divergent rather than convergent thinking. Although there is general consensus in creativity research that both processes are necessary to secure successful creative performance, divergent thinking has received more attention and remains a key topic in creativity literature.

Over the past 50 years, numerous studies have provided evidence for the ability of divergent thinking tests to predict certain aspects of creative problem-solving performance and real-world creative achievement. Kim (2008) performed a meta-analysis of 27 studies (with 47,197 participants) that established the correlation coefficients between divergent thinking test scores and creative achievement. Despite the differences in divergent thinking tests, creative achievement types, predicted time periods and creativity subscales, she found a significant relationship between divergent thinking performance and creative achievement ($r = 0.22$). Nevertheless, there is a meaningful argument that questions this relationship. For example, some researchers argue that the validity of divergent thinking tests may depend, in part, on the scoring procedures being applied (Runco & Mraz, 1992). Other researchers argue that divergent thinking tests are weakly related to other kinds of creativity ratings and therefore measure only a small portion of creativity (Hocevar, 1981). Still others question the nature of divergent thinking tests as the measures of creativity at all. They argue that this relationship is rather between divergent thinking and other types of cognitive capacities such as intelligence (Sternberg & O'Hara, 1999). In a broader sense, Barron and Harrington (1981) criticized the idea that eminent creative performance can be explained by mundane cognitive processing such as divergent thinking. They noted that there was remarkably little evidence revealing divergent thinking abilities in highly creative people.

This skepticism, however, is answered by researchers identifying the traces of divergent thinking in eminent individuals. For example, Stokes (2000: 279) notes:

> Matisse, Picasso, and Calder displayed divergent thinking in using a multiplicity of styles and media. Think of the innovative paper sculptures made by Picasso during his Cubist period; of Matisse's late, great cut-outs, the culmination of his pursuit of an art of pure line and pure color; of Calder's whimsical, wire-constructed contour 'drawings' in three dimensions.

In the same fashion, Runco (1986) explored the relationship between divergent thinking test scores and creative performance in 96 gifted and 116 nongifted children. The criterion of creative performance was a self-report that estimated the quantity and quality of extracurricular activity in different domains (e.g. writing, art, music and science). He found that divergent thinking and creative performance scores were moderately related in the gifted sample but unrelated in the nongifted sample. In a more recent study, Vincent *et al.* (2002) examined the relationships among intelligence, expertise, and divergent thinking as they influence creative problem solving and performance in a sample of 110 military leaders. Divergent thinking was measured using Christensen *et al*'s. (1953) consequences test known to capture aspects of divergent thinking relevant to leaders' problem-solving efforts (Mumford *et al.*, 1998). In this study, divergent thinking correlated with idea generation and idea implementation more strongly than intelligence and expertise. The study suggested that divergent thinking has unique effects on creative problem solving that could not be attributed to the other cognitive capacities.

Thus, although as Runco (1991) argues, 'Divergent thinking is not synonymous with creative thinking' (p. ix), many researchers believe that divergent thinking is an important component of the creative process (see also Lubart, 2000). Therefore, a close scrutiny of individuals' divergent thinking performance may at least partially illuminate their creative functioning.

The identification of creativity with divergent thinking spawned an array of divergent thinking tests such as Alternative Uses (Christensen *et al.*, 1960), Consequences (Christensen *et al.*, 1953), Instances Test (Wallach & Kogan, 1965), Plot Titles (Berger & Guilford, 1969), Remote Associates Test (Mednick & Mednick, 1967), Uses of Objects Test (Getzels & Jackson, 1962) and Torrance Tests of Creative Thinking (Torrance, 1966). These tests were widely adopted by creative cognition researchers as the measures of creativity (see Plucker & Renzulli, 1999, for an overview). However, the construct validity of these tests remains disputable.

The major critique that divergent thinking tests receive in the literature is whether these tests indeed measure creative abilities. For example, Guilford and his colleagues assumed that divergent thinking is linked to creative behavior. Personality psychologists, likewise, suggested that some personality traits are linked to creative behavior. Others claimed that individuals' attitudes and intentions or their past experiences are related to creative behavior. Each of these approaches uses its own strategy of creativity assessment. Hocevar (1981: 450) listed 10 different types of creativity measurement: 'tests of divergent thinking, attitude and interest inventories, personality inventories, biographical inventories, teacher nominations, peer nominations, supervisor ratings, judgments of products, eminence and self-reported creative activities and achievements.' All of them were employed to identify creative talent. Therefore, as Hocevar (1981: 457) noted, 'Since each method is purported to be measuring creativity, it is reasonable to predict that they be correlated, thus satisfying a minimum condition of convergent validity.' However, these measures failed to show evidence of convergent validity. Specifically, divergent thinking tests revealed no strong correlation with other tests of creative abilities.

Davis and Belcher (1971) also found no significant correlation between divergent thinking tests and a biographical inventory and self-rating scores on several questions pertinent to creative activity. No significant correlation was reported in a study of art students whose creative abilities were obtained using eight divergent thinking tests, two teacher ratings, two personality inventories, grades and intelligence scores (Getzels & Csikszentmihályi, 1964). In another study of art students, Ellison (1973) found low and negative relationships between judged creativity on a pastel drawing, the Remote Associates Test (Mednick & Mednick, 1967) and the Barron–Welsh Art Scale (Barron & Welsh, 1952). Moreover, even in the studies that reported a significant positive correlation between divergent thinking and other creativity measurements (e.g. Bartlett & Davis, 1974; Wallbrown & Huelsman, 1975), the correlation was seldom higher than 0.30, suggesting that the two measures shared only up to 10% of the variance in common.

A specific case in the discussion of the construct validity of divergent thinking tests is made by researchers questioning whether these tools merely measure intelligence. To answer this question, attempts have been made to establish the correlation between measures of intelligence and divergent thinking skills. These studies indicated moderate positive correlations (in the 0.20–0.40 range) of divergent thinking tests, typically scored for fluency, with measures of intelligence (Barron & Harrington, 1981). The positive correlation suggested that there was some relationship between these two. However, a low correlation value indicated that measures of divergent thinking skills might capture a capacity distinct from intelligence or the one sharing only one component of intelligence. This argument was supported by Guilford and Christensen (1973) who proposed that the relationship between divergent thinking abilities and intelligence becomes weaker after one passed some threshold level in basic cognitive capacity. This position found empirical support in studies reporting the independence of these measures at the above-average intelligence levels. However, the value of the minimal intelligence threshold in these studies varied from 90 in Lehman et al.'s (1981) study to 132 in Torrance's (1962) study, which suggests that there is no definite intelligence level at which divergent thinking separates from intelligence. Furthermore, there is an argument that the magnitude of the divergent thinking–intelligence relationship depends on the heterogeneity of the sample being used, with larger correlations being obtained in more heterogeneous samples (Hattie, 1980; Metcalfe, 1978; Vernon, 1964). Others see the magnitude of this relationship as a function of the domain being examined, with stronger relationships between divergent thinking and intelligence in intellectually demanding domains (Barron & Harrington, 1981) such as management and engineering (Mumford *et al.*, 1999). Finally, a recent meta-analysis (Kim, 2008) revealed that creative achievements correlate significantly more strongly with tests of divergent thinking than with intelligence tests. Kim also reported research showing that the relationship between creative achievement and divergent thinking is independent from intelligence.

Another case was made against divergent thinking tests as an all-purpose creative thinking assessment. For example, Brown (1989) believes that failure of divergent thinking tests to provide a sufficient measure of creativity can be explained by the inability of this test to assess different aspects of creative potential. He says:

> We can see why the initial promise of divergent thought has not been fulfilled. Implicitly or explicitly, creativity theorists viewed divergent thought as a fairly general process that would account for a variety of creative activities. But several lines of research and theory [...] are converging on the conclusion that talent and creativity are domain specific whether by dint of 'natural' proclivity, extensive training, and/or education. (Brown: 22)

Indeed, for many years creativity researchers assumed creativity as a domain transcendent process. It was tempting to identify processes that can explain all kinds of creativity at once. However, a growing body of evidence suggests that creative performance is not general, but domain specific (e.g. Albert, 1980; Bloom, 1985; Runco, 1986). It presents a challenge to a common view that creative people should exhibit eminent performance in different domains (e.g. visual art, poetry and science). The evidence previously interpreted as supporting theories of general creativity actually provide little support for such an interpretation (see Baer, 1998, for a review). For example, in a series of studies with participants ranging in age from second grade through early adulthood, Baer (1993) found that, among all age groups, correlations of creativity ratings on various products (including poems, oral and written stories, mathematical puzzles and collages) were consistently low, even with correction for attenuation due to measurement error. Squaring these correlation coefficients, one finds that the amount of shared variance was almost always less than 5% in these studies. It seems that if any across-domain generality really exists, it must be limited in size to this tiny degree of shared variance, and it must therefore be vanishingly small. Thus, the hopes to find a universal mechanism of creativity failed, and contemporary creativity research has to face a problem of determining various cognitive mechanisms underlying creative thinking in rather narrowly defined content domains (Runco, 1989). In this view, divergent thinking tests cannot be perceived as an assessment of overall creativity and its application should be clearly specified. The present work is contextualized within the creative cognition paradigm (see above). It assumes that divergent thinking is a normative cognitive mechanism, intensified exploitation of which may result in increase in creative abilities. Therefore, divergent thinking tests can be employed to identify these mechanisms of normative cognition.

Divergent thinking assessment

This section presents a divergent thinking assessment tool that served as a prototype for a test utilized in studies of the relationship between bilingualism and creativity discussed throughout this book. The Torrance Tests of Creative Thinking (TTCT, Torrance, 1966) were developed to measure divergent thinking abilities in children. The TTCTs were the most widely used (Davis, 1991) and most referenced (Lissitz & Willhoft, 1985) tests of creativity that have been translated into more than 35 languages (Millar, 2002) and utilized in the educational field and the corporate world (Kim, 2006). Hakuta (1984: 64) expressed the rationale behind the TTCT: 'For Torrance, creativity is closely identified with divergent productions and transformations with the ability to take different perspectives and different approaches to a given problem'. This test consists of relatively simple verbal and figural tasks that tap into divergent thinking abilities as well as in other problem-solving skills. Guilford (1967) associated the properties of divergent thinking with four main characteristics: fluency (the ability to rapidly produce a large number of ideas or solutions to a problem), flexibility (the capacity to consider a variety of approaches to a problem simultaneously), elaboration (the ability to think through the details of an idea and carry it out) and originality (the tendency to produce ideas different from those of most other people). The TTCT utilized this description of divergent thinking and presented four-dimensional assessment including fluency (total number of relevant responses), flexibility (number of different categories of relevant responses), elaboration (amount of detail in the responses) and originality (the statistical rarity of responses).

The TTCTs were used in about three-quarters of all recently published studies of creativity involving elementary and secondary school children (Baer, 1993). Moreover, the TTCTs were employed in the studies conducted with individuals speaking different languages (e.g. Chinese–English and Malayan–English in Torrance et al., 1970; French–English in St. Lambert Project, see Lambert, 1975, for a review; Japanese–English in Konaka, 1997). The extensive evidence of the validity of the tests comes from Torrance's longitudinal studies with elementary and high school students initiated in 1958 and 1959. These studies have produced strong evidence of relationships between test performance and real-life creative achievement (see Torrance, 2000, for a review). However, there have been questions about the predictive validity of the tests with respect to adult creative achievement (e.g. Baer, 1994; Gardner, 1993a; Wallach, 1976). In particular, can children's high performance on the TTCT predict their creative accomplishments in adulthood? A relatively recent study by Plucker (1999) provided an answer to this question and additional support in favor of the TTCT. He used structural equation modeling to reanalyze Torrance's longitudinal data on predictive validity and found that creativity scores on the TTCT accounted for about half the variance in adults' publicly recognized creative achievements and participation in creative activities obtained several years later. This corresponds to a predictive validity coefficient of about 0.70, which suggests that the TTCT scores differentiate well between individuals who subsequently go on to achieve public acclaim as being creative and those who do not. Interestingly, the TTCT predicted about three times as much of the criterion variance as intelligence tests.

Since giving both the verbal and the figural forms of the TTCT often requires considerable testing time (45 minutes for the verbal and 30 minutes for the figural), Torrance and his colleagues developed an abridged version. The new test, the Demonstration Form of the Torrance Tests (Torrance *et al.*, 1980) consists of activities utilizing the same rationale as activities in the original TTCT, but in abbreviated form and requiring considerably less testing time. This test was found suitable for adult populations, including older adults (Horng, 1981; Torrance & Safter, 1999; Townsend *et al.*, 1981). This test was then converted to the current Abbreviated Torrance Test for Adults (ATTA, Goff & Torrance, 2002). The adult version contains three 3-minute verbal and figural tasks that are scored for fluency, flexibility, elaboration, and originality. This test was used by the author to assess creative performance of the college students in several distinct geographic locations. A detailed description of this test is presented in the fourth chapter.

Convergent Thinking

Reiterating, as a result of divergent thinking a large number of unrelated concepts from distant categories can be simultaneously activated. However, the mere generation of various solutions to a problem does not imply that these solutions will necessarily be original (i.e. satisfy the criteria of novelty) and result in creative production. Other processes should be applied to the activated conceptual representations to ensure successful creative accomplishment. These processes are likely to be characterized by convergent thinking. As Baer (2003: 132) puts it, 'We must both *diverge* to find many ideas and *converge* to select the best ideas.' Recall that for Guilford (1967), creative production involves multiple cycles of divergent and convergent thinking, and neglect of the latter largely limits creativity research. However, the convergent thinking is underrepresented in study of creativity. A generally accepted metaphor of divergent thinking as a core creativity process leads us away from other important aspects of creativity such as convergent thinking (Baer, 2003; Runco, 2003b).

The purpose of convergent thinking is to find the single best (or correct) answer to a clearly defined problem (Cropley, 2006). This cognitive function appears inevitable when a large pool of ambiguous divergent thoughts needs to be narrowed down to a single creative solution. These possible candidates should be explored, criticized and evaluated to select the best fit to the problem. The nature of these processes cast doubt on the adequacy of the term convergent thinking proposed by Guilford (1967). Indeed, creative thinkers do not only converge in their thoughts but they are also engaged in a whole range of cognitive functions such as exploration of generated ideas, evaluation and critical review of possible outcomes. Therefore, researchers suggested other terms as alternatives to convergent thinking, such as evaluative thinking (see Baer, 2003, for a discussion). This term was argued to better reflect cognitive skills required to evaluate a pull of alternatives and to extract a single solution that satisfies the criteria of creative product (novelty and utility).

Knowledge and intelligence seem to play a pervasive role in this type of thinking (Runco *et al.*, 2006). The evaluation process largely relies on the knowledge base as the alternatives should be compared with the previously generated solutions in order to secure the originality. An individual's experience provides a database against which the new ideas are assessed. Ability to manipulate these ideas to generate novel solutions to a problem may stem from intelligence. Runco and colleagues even argue that the tests of intelligence, in fact, measure an individual's convergent thinking. This is quite controversial perspective, however, as research provides mixed findings on the relationship between creativity and intelligence ranging from the view that there is no relation between these two to the view that one is a subset of the other (see Sternberg & O'Hara, 1999, for an overview). Nevertheless, a potential overlap in cognitive functioning between convergent thinking and intelligence should not be withdrawn from an account.

Following Cattell (1963), at least two types of intelligence can be identified. Fluid intelligence employs inductive and deductive reasoning, classification and concept formation to solve novel, complex problems; it addresses the ability to successfully reason in novel situations. Crystallized intelligence refers to knowledge already acquired, partially through fluid intelligence, from culture, education and other experiences. The cognitive mechanisms of fluid intelligence are of a particular interest for the present discussion. There is no doubt that crystallized intelligence plays an important role in creative thinking, because it ensures a sufficient knowledge base against which newly generated ideas can be checked. Moreover, it is reasonable to assume that extensive knowledge base might play an important role in divergent thinking as well. As Runco and his colleagues (2006) rightly note, the ideas generated during divergent thinking are not weaved from the air, they are being extracted from long-term memory. Therefore, an extensive knowledge base provides a greater variety of possible ideas produced as a result of this process. Nevertheless, this book focuses on the cognitive mechanisms underlying fluid intelligence. These processes seem to reflect the dynamic nature of human cognition that undergoes certain modification as a result of multilingual practice.

A large number of empirical studies assessing fluid intelligence utilize a standard Culture Fair Intelligence Test battery (CFIT, Cattell, 1973). The CFIT uses nonverbal stimuli and therefore intends to assess intelligence in such a way that the influence of verbal fluency, culture and educational level has the least effect possible. The nature of the CFIT hints to a possible cognitive process underlying fluid intelligence. Look at the sample CFIT task in Figure 1.1. At the left, there are four boxes; the last one is empty. Continuing along that row, you see five more boxes, one of which will fit correctly in the empty box. To select the correct answer, you need to identify the common features of the pictures and to select one that adheres to these features. Here the little bar is growing more and more in the first three boxes. Which one from those on the right does fit the empty box? Right, this is a bar in the second box, because it grows more than the one in the third box on the left and it has the same heights as the ones in the left boxes. That is, the CFIT assesses the ability to focus attention on the common features of the figures in the series and to extract the correct relationships between these features. Individuals with greater ability to focus on relevant information in the series' elements should be more efficient at extracting the regulations and therefore should show greater test performance. Therefore, selective attention could be the cognitive function underlying fluid intelligence. Brain imaging studies

Figure 1.1 Sample task of the CFIT

provide evidence supporting this idea. The measures of fluid intelligence were found to correlate with the executive control functions of the frontal lobes (e.g. Duncan *et al.*, 1996).

Thus, individuals' advanced mechanism of selective attention could be a good candidate to predict their greater performance on intelligence tests. In light of the previous discussion, if there is a parallel between intelligence and convergent thinking, the latter may also benefit from enhanced selective attention. That is, the efficient selective attention may support creative problem-solving at the stage where a conscious attention demanding process assists in narrowing a multitude of possible alternatives down to a single original solution. The role of selective attention in an individual's convergent thinking is further detailed in Chapter 4 in the context of bilingual creative performance.

Summary

In psychometric tradition, creativity is assumed as an essential property of normative human cognition, which is characterized by novelty and utility of the product. A large portion of creativity research perceives creative thinking as an ability to initiate multiple cycles of divergent and convergent thinking. The solutions generated during divergent thinking, which involves generation of numerous alternatives, are subsequently evaluated during convergent thinking, which narrows all possible alternatives down to a single novel solution. In spite of sound skepticism regarding equation of divergent thinking with creativity, many researcher employ divergent thinking tests as a measure of creative thinking. However, assuming divergent thinking as a core creativity process leads us away from other important aspects of creativity such as convergent thinking. There are some hints in the literature to a similarity of underlying processes in convergent thinking and intelligence. Therefore, it is plausible to propose that efficient selective attention, underlying fluid intelligence, may support creative problem-solving during convergent thinking.

The purpose of this chapter was to introduce the reader to the issues in creativity research pertinent to the theme of this book. So far, we have outlined the theoretical framework in which the relationship between multilingualism and creativity will be considered. This is creative cognition paradigm approaching creativity from a perspective of normative human cognition. Divergent and convergent thinking as well as fluid intelligence and its underlying selective attention were introduced as key cognitive functions contributing to an individual's creative capacities. The following chapter presents another side of the book's theme, the research in multilingualism.

2 Multilingual Cognition

Overview

During the past few decades, research in the area of multilingual cognitive development has made tremendous progress and provided evidence supporting the notion that speaking more than one language extends rather than diminishes an individual's cognitive capacities. There is a strong argument in the literature that multilingual development may result in establishing specific architectures of the mind that are likely to promote later cognitive advantages. On the other side, according to creative cognition approach discussed in Chapter 1, creativity is considered a product of normative cognitive functioning. The author assumes that if multilingualism facilitates general cognitive functioning, it may also facilitate creative functioning. Therefore, before we plunge into the realm of multilingual creative cognition, let us review the findings in multilingual normative cognition. These findings will allow us to identify important determinants that need to be investigated with regard to multilingual creativity.

This chapter deals with issues in multilingual cognitive functioning that in the author's opinion may be pertinent to multilingual creative functioning. The review of studies on the role of multilingualism in an individual's cognitive and linguistic development reveals interesting tendencies: multilingual individuals demonstrated apparent advantages on cognitive tasks presented in a nonverbal context. These advantages are explained by specific cognitive functions that might benefit from multilingual practice, specifically metalinguistic awareness and executive control. A logical continuation of this discussion presents several factors in multilingual development that may have an impact on an individual's cognition. These factors tap into one's experience with different languages and sociocultural settings. Furthermore, it is hypothesized that the influence of these factors on an individual's cognitive functioning may be due to specific structure of bilingual memory. In other words, cross-linguistic and cross-cultural developmental factors have a particular impact on structures and/or functions in bilingual memory, which may result in a specific organization of this memory. The latter may facilitate an individual's cognitive capacities. The chapter ends with a detailed description of the architecture of multilingual memory and the effect of multilingual developmental factors on its structure.

Multilingualism and Cognitive and Linguistic Development

One of the widely discussed topics in the research on bilingualism comes from the pedagogical considerations of how to raise bilingual children (see August & Shanahan, 2006, for an overview), and possible consequences of bilingual development (see Bialystok, 2009; Nicoladis, 2008, for an overview). In this regard, several questions concerning the linguistic and cognitive consequences of bilingualism have been raised. Does bilingualism delay or accelerate language development? Does the possession of two languages hinder or facilitate the effectiveness of linguistic and thinking processes? Do bilinguals, operating in two linguistic systems, have more or fewer linguistic and cognitive advantages? Do bilinguals receive, transfer, store and reproduce thoughts differently from monolinguals? The opinions on these questions are divided as a growing body of empirical data provides support for both bilingual advantages and disadvantages (see Cook, 1997, for a review). On one side, evidence suggests that bilingual development causes a deficiency in the processing of first (L1) and second (L2) languages (e.g. Gollan et al., 2002; Ivanova & Costa, 2008; Rosselli et al., 2000). On the other side, speaking two languages is shown to extend rather than to diminish an individual's cognitive capabilities, which is also supported by a growing number of empirical studies (see Bialystok, 2009, for an overview).

An interesting tendency observed in this discussion is that the aforementioned studies showing bilinguals' disadvantages focus on their verbal abilities, whereas the ones supporting the opposite perspective emphasize bilinguals' greater performance on nonverbal cognitive tasks. These studies show three major tendencies in bilingual development: (1) bilingualism negatively affects an individual's skills in both languages, (2) limited linguistic skills of bilinguals impair their performance on the cognitive tasks presented in verbal context and (3) if the task is presented in nonverbal context, bilinguals show greater cognitive performance than monolinguals do.

Empirical evidence demonstrates bilinguals' disadvantage on linguistic tasks, in particular in language production. Oller and Eilers (2002) reported vocabulary deficits in fluent bilingual children. Researchers who have investigated the tip-of-the-tongue phenomenon in different languages (e.g. Gollan et al., 2005; Gollan & Silverberg, 2001) revealed a tendency for bilinguals to produce more tip-of-the-tongue states than monolinguals even when tested in their dominant language exclusively (Gollan & Acenas, 2004). Finally, Kohnert et al. (1998) found that bilinguals scored below the monolingual norms on the Boston Naming Task in both their languages.

Boston Naming Task (Kaplan *et al.*, 1983) is a test of productive vocabulary, in which participants have to name pictures of objects and animals presented in the order of word frequency and grade of difficulty. This finding was confirmed by Roberts *et al.* (2002) who found that bilinguals produced more errors in picture naming than monolinguals. Moreover, Gollan *et al.* (2005) reported that bilingual adults required more time to name a picture than their monolingual counterparts. Another study utilizing picture-naming test similar to the Boston Naming Task also revealed a monolingual advantage on this measure (Kharkhurin, 2010a). Thus, all these studies indicate that bilingualism seems to have a negative impact on individuals' linguistic performance even in their dominant language.

Research also demonstrates that bilinguals' limited linguistic skills seem to have an impact on their performance in other cognitive domains as well. For example, Frenck-Mestre and Vaid (1993) found that bilinguals verified simple arithmetic problems most quickly and accurately when the problems were presented as digits, slower when presented in word format in their L1, and slower again in their L2. They concluded that arithmetic ability is compromised for bilinguals in their L2. The fact that bilinguals in this study were late language learners with a lower proficiency in their L2 than L1 suggests that this effect can be attributed to their linguistic abilities rather than to mathematical ones. At the same time, the presentation of the cognitive task in bilinguals' dominant language may annihilate this linguistic effect. Morales *et al.* (1985) found that when the problem was presented in dominant language, both bilinguals and monolinguals showed similar performance on problem-solving tasks. However, this claim faces a meaningful counterargument that the processing of two languages may increase demands on the cognitive system, thereby decreasing bilinguals' performance on problem-solving tasks (e.g. Ellis, 1992). All these findings provide mixed results, but there is at least one apparent conclusion: although bilingualism per se does not impair individuals' problem solving, the linguistic context of the problem may impose certain limitations on the cognitive system, thereby interfering with their performance (Bialystok, 2005). In other words, framing a nonverbal problem in a verbal context may require additional cognitive efforts which cause deficiency in bilingual problem solving.

In contrast, research in bilingual cognitive development provides evidence that bilingualism extends rather than diminishes an individual's cognitive capacities in nonverbal domains. Specifically, bilinguals were found to outperform their monolingual counterparts on the nonverbal tasks requiring control processes such as selective attention to relevant aspects of a problem, inhibition of attention to misleading information, and switching between competing alternatives (see Bialystok, 2005, 2009, for an overview). Bilingual children tended to solve problems that contain conflicting or misleading cues at an earlier age than monolinguals (Bialystok & Martin, 2004). They were also better in identifying the alternative image in reversible figures (Bialystok & Shapero, 2005). Moreover, studies with older bilinguals show that this cognitive advantage persists into adulthood. Bilingual young adults needed less time than their monolingual counterparts to resolve the conflict between the target stimulus and the to-be-ignored flanker information (e.g. Costa *et al.*, 2008). Bilingual older adults demonstrated the offset of age-related losses in executive processes (e.g. Bialystok *et al.*, 2008a; Craik & Bialystok, 2010).

Summarizing the reviewed studies, speaking two languages seems to be a double-edged sword. On the one hand, bilinguals show a lower proficiency in their languages compared to their monolingual counterparts. Bilinguals' relatively lower language skills seem to impede their performance both on linguistic tasks and on cognitive tasks if they are presented in the verbal context. On the other hand, bilinguals demonstrate greater performance on nonverbal cognitive tasks involving executive control and inhibition of irrelevant information. These findings lead to a logical question that taps into the nature of the processes underlying bilingual advanced cognitive functioning. The following section answers this question by discussing two cognitive processes that are supposedly facilitated by multilingual practice: metalinguistic awareness and executive control. These processes are believed to facilitate both cognitive and creative functioning. Therefore, they are of great importance for the later discussion of bilingual creative capacities, which forms the core of this book.

Multilingual Cognitive Advantages

There is a sound opinion in the literature that the positive effect of bilingualism on an individual's cognitive abilities can be attributed to metalinguistic awareness. The latter can be described as the conscious awareness of structural properties of one's language, the awareness of language itself, independent of the message it is conveying (see Reynolds, 1991). The development of metalinguistic awareness is closely associated with language development in general (e.g. Cheung *et al.*, 2010; Francis, 2002; Jessner, 2008). One requires substantial linguistic skills to develop this capacity. Young children fail to demonstrate metalinguistic awareness because it develops quite late in the process of language acquisition. For example, Bruce (1964) showed that children under 6 years are not aware of phonological units. Similarly, Zhurova (1971) demonstrated that children were unable to say the first letter of visually presented objects until they were 5 or 6 years of age. Another study revealed that children have difficulties understanding that words are decomposable into sounds (Fox & Routh, 1975), an important ability in learning to read using an alphabetic writing system. It is also argued that L2 learners increase their knowledge about the ways languages differ, which consequently boosts their metalinguistic awareness. A number of studies with bilingual children revealed a positive effect of knowing another language on metalinguistic abilities, such as understanding the word-referent distinction (Ianco-Worrall, 1972), sensitivity to language structure and details (Ben-Zeev, 1977), and correction of ungrammatical sentences and detection of language mixing (Diaz, 1985). Even partial L2 proficiency is likely to affect metalinguistic knowledge which, in turn, may aid in language acquisition, including the acquisition of any other language that the learner might encounter.

There is debate in the literature regarding the effect of bilingualism on metalinguistic awareness. Evidence for a facilitating effect (Bialystok, 1988), an inhibiting effect (Palmer, 1972) and no effect (Rosenblum & Pinker, 1983) of speaking more than one language have been reported. Some investigators found both positive and negative effects when studying different samples of bilingual children (e.g. Ben-Zeev, 1977; Cummins, 1978a). A positive effect of bilingualism on metalinguistic abilities appears in understanding the word-referent distinction and the arbitrariness of language. Bilinguals know that the same object can have different names; therefore, they can detach the name from the object much more easily. As a result, bilinguals have to conceptualize things in their general properties rather than relying on their linguistic symbols. In a typical metalinguistic awareness experiment with 4–9-year-old children, Ianco-Worrall (1972) reported that more than twice as many bilingual participants as monolingual ones agreed that a dog could be called *cow* and a cow called *dog*. Having two labels will force an early separation of a word from its referent, demonstrating the awareness of the arbitrariness of language. This may lead to a more analytic orientation, flexibility in thinking and superiority in concept formation. The metalinguistic awareness, therefore, may ensure bilingual children's greater cognitive performance. Moreover, a trait such as flexibility in thinking may be highly suitable in situations requiring nontrivial manipulation of existing cognitive structures; that is, it may have a positive impact on an individual's creative thinking.

Another potential explanation for bilinguals' cognitive superiority stems from their extensive practice with two active language systems. The findings show that both languages become activated during bilingual language processing (see Costa, 2005, for an overview).[1] When bilinguals use a target language, the linguistic representations of the other language are still active and interfere with the target ones. Simultaneous activation of both languages makes bilinguals constantly focus on one language, inhibit another language or switch between languages (Bialystok *et al.*, 2005). The executive control functions ensure noninterruptive processing in the target language by attending to the representational system corresponding to this language and disregarding the system associated with a nontarget language. Thus, an extensive practice with at least two active language systems may facilitate executive control engaged in solving the conflicts in lexical retrieval as was demonstrated by empirical research (reviewed in Bialystok, 2005, 2009). These findings were supported by the results of the brain imaging studies revealing that experience with two languages leads to systematic changes in frontal executive functions (e.g. Bialystok *et al.*, 2005). Due to cross-linguistic practice, bilinguals exercise crucial cognitive skills that enhance the problem-solving abilities requiring attentional control to focus on relevant and to ignore misleading cues. This type of control was described by Bunge *et al.* (2002) as 'interference suppression.' That is, individuals with everyday multilingual practice routinely engage in interference suppression, which develops their attentional control to a greater extent (Bialystok, 2001; Green, 1998). In a similar fashion, although unrelated to bilingualism per se, Kiesel and her collegues (2010) presented a review of the research utilizing task-switching paradigm to study cognitive control and task interference. These studies also converge on the notion that the ability to control the switch encouraged by well-developed executive control function seems to facilitate an individual's cognitive performance.

One of the most widely used tests, which implicates selective attention and response inhibition is the Stroop task (Stroop, 1935). This test exploits the conflict between an automatic behavior (i.e. reading) and a decision rule that requires this behavior to be inhibited. The task taps into the ability to inhibit inappropriate responses and resist interference (Stroop effect). This effect arises from two processes working in opposite directions: facilitation and inhibition. The assessment of these processes provides a more detailed description of the attentional control. Facilitation taps into ability to focus on the information when it is helpful, and inhibition refers to the ability to ignore the information when it is misleading. The most typical Stroop paradigm presents color names printed in different color fonts, and asks participants to name the color in which a word is printed. The automatic behavior (reading of the word for a color name) interferes with the decision rule (naming of the font color), and this behavior needs to be suppressed. The Stroop test was used in different modalities in a large number of clinical (e.g. Macniven *et al.*, 2008; Richards *et al.*, 2007), neuroimaging (e.g. Gruber & Yurgelun-Todd, 2005; Mitchell, 2005) and bilingualism studies. In the latter, the test was utilized to assess cross-language interference (e.g. Altarriba & Mathis, 1997; Costa *et al.*, 2008; Miller & Kroll, 2002) and inhibitory mechanism of selective attention (e.g. Martin-Rhee & Bialystok, 2008; Sutton *et al.*, 2007; Zied *et al.*, 2004). Bialystok and coworkers (2008a) used a version of the standard Stroop color-naming task to compare the rate of interference suppression in young and old bilinguals and monolinguals. They reported a bilingual advantage on the Stroop task for both age groups. Bilinguals showed stronger inhibition (termed 'cost' in their study) than monolinguals. These findings were expanded by the author's study (Kharkhurin, 2011) showing that interference suppression is more evident in more proficient bilinguals. In that study, bilinguals with greater vocabulary knowledge demonstrated a weaker Stroop effect (more interference suppression) and a stronger inhibition than their less proficient counterparts. On the other side, bilinguals with moderate vocabulary knowledge revealed a greater facilitation effect. The stronger inhibition in highly proficient bilinguals can be explained by their greater need to efficiently suppress the interference from one language to ensure noninterruptive processing of the other language. Both of their highly developed languages interfere with each other, which imposes a greater demand for more efficient interference suppression. The explanation for stronger facilitation in less proficient bilinguals can be rooted in a sound opinion that during early stages of L2 acquisition, the learners access the meaning of L2 words through L1 (cf. revised hierarchical model of bilingual memory discussed by Kroll & Tokowicz, 2005). Successful L2 processing, therefore, may be contingent on an ability to keep both languages active and use all available linguistic cues. An efficient facilitation in unskilled language learners would enhance this process. Conversely, as learners become more proficient in L2, they begin to develop direct conceptual processing of this language. The L1–L2 route becomes less exploited and the connection between the languages becomes weaker. However, they still may interfere with each other's processing along this route (cf. language nonselective access in bilingual memory demonstrated by Dijkstra, 2005). Therefore, less advanced L2 learners may employ facilitation mechanism to maintain the link between both languages, whereas more advanced L2 learners may employ the inhibition mechanism to suppress the interference of one language during the processing of the other.

Thus, multilingual practice enhances executive control functioning that encourages an advanced performance on the tests requiring inhibition of irrelevant and facilitation of relevant information. Moreover, Bialystok and Feng (2009) suggest that bilinguals' greater executive control may compensate for weaker linguistic skills and allow them to show equal or greater performance than monolinguals on the tasks involving a verbal component (such as proactive interference task).

The reviewed research demonstrates bilingual advantages on the cognitive tasks assessing metalinguistic awareness and executive control. These studies suggest that bilinguals may develop certain cognitive functions to a greater extent than their monolingual counterparts. Why would an individual's practice with more than one language elicit these cognitive advantages? An answer to this question seems to be rooted in the factors characterizing multilingual development.

Multilingual Developmental Factors

The reader should not be surprised that multilingual individuals are as normal as every other human being, and they undergo the same course of development as everyone else. However, by mere fact of exposure to different languages, they obtain additional facets that may have implications in their linguistic and cognitive development. These developmental aspects can be related either to their direct experience with different languages or to their experience with cultural settings that accompanies language acquisition. A growing body of empirical evidence identifies two factors of cross-linguistic experience that play a pervasive role in development of cognitive functions in bilinguals: language proficiency and age of language acquisition. The third factor is inferred from specific features of published bilingual studies, which focus on individuals who have acquired their languages in different cultural contexts. These studies suggest that language acquisition is accompanied by cross-cultural experience, and the latter has a measurable impact on one's cognitive development. There, it is prudent to discuss a potential impact of cross-linguistic and cross-cultural factors in multilinguals' development on their cognitive abilities. Again, the author assumes that these factors play a pervasive role in both cognitive and creative development. Therefore, it is essential to elaborate on these factors to provide a sufficient ground for further discussion of their influences on one's creative potential.

The first developmental factor implicated in the cognitive abilities of multilinguals is the level of their proficiency in the languages they speak. Lambert (1955) drew a distinction between two types of bilinguals based on their degree of relative linguistic proficiency. Balanced bilinguals, he argued, are equally competent in both languages, whereas dominant bilinguals speak one language better than the other. A number of empirical studies identified the degree of language proficiency as a reliable predictor of bilinguals' cognitive capacities. Bialystok (1988) reported two studies in which French–English bilingual children differing in their level of language proficiency were given metalinguistic problems that made demands on either analysis of knowledge (i.e. the way in which the language is represented in the mind) or control of processing (i.e. the selection of information for use). She found that fully bilingual children performed better than partially bilingual children on tasks requiring high levels of analysis of knowledge. Lemmon and Goggin (1989) compared performance of undergraduate Spanish–English bilinguals and English monolinguals on cognitive ability tasks that required concept formation, mental reorganization, abstract and divergent thinking and mental flexibility. They revealed that monolinguals tended to outperform bilinguals on most of the measures of cognitive skill, but subsequent comparison of the monolingual group with high- and low-proficiency bilingual subgroups (divided on the basis of their proficiency in Spanish) suggested that the effect was attributable to bilingual participants with low language proficiency. Harris *et al.* (1995) compared balanced and dominant Spanish–English bilingual and English monolingual adults on learning and memory tests. They reported that dominant bilinguals retained fewer words in English (their L2) than did balanced bilinguals and monolinguals in this language. The difference between bilingual groups disappeared, however, when bilinguals were tested in Spanish (their L1). In a recent study, Bialystok *et al.* (2008b) investigated lexical access in college students speaking English and various native languages, and those speaking only English. Monolinguals obtained higher letter fluency scores than bilinguals. The letter fluency task required participants to produce as many words as possible that started with a given letter within one minute. However, this difference disappeared when vocabulary size was taken into account. A follow-up study utilized letter fluency task with higher demand for executive control, in which participants were required to exclude names of people, places, numbers and verbs with different endings from a list of words that started with a given letter. In this study, highly proficient bilinguals outperformed their monolingual counterparts, whereas bilinguals with lower proficiency performed at the same level as monolinguals.

The reviewed studies converge in the findings that bilinguals with different levels of language proficiency may vary in their cognitive performance. The threshold hypothesis (Cummins, 1976) explains these results by stating that bilinguals need to achieve a minimum (age-appropriate) proficiency threshold in both of their languages before bilingualism can promote cognitive advantages. This theory was supported by studies with children (e.g. Diaz, 1985) showing that participants who did not reach a certain proficiency level in each of their languages performed poorer on a variety of cognitive tasks compared to monolinguals. For example, Ricciardelli (1992a) tested this theory with Italian–English bilingual and English monolingual children and found that only those bilinguals who scored high on both English and Italian versions of the Peabody Picture Vocabulary Test (Dunn, 1965) showed superior divergent thinking and metalinguistic abilities. Those bilinguals who had low proficiency in either one or both languages were statistically indistinguishable from the monolinguals. Another explanation is put forward by the research on executive control (see previous section) that argues that due to more extensive cross-linguistic practice (i.e. greater language proficiency) bilinguals acquire cognitive skills that can be constructively used in other nonlinguistic domains. Remarkably, this theory can at least partially explain the threshold hypothesis. Two highly developed language systems would interfere with each other to a greater extent than two unequally developed systems. Therefore, those bilinguals who attained high level of linguistic proficiency in both languages face the problem of interference suppression to a greater extent than their less proficient counterparts. As a consequence, they develop more efficient executive control mechanism, which facilitates their performance on the cognitive tasks.

The second factor in bilingual development that may have a potential impact on individuals' cognitive abilities is the age at which each of their languages was acquired. Traditionally, the distinction is made between simultaneous and sequential bilinguals (McLaughlin, 1984). The simultaneous bilinguals learn both of their languages from the onset of language acquisition. The sequential bilinguals learn their L2 after age of five, when the basic components of L1 are already in place. The sequential bilinguals are further divided into early and late ones, reflecting the age at which L2 acquisition occurred (Genesee, 1978).

The view that the age of acquisition of bilinguals' languages can predict their cognitive performance originates in Lenneberg's (1967) critical period hypothesis. In this framework, L1 acquisition must occur before cerebral lateralization is complete, at about the age of puberty. One prediction of this hypothesis is that L2 acquisition will be relatively fast, successful and qualitatively similar to L1 only if it occurs before the age of puberty. This prediction was tested in a number of studies (e.g. Harley & Wang, 1997; Yeni-Komshian et al., 2000), demonstrating that individuals who have acquired L2 before age 12 show stronger linguistic skills than those who acquired L2 later. For example, Johnson and Newport (1989) tested native Korean or Chinese speakers who had arrived in the United States at ages 3–39 years and who had lived in this country between 3 and 26 years at the time of testing. The results indicated that early arrivals performed significantly better on an English grammaticality judgment task than late arrivals. Moreover, test performance of early arrivals was linearly related to age of arrival, whereas late arrivals' performance was highly variable and unrelated to age of arrival. Obviously, the age of arrival in this study indicated the age at which the migrants were exposed to English (their L2). These findings correspond to the reports of bilingual children's performance in the early French immersion programs in Toronto and Ottawa (Canada) conducted in the 1970s (see Swain & Lapkin, 1982, for a listing of published reports). These studies showed that the age of entering the program could be an essential factor in predicting bilingual children's cognitive development.

Thus, it is plausible to acknowledge the advantages of early language acquisition. Lenneberg (1967) related them to the fact that language learning occurs before lateralization is complete. The brain at an early age is still flexible and therefore allows more detailed analysis of incoming linguistic information, which may result in a greater level of attainment in language acquisition (cf. 'less is more' hypothesis, Newport, 1990). Later on, as the person matures and learns various cognitive strategies, this early advantage may be lost. The studies with connectionist networks provide evidence for the maturation hypothesis. Elman (1993) demonstrated that the training of a recurrent connectionist network with complex grammatical rules fails if the model is fully formed and equipped with adult-like capacity from the onset. However, learning is successful if the model initially has a restricted child-like capacity that gradually matures into an adult-like one. In the same fashion, the findings of the acquisition of verbs' past tense with a connectionist model simulation (Marchman, 1993) revealed that the more the networks learn, the less flexible they become.

The evidence showing age-related decline in language functioning is paralleled by the findings demonstrating that other cognitive capacities decrease with age. These findings reveal an age-related decrease in the ability to learn paired associates (Salthouse, 1992), increased difficulty encoding new information (Craik & Jennings, 1992; Rabinowitz et al., 1982), reduced accuracy in recalling detail as opposed to the broader picture (Hultsch & Dixon, 1990) and changes in working memory capacity, cognitive processing speed and attention (Kemper, 1992; Kharkhurin et al., 2001). Age-related deficiencies were also reported for implicit learning abilities (e.g. Curran, 1997; Fischman, 2005; Howard & Howard, 2001). The decline in cognitive functioning can be explained to some extent by age-related changes in cognitive structures and/ or processing that occur as the person matures.

As discussed above, bilingual cognitive advantages are traditionally associated with the virtue of developing two linguistic systems. However, there is an alternative view gathering strength in that this effect can be attributed not to the cross-linguistic variations, but to the cross-cultural values adopted in parallel with language acquisition (e.g. Leung et al., 2008). The term culture has numerous overlapping meanings that sometimes are misleading and provide 'fuzzy' definitions (Appel, 2000; Francis, 2000). Traditional associations with the word 'culture' refer to the art and knowledge and sophistication gained through exposure both to the art exemplars and to the artistic and literary heritage of a particular nation. In this work, however, culture reflects rather social and anthropological aspects of human behavior.

It is defined as a set of beliefs, moral norms, customs, practices and social behaviors of a particular nation or a group of people whose shared beliefs and practices identify the particular place, class or time to which they belong. A set of common mental models, cultural scripts and 'interpretive frames' (Pavlenko, 2000) characterize these people and suggest strategies in solving problems and dealing with a variety of situations in a culture-specific way. The studies on the effect of multilingualism on cognitive abilities generally disregard the fact that most participants in the target samples experience and participate in more than one culture. These individuals are primarily immigrants, migrant workers, members of the minority groups or foreign students exposed to different educational systems. They acquire each of their languages in the respective cultural environments where different cultural cues are available (Pavlenko, 2000). Therefore, in addition to acquiring several languages, they could adopt a range of multicultural values. Acculturation studies support this view by demonstrating that language acquisition is often accompanied by adoption of the cultural values of the country in which this language is acquired (e.g. Birman *et al.*, 2002; Gordon, 1964). For example, Schumann's (1978) acculturation theory assumes that language is one aspect of culture. His model proposes that the degree to which individuals acculturate within a new linguistic community predicts their abilities to acquire L2.

The important role of cross-cultural experience can also be inferred from a discussion in the literature regarding the context of language acquisition. Pavlenko (2000) argues that bilinguals who acquired their L2 in a decontextualized environment (e.g. in classroom setting) should be differentiated from those who acquired this language in environment where they used this language in everyday life and map it onto culture-specific events. She believes that the presence of the cultural cues may modify bilingual conceptual system. This view received support in the literature on bilingual conceptual representations, which shows that bilinguals may undergo conceptual changes due to their experiences within different cultural settings (e.g. de Groot, 2000; Paradis, 2000; Pavlenko, 2005). These researchers argue that the conceptual system of individuals who acquire more than one language inevitably undergoes adaptations that are influenced by the cultural and social contexts in which these languages were learned. Since cultural experience is deeply rooted in higher order linguistic structures such as polysemy, metaphor, irony and other nonliteral aspects of language, successful language acquisition is likely to be accompanied by the acquisition of cultural knowledge (in the form of schemas and frames), which modifies conceptual representation and organization in bilingual memory (Vaid, 2000). New connotations, even entirely new meanings, may develop through acculturation. De Groot (2000) illustrates this with the example of a turkey.

The conceptual features of TURKEY in non-North American culture-specific conceptual system have no association with great festivities taking place only in North America. However, for newcomers to North America the concept THANKSGIVING develops over a series of Thanksgiving experiences and includes turkey as an attribute of the festival. As a result, a conceptual representation of a turkey may change over time as a function of experience with the L2 culture. In particular, the conceptual representation of a turkey may become extended once it includes additional celebration-related features.

It is important to note that the structure of bilingual conceptual system is not just a combination of two monolingual ones with separate culture-specific conceptual representations. The experience of bilinguals varies depending on their isolation or participation in the new culture and in a bilingual community. For example, Ervin-Tripp (2000: 11) notes that 'American Nisei have not learned Japanese speech etiquette and are seen as rude in Japan, and American Lebanese may lack classical Arabic allusions for formal situations.' For this reason, she continues:

> We cannot expect to find a simple match between bilingual and monolingual cognitive or semantic features. [...] Bilinguals have a different access to experience; they can observe in more than one community, so we cannot expect their concepts to be matched to monolinguals at all times. (Ervin-Tripp, 2000: 11)

Moreover, two individuals who speak different languages and participate in different cultures could have developed different conceptual systems as a result of multicultural experience. Russians in Russia, for example, will interpret an event in the light of conceptual representations developed in Russian ways of thinking; North Americans will have another interpretation of the same event in accordance with American ways of thinking, whereas Russian immigrants in America will have their interpretation depending on the degree of acculturation into a new culture, that is, the extent to which they have been exposed to the new culture and adopted the new values relative to the old ones (Pavlenko, 1999).

Thus, experience with two different cultures may cause modifications in the bilingual conceptual system that reflects cross-cultural diversity in conceptual representations. In turn, newly developed conceptual representations may allow bilinguals to see the same phenomenon from different perspectives. Bilingual individuals who experience and participate in two cultures may well perceive the world through the amalgam of two different conceptual prisms and view events with a wider range of enriched experiences (Okoh, 1980). As Peal and Lambert (1962: 20) put this 50 years ago, a bilingual individual

> whose wider experiences in two cultures have given him advantages which a monolingual does not enjoy. Intellectually his experience with two language systems seems to have left him with a mental flexibility, a superiority in concept formation, a more diversified set of mental abilities.

In this framework, it is not the 'experience with two language systems,' but the experience with two systems of cultural meanings that may have an impact on bilingual cognitive functioning. Therefore, the mere fact of the acquisition of a new language in a sociocultural context of this language may have certain ramifications for bilingual cognitive development. Thus, the peculiarities of the cultural environments to which an individual is exposed during language acquisition should be taken into account. In the framework of creative cognition adopted in this book, a question that needs to be answered is what sociocultural cues might have an effect on the conceptual changes that presumably influence an individual's cognitive capacities.

The discussion of cross-linguistic and cross-cultural developmental factors would not be complete without recognizing their confounding nature. Research shows that bilinguals' age of acquisition of a new language, their exposure to the cultural environment of that language and success in the acquisition of this language are intimately intertwined. For example, Kharkhurin (2008) found that participants' age of L2 acquisition significantly correlated with their mastery in this language. Russian–English bilinguals who learned English earlier in life revealed greater English proficiency. This finding overlaps with the argument in the language acquisition literature that language learning abilities decline with age (e.g. Krashen, 1973; Lenneberg, 1967; Pinker, 1994). The same study revealed that participants' L2 cultural experience (assessed in terms of age of arrival and the length of residence in L2 country) was related to their L2 proficiency. Individuals who were exposed to the North American cultural environment earlier and for a longer time tended to show greater linguistic skills in English. This finding is in line with the prediction of the acculturation studies that show that successful language acquisition goes hand in hand with cultural adaptation (e.g. Birman *et al.*, 2002; Gordon, 1964). More extensive exposure to the L2 cultural environment is likely to result in a greater rate of acculturation, which may indirectly facilitate L2 acquisition (e.g. Johnson & Newport, 1989).

The evidence of the interlacing effect of the various factors in multilingual development lends support to the appealing argument in the literature that multilingualism should be studied not only in the context of an individual's linguistic abilities but also in a sociocultural context. In studying the psychological effects of multilingualism, the time and circumstances of an individual's experiences with different languages and sociocultural settings should be carefully examined. Ignoring the combination of linguistic and sociocultural factors would degrade research of multilingual cognition.

Recall that in this chapter we analyze research in multilingual cognition to identify potential candidates to explain multilingual creative behavior. So far, we discussed cross-linguistic and cross-cultural factors in an individual's development that may have potential impact on one's cognitive capacities. A logical continuation of this discussion would be a sketch of a theoretical framework which explains how these factors may influence multilingual cognition. Specifically, what may happen in an individual's mind as a result of multilingual development? The answer to this question in the author's opinion is related to the architecture of bilingual memory. As a result of multilingual development, this memory undergoes particular changes that in turn may have impact on one's cognitive performance. This theme is presented in the next section.

The Architecture of Bilingual Memory

Let us take a look at the multilingual brain. Is the brain of a multilingual individual different from the one of a monolingual one? A growing number of brain studies provide evidence that bilinguals have broader hemispheric involvement in language processing than monolinguals. In response to L2 acquisition and use, the human brain undergoes cortical adaptation to accommodate multiple languages either by recruiting existing regions used for the native language or by creating new cortical networks in distinct adjacent areas of the cortex to handle certain functional aspects of L2. These studies suggest that bilinguals might develop a different brain structure to accommodate multiple languages.

In spite of apparent controversy in these findings, if we accept the notion that multilingual brain might be different from the monolingual one, can we identify those factors in multilingual development that play here an important role. Indeed, one of the central questions in cognitive research of multilingualism focuses on specific developmental factors that influence the formation of multilingual mind. Do different types of multilinguals with different history of language acquisition show distinct cortical involvement? The previous section reviewed empirical evidence emphasizing the role of cross-linguistic and cross-cultural experiences in multilingual cognition. The cognitive advantages of individuals speaking more than one language were related to their language proficiency, age of language acquisition and exposure to multicultural settings. The behavioral research is complemented by the findings of the brain studies revealing different patterns of cortical involvement in bilinguals with various levels of expertise in both languages and with different ages of acquisition of these languages. They show that bilingual hemispheric involvement differs as a function of the degree of proficiency in each language (e.g. Moreno & Kutas, 2005; Vaid & Genesee, 1980). For example, Mägiste (1992) presented a dichotic listening task of stepwise addition to German–Swedish bilinguals. She found that German-dominant group had more left-hemispheric involvement in both languages, whereas a balanced group indicated about equal left- and right-hemispheric involvement. Similarly, Perani *et al.* (1996, 1998) and Rodriguez-Fornells *et al.* (2002) reported L2 proficiency effect on cortical activation during linguistic activity. Moreover, they argued that the differences in cortical representation could be attributed to bilinguals' language proficiency rather than to the age of L2 acquisition. Perani *et al.* (1996) asked Italian–English dominant bilinguals to listen to the stories in both languages. The positron emission tomography showed that auditory processing of stories in L1 (Italian) engaged the temporal lobes and temporoparietal cortex more extensively than L2 (English). However, the fact that participants had relatively low command of L2 and acquired this language late suggested that the effect could be attributed to the age of language acquisition. In the follow-up study, Perani *et al.* (1998) used the same paradigm to test two groups of bilinguals highly proficient in both languages. One group included Italian English bilinguals who acquired L2 after the age of 10 (late bilinguals) and another group consisted of Spanish–Catalan bilinguals who acquired L2 before the age of 4 (early bilinguals). The findings revealed that the differing cortical responses to L1 and L2 of the dominant bilinguals in the previous study were not found in either early or late bilinguals in this study. In addition, several brain areas, similar to those observed for L1 in the previous study, were activated by L2 in the present study. The latter study, however, may suffer from methodological flaws. The criterion for inclusion in the late bilingual group (after the age of 10) considered individuals who acquired L2 during the critical period of language acquisition (see discussion in the previous section) as late bilinguals. Also, early and late bilinguals spoke different pairs of languages, which potentially could have an impact on their cortical activity.

Furthermore, Moreno and Kutas (2005) provide evidence that both language-related developmental factors may influence the brain activity. They measured the brain response to semantic anomalies in Spanish–English and English–Spanish dominant bilinguals by recording event-related brain potentials to semantically congruent and incongruent words completing written sentences. The brain responses were found to be significantly slower in the nondominant than the dominant language. The findings also revealed that both vocabulary proficiency and age of exposure to L2 predicted the timing of semantic integration effects during written sentence processing. The age of L2 acquisition was related to variation in memory structures in other studies as well (e.g. Dehaene *et al.*, 1997; Simos *et al.*, 2001). Kim *et al.* (1997) used functional magnetic resonance imaging to determine the spatial relationship between L1 and L2 in the cortex of early (learned both languages during infancy) and late (learned L2 in early adulthood) bilingual adults. The task was to silently describe previously occurring events using both languages. All participants were equally fluent in both languages. Findings showed that within the frontal-lobe language-sensitive regions (Broca's area), L2 acquired in adulthood was spatially separated from L1. However, L2 acquired during the early language acquisition stage of development tended to be represented in common with L1 frontal cortical areas.

Thus, the reviewed data suggest that experience with multiple languages may result in a distinctively different brain structure and/or functions that are modified to adopt these languages. An individual's cross-linguistic and cross-cultural experiences may have impact on his or her brain development. These modifications may result in employing certain cognitive mechanisms differently and thereby facilitating multilingual information processing. A particular utilization of these mechanisms may lead to increase in cognitive and creative performances. This book adopts a structural model of bilingual memory to address modifications in the brain resulted from multilingual experiences. This model will be utilized in the later discussions of multilingual creative capacities.

One of the central issues in psycholinguistic research of bilingual memory revolves around the levels of representation of bilinguals' languages and their underlying concepts. This issue can be formulated in terms of two problems that are widely discussed in contemporary research. One problem is concerned with conceptual and lexical levels of representation. It is pertinent to both bilingual and monolingual minds and can be addressed with the following question: Are conceptual and language systems stored separately, and if so, how do they connect? Another problem is specific for bilingual memory: do we have separate conceptual and language systems for each language or are they shared across languages?

First, we discuss the issue of the conceptual and lexical representations in one's memory. It is evident that conceptual representations refer to our concepts or ideas, whereas the lexical representations refer to their signifiers in our language(s). For example, a conceptual representation of a dog consists of a number of conceptual features such as four paws, tail and barking (see discussion in Chapter 1). A lexical representation of a dog consists of linguistic characteristics of a word 'dog' in English or 'der Hund' in German or 'sobaka' in Russian. These characteristics may include syntactic, morphological and phonological features of this word. Most models of bilingual memory converge on the notion that lexical representations and their conceptual referents are stored separately (e.g. Francis, 2005; Kecskes & Papp, 2003). Paradis (2000) supports this claim by presenting evidence from neurolinguistic research, which shows that the concepts remain intact when language is lost, as in the case of paroxysmal and global aphasia. Due to language loss, aphasia patients cannot trigger conceptual representations that under normal circumstances could be accessed through language. Nevertheless, they can still access the concepts by activating their nonverbal representations. Indeed, conceptual features can be activated by impulses coming from nonverbal sensory experience (such as auditory, visual, somesthetic and olfactory) or may be self-activated during an act of thinking in the absence of any stimuli. Paradis (2000: 22) concludes:

> Hence, when language is no longer available to a patient with global aphasia, the concept for the word *mug*, as such, is no longer available, but the conceptual features that correspond to the patient's perception and needs will make him select a mug rather than a cup in a store, based on his familiarity with the object (for which he has a non-verbal multisensory mental representation).

Therefore, the conceptual system may contain language-independent elements.

At the same time, our everyday experience is inseparably related to the linguistic practice. A large portion of this experience that leaves an imprint on our mental representation is gained through language (verbal communication, mass media, literature, etc.). Many researchers consider the conceptual system as a dynamic model that undergoes qualitative modifications determined by an individual's history of language learning and use (e.g. Ervin-Tripp, 2000; Grosjean, 1998; Pavlenko, 2000). For example, the contemporary version of Whorf's linguistic relativity argues that cultural experience may have an impact on the conceptual system, and this experience is language mediated (see also Pavlenko, 2005, for an overview). In other words, although conceptual and lexical representations are assumed to have separate storages, the conceptual development is likely to be language mediated. Thus, a close link between conceptual and linguistic systems is suggested. Language-driven input and knowledge obtained through language practice directly or indirectly modify conceptual representations and thereby keep this link constantly active.

This view can be illustrated with an example of a representation of a bird in one's memory. A mental representation of the concept BIRD can be seen as a pattern of activation over a set of conceptual features that represent the properties of the category, bird (e.g. the ability to fly and to lay eggs and the possession of wings), examples of birds (e.g. sparrow, pigeon and eagle), our personal experience with actual birds and our experience with using the word 'bird.' The former conceptual features are language independent, whereas the latter establishes close connections with linguistic features and can be triggered by presenting the word 'bird.' Thus, in this perspective, the memory system may include independent conceptual and lexical stores that are linked through a set of language-related conceptual features (Masson, 1991), which in turn are influenced by the linguistic experience.

Indeed, linguists and psycholinguists tend to distinguish between two levels of meaning representation. One level represents information that includes real-world knowledge and the meanings of the objects and events to which words refer. The other contains semantic specifications that form a part of the lexical representation and serve to constrain the way in which the word meanings are accessed for the purpose of processing syntactically well-formed utterances (Kroll & de Groot, 1997). In this view, in addition to the conceptual and lexical levels, a third level of representation is proposed to handle language-specific units of meaning that bear some lexical-semantic functions. This level is presented as the lemma level in Kroll and de Groot's distributed lexical/conceptual feature model, the semantic system in Pavlenko's (1997) model and lexical meaning representations in Paradis's (2000) three-store model (for a comprehensive review of research on semantic and conceptual representations in bilinguals, see Francis, 2005 and in monolinguals see Kroll & de Groot, 1997). In spite of some disagreement about the exact functioning on the lexical-semantic level (see discussion in the special issue of *Bilingualism: Language and Cognition*, 3(1), published in 2000), this level is generally assumed to include some information of both syntactic and semantic nature. Clinical studies also supply evidence that certain types of aphasia that affect lexical-semantic representations do not necessarily affect conceptual representations (Paradis, 2007). Thus, an individual's memory consists of three levels of representation: conceptual, lexical and lexical-semantic. Note that the former level is a part of the conceptual system, whereas the latter two are parts of the language system. The three-store model makes a distinction between the conceptual representations, which are language independent, and the word meaning representations that are language bound. These two types of representations are often confused in two-store models (see Francis, 2005, for a discussion of the confusion). As a result, these models address only a limited scope of empirical findings.

Second, we discuss the configuration of conceptual and language systems for different languages. The early models of bilingual memory accentuated the distinction between separated and integrated lexical and conceptual representations in both languages (see overview in Kirsner *et al.*, 1984). One class of models argues that lexical and conceptual systems for each language are stored separately. These models differ in the degree of cross-language connectivity. One model assumes that lexical and conceptual representations for each language are separated and there is no interaction between them. The other assumes the cross-language links between translation equivalents. The third model establishes these links not only between the translation equivalents but also between the associated words across languages. Another class of models supposes that lexicons and conceptual systems of both languages are integrated. One of these models takes the extreme position that lexical and conceptual representations are shared within and across languages. The other assumes shared conceptual representations but separate lexicons for each language.

All these models have a limited scope of application for they do not address many important aspects of language processing. In particular, they do not differentiate between orthographic and phonological aspects of lexical form. That is, these models distinguish between conceptual and lexical representations in one or both languages, but they do not specify how different lexical forms are linked to each other. For example, German–Dutch bilinguals may have shared phonological representation due to the fact that these languages have similar phonological composition, whereas their English–Chinese counterparts may have separate phonological representations. These models also do not specify how the words with no precise translation across languages are represented. Furthermore, they do not distinguish between initial access from word to concept in comprehension and later lexicalization from concept to word in production. More generally, the selectivity of lexical access is not taken into account. Finally, these models do not take into account the history of language learning and how the relationship between lexical and conceptual systems would change as a function of language development. These issues have been addressed in recent models that take more specialized account. They focus on particular aspects of representation and specify which of them are shared across languages and to what extent access to them is selective. Moreover, these models look at how cross-language interactions change in different language modalities under specific task conditions. Last but not least, they spell out what functional and structural changes accompany L2 acquisition, and how different factors in bilingual development stipulate these changes. The book omits a detailed discussion of the contemporary models of bilingual memory, and suggests the reader to refer to their elaborate overview by Kroll and Tokowicz (2005). Instead, this book presents a review of three models, whose principles serve as a theoretical framework for discussion of bilingual cognitive and creative advantages.

Potter *et al.* (1984) proposed two models of bilingual memory. The word association model claims that in order to access the underlying concept, the L2 word needs first to activate L1, which in turn triggers the conceptual representation; that is, L2 lexical access is L1 mediated. In contrast, the concept mediation model assumes that words in both languages are directly connected to the underlying concepts. The principal difference between these models is that the former assumes a direct connection between language systems, whereas the latter assumes that they are linked through the shared conceptual representations. In the course of empirical investigation of these models with bilinguals at different stages of L2 acquisition (Chen & Leung, 1989; Kroll & Curley, 1988; Potter *et al.*, 1984), it was observed that at the earlier stages of language learning there is more reliance on translation equivalents between L1 and L2, whereas at the later stages direct concept mediation is possible. This transition depends on the linguistic skills in L2. As a result, Kroll and Stewart (1994) proposed a revised hierarchical model, which assumes that both language systems are interconnected and linked to the conceptual system. During early stages of L2 acquisition, the connection from L1 to the concepts is stronger than the one from L2, and learners rely on L2–L1 connection to access meanings in L2. As learners become more proficient, the connection between L2 and conceptual system intensifies so that they rely more on this connection rather than on the one mediated by L1. The reinforced L2–concept connection weakens L1–L2 connection. The communication principles of the revised hierarchical model were implemented in distributed lexical/conceptual feature model (see Kroll & de Groot, 1997, for a detailed description) that is employed in this book to explain the facilitation effect of the specific structure of bilingual memory on cognitive and creative abilities.

The distributed lexical/conceptual feature model (see Figure 2.1) presents bilingual memory as a dynamic system with three levels of representation: (a) a conceptual features level that consists of representations of meaning, (b) a lexical features level that does not include word meanings, but only aspects of word form and (c) a language-specific lexical-semantic (lemmas) level that mediates the word forms and their meanings. Both conceptual and lexical features levels are language nonspecific (i.e. shared across both languages), and the lemmas level is specific for each language. The conceptual features level contains distributed conceptual representations; that is, representations of knowledge and meanings stored in conceptual memory. The characteristics of the latter were discussed in Chapter 1 with respect to the structure of

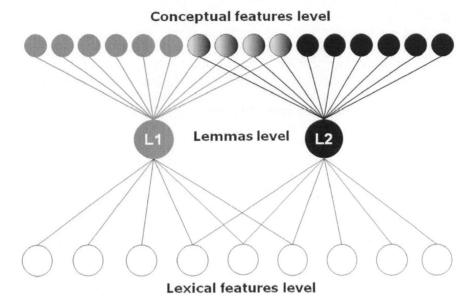

Figure 2.1 The distributed lexical/conceptual feature model of bilingual memory consists of three levels of representation: A conceptual feature, a lexical feature and a lexical-semantic (lemma). Adapted from Kroll & de Groot (1997)

conceptual system that presumably facilitates divergent thinking. The lexical features level contains distributed lexical representations. The distributed nature of the lexical features presumes that the same word forms can be shared by words in both languages. For example, a word 'marker' in English shares phonological features with a Russian word 'marka' /stamp/ (Spivey & Marian, 1999). This is a particularly important notion for understanding a phenomenon of a language-mediated concept activation discussed in Chapter 4. Note that throughout the discussion of bilingual memory, the terms *lexicon* and *lexical* refer to the lexical-semantic system including language-specific units and more generally to bilinguals' languages. On the other side, the term *lexical feature* refers to specific lexical feature system that contains only the aspects of word form such as phonological or orthographic representations. The lexical-semantic level contains language-specific lemmas. Lemma can be seen as an abstract lexical unit that mediates conceptual representation and word form. In language production, lemma is selected after the word has been retrieved mentally, but before any information about the word form is accessed. The lemma contains some information about the meaning and syntactic role of a word, but not about its form (Kroll & de Groot, 1997). The spreading activation is assumed as a communication mechanism between all three levels. On one side, this mechanism supports the distributed feature representation at each level, and on the other side it encourages parallel processing and communication between the features at different levels. Several important considerations for the future discussion of multilingual creativity stem from this structure of bilingual memory.

First, according to the discussion in Chapter 1, the distributed nature of the conceptual level suggests that the same conceptual features may be part of the representation of different concepts. Therefore, consideration of one concept may result in activation of a common set of features characterizing another concept, which entails mental consideration of that concept as well (see previous example of a cat and a dog). As a result, multiple associations with a given idea can be established simultaneously.

Second, the bidirectional lexical access takes place through direct links from L1 and L2 lemmas to the conceptual system. Experience with L2 stipulates the asymmetry in lexical access: L2 lemma–concept connections become stronger during L2 acquisition. The cross-language communication is established at the lexical feature level due to assumption that the word forms for both languages are shared. Activation of common word forms results in activation of lemmas from both languages (see example of English 'marker' and Russian 'marka' above). Following the concept mediation model, the translation equivalents in L1 and L2 lexicons activate each other through the corresponding conceptual units. For example, the word 'cat' in English and its German translation equivalent 'die Katze' share the same set of conceptual units (such as four paws, a tail, an animal, a meow, etc.) that mediate between lexical units in these two lexicons. A bilingual variant of primed lexical decision task supports this notion by showing that translation equivalents in different languages prime each other (e.g. Kroll & Tokowicz, 2005; Zeelenberg & Pecher, 2003).

Third, although translation equivalents share some common conceptual features, they may also have language-specific ones that differ in their lexical-semantic constraints. Paradis (1997) illustrates this with an example of a French word *balle* generally assumed as the translation equivalent of the English word *ball*. He argues that if the word *balle* would activate the same mental representations, 'bilingual speakers would not respond appropriately to the request to bring all the *balles* from the gym closet. They would erroneously bring the basketballs and footballs along with the tennis balls – only the latter being *balles* (1997: 335).

Fourth, due to the time and circumstances of acquisition of both languages, there are conceptual features that can be accessed through both languages or through one language only (Paradis, 2000). For example, bilinguals who learned fundamental mathematic principles (e.g. mental arithmetic) in L1 experience difficulties using them in L2 (Ellis, 1992; Marsh & Maki, 1978) and vice versa. In the same fashion, the author observed bilingual immigrant college students who were fluent in L1, but were uncomfortable to communicate in this language certain topics in school curriculum that were acquired in L2. The studies on bilingual autobiographical memory provide similar findings showing that when triggered in a particular language, bilinguals tend to recall events related to geographic and/or sociocultural context of this language (e.g. Aragno & Schlachet, 1996; Marian & Neisser, 2000).

Finally, the author proposed that in addition to concept-mediated language activation, there is a language-mediated concept activation (LMCA; Kharkhurin, 2007) that establishes a mutual communication between distant conceptual and lexical units in both languages. This mechanism is based on the previously discussed assumptions that translation equivalents activate each other through shared conceptual representations, and some of these representations are not identical. Due to this mechanism, conceptual representations from distant categories can be activated through shared lexical units. This, in turn, may encourage cognitive flexibility and facilitate multilingual cognitive and creative performance. The detailed description of this mechanism is presented in Chapter 4.

At this point, we conclude the presentation of bilingual memory. It appears as a three layer structure with distributed language nonspecific conceptual and lexical representations mediated by language-specific lemma representations. Now, we utilize this model as a theoretical framework to explain how different aspects of multilingual development influence one's cognitive abilities. The major purpose of this discussion is to fertilize the soil for the presentation of the impact of multilingual development on an individual's creative potential presented in Chapter 5.

The Effects of Multilingual Developmental Factors in the Framework of Bilingual Memory Model

In the framework of bilingual memory proposed in this book, cross-linguistic and cross-cultural experiences are theorized to have an influence on the structure and functioning of this memory. Extensive cross-linguistic experience is believed to establish stronger and more efficient connections between conceptual and lexical representations. Enriched cross-cultural experience may modify the conceptual representations. These changes are expected to promote a greater activation flow and to improve bilingual cognitive abilities. This subsection discusses the possible influence of the age of L2 acquisition, language proficiency and multicultural experience on bilingual memory. Note, however, that these assumptions are speculative and serve merely for the purpose of theoretical considerations.

If the acquisition of new language results in certain changes in bilingual memory (de Groot, 2000), then the age of this acquisition may determine the specificity of these changes (e.g. Brysbaert *et al.*, 2000; Kroll & de Groot, 1997; Silverberg & Samuel, 2004). Individuals who acquired both of their languages early in life may develop greater sensitivity to underlying concepts and more refined connections between lexical and conceptual representations. If bilinguals acquired both of their languages early and underwent an equal development in both languages, they might be able to establish equally strong direct links from both lexicons to the conceptual system. These links can be reinforced by a constant exposure to both languages in combination with frequent language switching. Thus, bilinguals who acquired their languages early in life would have two equally developed lexical systems connected to a shared conceptual one. This presumably fosters LMCA (described in detail in Chapter 4) by providing fast routing of informational exchange between both the lexicons and the concepts. On the other hand, individuals who acquired their L2 later in life first establish the links between their L1 lexicon and conceptual system. During L2 learning, they initially access the meanings for L2 words through L1 and only later become able to conceptually mediate L2 directly. The shift from reliance on L1 to direct conceptual processing of L2 may result in creating an asymmetry in lexical access (Kroll & de Groot, 1997). Late bilinguals would have more lexical–conceptual connections from L1 than from L2, and the strength of these links would be different for first and second languages. Due to lexical access asymmetry, more conceptual features can be accessed through L1 than through L2. Since the vast majority of the conceptual system in late bilinguals was established during L1 acquisition, and since L2 lexical features were mapped to the conceptual features through the L1 lexical–conceptual route, there might be fewer shared conceptual features that have direct links from both lexicons in the memory of individuals who acquired L2 later in life. This may result in a less efficient LMCA, and consequently in poorer cognitive performance. Cross-language priming studies support this notion. For example, Silverberg and Samuel (2004) demonstrated that early and late bilinguals showed different patterns of performance in the bilingual lexical decision priming study. In this study, semantic and mediated form primes produced priming effects for bilinguals who acquired their L2 early, but not for those who acquired L2 late. Thus, bilinguals who acquired their languages in different periods of life might have qualitatively different communication routes between lexical and conceptual systems. This assumption accords with maturational and critical period hypotheses discussed above. The changes in lexical-conceptual routes could result from the maturational changes that take place during the critical period of language acquisition (Johnson & Newport, 1989; Long, 1990).

The influence of the age of L2 acquisition on modifications in bilingual memory can – at least theoretically – be complemented by the effect of language proficiency. If the age of L2 acquisition can determine the directions of lexical–conceptual routes, the proficiency in L1 and L2 can determine the strength of connections between the lexical and the conceptual systems. The degree of linguistic skills may influence the intensity of lexical access: greater language proficiency may result in establishing stronger and more elaborate links to the conceptual system. As a result, more concepts become readily available for the LMCA. Following this assumption, bilinguals who attained high expertise in both languages would have stronger and more efficient links between lexical and conceptual levels than those who were not able to develop any of their languages to a high degree. Thus, bilinguals highly proficient in both languages would employ the LMCA mechanism more effectively and therefore may show greater cognitive performance compared to their less proficient counterparts.

Altogether, both factors in cross-linguistic experience are theorized to influence connections between lexical and conceptual representations in bilingual memory. Early bilinguals may develop equally elaborated direct links between the L1 and L2 lexicons and the conceptual system, whereas late bilinguals are likely to develop an asymmetrical system, in which L1-mediated route is more elaborate than L2-mediated one. In the same fashion, bilinguals with greater expertise in both languages would establish stronger links between the L1 and L2 lexicons and the conceptual system compared to their linguistically less proficient counterparts. The highly developed lexical–conceptual routes may facilitate the LMCA, which in turn, as proposed above, may promote cognitive advantages.

As discussed earlier, the process of learning two languages may be accompanied by the acquisition of different categories of concrete objects and abstract notions that reflect cross-cultural differences. An individual's experience with different cultural settings may result in qualitative modifications in the conceptual system (e.g. de Groot, 2000; Paradis, 2000). Pavlenko (2000) suggests that the conceptual changes may include the internalization of new concepts, convergence of the concepts and restructuring, attrition and/or substitution of previously learned concepts by new ones and shift from one conceptual domain to another. In the example of turkey discussed above, once the new celebration-related features are acquired, they expand the conceptual representation. Moreover, since bilingual conceptual system is not merely a combination of two monolingual ones, it may embed these new representations in a manner qualitatively different from that in a monolingual memory. Note that the conceptual system is shared across both languages, each of which would have access to the expanded conceptual representation. In our example, once the additional knowledge about the Thanksgiving modifies the conceptual representation, the word 'turkey' in both L1 and L2 would address these new conceptual features. Therefore, a word in a bilingual speaker's lexicon might initiate a different pattern of activation in the conceptual system compared to the same word in a monolingual speaker's lexicon. The qualitatively modified conceptual system may promote the integration of different, often contradicting, concepts, which may increase cognitive flexibility.

Summary

Human creativity is assumed as a special case of general human cognition. Therefore, the investigation of the relationship between multilingualism and creativity should start with understanding the relationship between multilingual practice and cognitive development. This chapter provided an overview of the bilingualism and cognition research pertinent to the theme of the book. It revealed bilingual advantages in nonverbal cognitive task. These advantages seem to be stipulated by bilinguals' greater metalinguistic awareness and executive control functions. Cross-linguistic and cross-cultural factors in bilinguals' development appear as important determinants of their cognitive capacities.

A particular attention was paid to the architecture of bilingual memory. Bilingual memory was presented as a dynamic system that consists of one common conceptual store in the form of the conceptual feature network and two integrated lexical stores that are linked to the conceptual one. Some of the conceptual features can be accessed from both lexicons, whereas others can be accessed from one lexicon only. In the same fashion, some of the lexical features are common to both lexicons, whereas others are language specific. This latter property is assumed by dividing lexical stores in two layers: one contains word forms shared by both languages and the other contains language-specific lemmas. All three stores communicate by means of the spreading activation mechanism that distributes the signal within and between different levels of representation. The structure and the processing of the conceptual network can be modified by an individual's experience, including the culture-related experience. The communication between lexicons as well as between lexical and conceptual systems may be determined by language-related factors in bilingual development (such as fluency in two languages and age of acquisition of these languages). Thus, an individual's cultural and linguistic experiences may both influence the information processing in the bilingual memory. Bilingual individuals with a different history of language acquisition and cross-cultural experience may develop the links between all three stores differently and therefore exhibit various patterns of information processing. These differences may explain the variations in findings on cognitive performance between different types of bilinguals and monolinguals.

Bilinguals' cognitive advantages may reflect in their greater creative performance. This idea is elaborated in the following chapters, in which the findings in bilingual cognition are tested with respect to bilingual creative cognition. The roles of cross-linguistic and cross-cultural factors as well as specific architecture of bilingual memory are discussed in terms of bilingual creative abilities.

Notes

(1) This integrated lexicon approach to the bilingual memory is contrasted with an alternative view that advocates a language-specific access system in which both languages are stored separately and activation of one language does not entail the activation of the other (Gerard & Scarborough, 1989; Soares & Grosjean, 1984).

3 Multilingual Creativity

Overview

The major theme of this book appears at the intersection of two large fields of scientific inquiry: creativity and multilingualism. The previous chapters pointed out research areas in these fields, which in the author's opinion fall within this overlapping region. Now, it is time to present the reader with the findings of bilingualism and creativity research. As was mentioned in the preface, these findings are thin on the ground for very little attention has been paid to potential impact of multilingual practice on an individual's creative potential. Nevertheless, it is important to review all existing data to make knowledgeable conclusions and to prevent potential drawbacks in the future studies.

The overview of existing findings is divided into two parts. First, we discuss the outcomes of the historiometric research, which looks at eminent creative individuals in various linguistic and sociocultural communities. The Nobel Prize award is used as an indicator of exceptional creative capacities. We reason as the following: if multilingual practice has an impact on creativity, then the proportion of Nobel Prize laureates should be greater in the geographic locations where multilingualism is more common. Another observation that should not be overlooked is that a large portion of multilingual individuals have extensive multicultural experience. Acquisition of foreign language can take place in a classroom setting where an individual learns grammar and vocabulary of this language without its sociocultural context. Alternatively, it can take place in a country where this language is spoken and therefore the learner is exposed to the sociocultural environment of this language. In this case, multilingual individuals learn L1 in one country and acquire a particular set of sociocultural values, then they learn L2 in another country and acquire a different set of sociocultural values and so on. Since sociocultural experience parallels language acquisition, it seems to be difficult to disentangle the effect of one from another. Therefore, it is prudent to look at eminent people who are largely exposed to different sociocultural settings: the ones with history of migration and those who live in ethnically and culturally defragmented areas.

Second, we discuss the findings of the psychometric research, which looks at creative performance of bilingual and monolingual individuals. A blueprint for these studies constitutes a comparative analysis of a group of individuals indentified as bilinguals and their counterparts identified as monolinguals. If multilingualism has an impact on creative abilities, then those individuals who speak more than one language should demonstrate greater performance on the creativity tests compared to their monolingual counterparts. In these studies, participants' creative performance was assessed with various creativity tests, most of which were divergent thinking tests described in Chapter 1. A large majority of these studies were conducted with children and only a few recent studies made an attempt to engage adults. Getting ahead of ourselves, the studies with bilingual children indicated that bilingualism facilitates an individual's creative potential. The advantages of bilingual children extrapolated from this research were supported by the studies with adults.

A logical question emerging from these findings taps into the reasons for multilingual individuals to demonstrate greater creative performance. The following premises may be used to establish a theoretical foundation for multilingual creative advantages. Recall from the previous chapter that bilingualism studies show that speaking multiple languages extends one's cognitive capacities. Following creative cognition approach discussed in Chapter 1, creativity can be explained by enhanced normative cognition. That is, multilingual practices may strengthen certain cognitive mechanisms, which in turn may increase one's creative potential. Therefore, the facilitatory effect of speaking multiple languages on individuals' cognition may also manifest in their enhanced creative performance.

Interpreting the findings of bilingual creative advantages, one is tempted to draw a conclusion, which assumes bilingual eminent creativity. That is, the mere fact of speaking multiple languages guarantees one's eminent creative capacities. However, this assumption would be quite premature considering the lack of systematic examination of multilingualism–creativity relation outside a laboratory setting. Due to the fact that the psychometric research deals with mundane rather than eminent creativity, the real-life creative accomplishments of multilingual individuals have not been tested. Yet no historiometric study to date has directly investigated the relationship between multilingualism and eminent creativity. Moreover, the real state of affairs in multilingual countries discourages from making too optimistic assumptions. In spite of the fact that most nationals of these countries are multilingual, we do not find an overall higher level of creativity in these countries compared to predominantly monolingual countries. Even the *List of Nobel laureates by country per capita* shows that traditionally monolingual countries such as the United States of America and the United Kingdom have a greater number of Nobel Laureates per capita than traditionally bilingual countries such as Canada and Belgium (1.04 and 1.88 vs. 0.53 and 0.93, respectively). Several possible explanations can be advanced to account for the contradiction between empirical findings showing bilingual advantages on the creativity tests and the real-life observations showing no remarkable differences in creative performance between multilingual and monolingual populations. These explanations serve as a framework for methodological considerations of the research in the field.

Specifically, it is argued that psychometric research in bilingual creativity reveals a substantial amount of methodological weaknesses. These can be related to the assessment of both creative capacities and language proficiency, to inappropriate selection and assignment of participants to bilingual and monolingual groups and to disregarding the confounding nature of multilingual and multicultural experiences. Another complication can arise from research design employed in these studies. These issues can be related to participants' age, dispersion of their linguistic and geographic backgrounds, limited combination of tested languages and their histories of language acquisition and cultural experience. Moreover, most of these studies primarily compared bilingual and monolingual groups disregarding the differences between different types of bilinguals. The discussion of the methodological drawbacks concludes the chapter and suggests the directions for improvement that have been considered by the author in his longitudinal project presented in Chapter 4.

The Relationship between Bilingualism and Creativity

The previous chapter presents research in the area of bilingual cognitive and linguistic development, which shows evidence supporting the argument that speaking more than one language extends, rather than diminishes, an individual's cognitive capacities. In the framework of creative cognition discussed in Chapter 1, increase in general cognitive functioning may facilitate an individual's creative abilities. One's creative performance can be understood in terms of the use of specific processes, and the richness and flexibility of stored cognitive structures to which these processes are applied (Ward *et al.*, 1997). If multilingualism results in more elaborate cognitive structures and/or functioning, then it follows that it should also facilitate creativity.

Unfortunately, the relationship between multilingualism and creativity has not received adequate consideration in the scientific community. The reasons for this oversight can be inferred from the discussions in the previous chapters. First, both theoretical constructs are fuzzily defined and researchers still struggle with a precise description of these phenomena (Simonton, 2008). Second, the impact of multilingualism on creativity is mediated by the effects of multicultural experience. On the one side, the term 'culture' has numerous overlapping and misleading meanings, which hampers adequate quantitative analysis of its relation to one's cognitive functioning. On the other side, the influence of sociocultural context on an individual's creative abilities has received in itself substantial attention in the scientific community (e.g. Kaufman & Sternberg, 2006; Lubart, 1999; Niu & Sternberg, 2001). Third, the research into creativity has virtually no overlap with that of bilingualism. As one can see in the first two chapters, each of these fields is largely developed and has received a substantial amount of empirical investigation. However, the studies focusing on the intersection of these two areas are few in number. In her seminal review paper, Ricciardelli (1992b) reported 24 studies that took place between 1965 and 1992. In the following decade, this scarce research has been complemented by six dissertation works (Fleith, 1999; Garcia, 1996; Konaka, 1997; Martorell, 1992; Stephens, 1997; Stone, 1993), six peer-reviewed journal articles (Burck, 2004; Fleith et al., 2002; Garcia, 2003; Karapetsas & Andreou, 1999; Paduch, 2005; Palaniappan, 1994) and one book (Calderón & Minaya-Rowe, 2003), which rather addressed the theme in the context of bilingual education and its potential impact on students' creativity. Altogether, bilingual research in creativity delivered approximately 40 studies over 40 years of work. Only recently was this theme resuscitated and received systematic empirical investigation in the author's longitudinal project studying cognitive processes underlying bilingual creativity (Kharkhurin, 2005, 2007, 2008, 2009, 2010a, 2010b, 2011). After that, four more studies addressing the relationship between bilingualism and creative and insightful problem solving appeared in various publications (Cushen & Wiley, 2011; Hommel et al., 2011; Lee & Kim, 2011; Leikin, in print). Two more studies (Aguirre, 2003; Granada, 2003) focus on bilingual and gifted population. The concern of these works, however, appears with how to educate students who have been identified as bilingual and gifted. This chapter provides an overview of historiometric and psychometric research supporting the notion of a positive relationship between multilingualism and creativity. The focus of this research is primarily on the creative performance of bilingual and monolingual children and adults.

Historiometric Research

There is no direct historiometric evidence showing that individuals speaking more than one language have apparent creative advantages. However, indirect evidence favoring bilingual creative advantages can be inferred. The analysis of Nobel Laureates in countries with population over 1 million (*List of Nobel laureates by country per capita*) revealed that the multilingual nations deliver the largest number of the laureates per capita. Switzerland, with four official languages (German, French, Italian and Romansh), tops the list, three top ten countries (Ireland, East Timor and Israel) have two official languages and the nationals of five other top ten countries (Sweden, Austria, Denmark, Norway and Germany) reported high fluency in foreign languages (with on average over 70% of citizens indicating an ability to speak a language different from their native tongue; European Commission, 2006).

Another line of indirect evidence favoring bilingual creative advantages comes from a discussion in the previous chapter emphasizing that most bilingual individuals engaged in cognitive research have extensive multicultural experience. The factors of cross-linguistic and cross-cultural experiences are intimately intertwined, and contemporary research cannot separate their effects on creative potential (Simonton, 2008). Creativity literature reports observations of the increase in creative potential in the groups largely exposed to different cultural settings. Creativity is boosted in geographic areas that are ethnically diverse and politically fragmented and after civilizations open themselves to outside influences (Simonton, 1997). The study of the distribution of eminent creators and leaders in Japanese civilization shows that a higher distribution of exceptional people was observed in times of 'cultural heterogeneity' (Simonton, 2003). After Japan was opened to foreign influences, foreigners traveled to Japan and eminent Japanese traveled abroad, which together introduced various elements of foreign lifestyle and education to the previously closed Japanese society. Simonton (2008) associates these tendencies with increased number of bilingual individuals. However, it is entirely possible that the mere fact of exposure to alien cultural values may have stipulated the clustering of creative geniuses after this important milestone in Japanese history.

Further research shows that first- and second-generation immigrants as well as ethnically diverse or marginalized individuals reveal relatively high rates of creativity (Lambert *et al.*, 1973; Simonton, 1997, 1999). As many social scientists have speculated, migrants show exceptional creative abilities as a result of being on the edge of different cultures they were exposed to through migration (e.g. Campbell, 1960; Park, 1928). This speculation received support from historiometric studies overviewed by Simonton (2008). For instance, Goertzel *et al.* (1978) revealed an unusually high percentage of first- or second-generation immigrants among 300 eminent 20th century personalities. Similarly, an investigation of the Nobel Laureates showed that almost all 'have carried out study courses abroad, either as students, research workers, or professors' (Moulin, 1955, as cited in Simonton, 2008:

149). In the same fashion, a recent study of famous US scientists in the physical and life sciences revealed that 'individuals making exceptional contributions [...] are disproportionately drawn from the foreign born' and 'are also disproportionately foreign educated, both at the undergraduate and graduate level' (Levin & Stephan, 1999, as cited in Simonton, 2008: 150). Here again, Simonton interprets these findings as indirectly supporting the notion of bilingualism–creativity association. Individuals who resided abroad for an extensive period should have acquired the language of the host country and therefore could be considered to be multilingual. However, the only reliable conclusion that can be inferred from these findings is that an individual's experience with different cultures might be an important contributor to the development of their creative potential.

Psychometric Research

Psychometric research provides evidence favoring bilinguals' creative abilities. Most of the studies have been conducted with children and only recently were they complemented by research with college students. In most of these studies, creativity was assessed by divergent thinking tests, and the comparison was made between bilingual and monolingual groups.

The majority of studies investigating the relationship between bilingualism and creativity in children reported bilingual advantages on various verbal and nonverbal divergent thinking tests (Garcia, 1996; Konaka, 1997; Stone, 1993; see also Ricciardelli, 1992b, for an overview of the earlier studies). Bilingual children outperformed their monolingual counterparts on divergent thinking traits such as fluency (e.g. Carringer, 1974; Jacobs & Pierce, 1966; Ricciardelli, 1992a), flexibility (e.g. Carringer, 1974; Konaka, 1997), elaboration (e.g. Srivastava & Khatoon, 1980; Torrance et al., 1970) and originality (e.g. Cummins & Gulutsan, 1974; Konaka, 1997; Okoh, 1980). In a recent study, Lee and Kim (2011) demonstrated a positive correlation between the degree of bilingualism and the degree of creativity in a sample of Korean–English bilingual students attending Atlanta Korean American School. This rather encouraging finding, however, should be interpreted with a note of criticism due to the fact that participants' language proficiency was measured by the Word Association Test (also used by Cummins & Gulutsan, 1974; Peal & Lambert, 1962). This test required participants to produce as many associations as possible in response to a word presented in one or another language. The number of responses produced in each language was used to assess their degree of bilingualism. The nature of this procedure, however, seems to tap into one's fluency in divergent thinking (ability to generate associations) rather than one's linguistic skills. Not surprisingly, this study showed a high correlation of this measure with the measures of divergent thinking.

Only a few studies reported a different pattern of findings (e.g. Garcia, 1996; Gowan & Torrance, 1965). Whitney (1974) found no differences in the verbal TTCT scores obtained by 12- and 14-year-old German–English bilinguals and English monolinguals. Similarly, Stephens (1997) reported no TTCT performance differences between Spanish–English bilinguals and their monolingual counterparts, although the former indicated greater social problem-solving abilities (assessed by the Interpersonal Problem-Solving Scale). In the same fashion, Fleith and her colleagues (2002) revealed that placement in Portuguese monolingual or English bilingual classrooms was not related to Brazilian third to fifth grade students' TTCT performance. Finally, Torrance *et al.* (1970) compared Chinese and Malayan-English bilingual and Chinese and Malayan monolingual children on figural TTCT. They found monolingual superiority on the fluency in different grades and flexibility in third and fourth grades. The potentially negative effect of bilingualism on creativity could be explained by a variation in Cummins's (1976) threshold effect discussed in the previous chapter. According to this theory, bilingual cognitive advantages are not likely to be expressed until a minimum age-appropriate threshold of proficiency in both languages is achieved. If this applies to creative abilities as well, we should not expect to find creative advantages in bilinguals with moderate language skills. Indeed, Ricciardelli (1992a) found that only those Italian–English bilingual children who had high proficiency in both languages showed greater divergent thinking abilities compared to their English monolingual counterparts. Therefore, negative effects of bilingualism on creativity reported in studies mentioned above could be explained simply by bilinguals' poor linguistic fluency in one or both languages. Unfortunately, this assumption cannot be confirmed due to the fact that many of these studies did not report what language assessment tools they employed.

Summarizing the studies with bilingual children, one can make a preliminary conclusion that bilingualism facilitates an individual's creative potential. In the rare cases where monolinguals outperformed bilinguals, it was argued that the latter were not sufficiently fluent in either of their languages for creative advantages to occur. These conclusions, however, are unreliable due to the fact that most of these studies suffered from various methodological drawbacks; specifically the ones related to language proficiency assessment in both bilingual and monolingual groups (see discussion of this issue in the last section of this chapter). Moreover, these conclusions cannot be fully trusted until the findings of bilingual children's creative advantages were generalized to adult population.

The studies of the relationship between bilingualism and creativity in adults are really thin on the ground. In her review paper of the early studies in the field, Ricciardelli (1992b) reported only one study conducted with adults. Lemmon and Goggin (1989) compared performance of undergraduate Spanish–English bilingual and English monolingual college students on cognitive ability tasks that required concept formation, mental reorganization, abstract and divergent thinking and mental flexibility. The monolingual participants tended to score higher than their bilingual counterparts on most of the measures of cognitive skill. However, subsequent comparisons of the monolingual group with high- and low-proficiency bilingual subgroups (divided on the basis of their picture-naming score in Spanish) indicated that this effect could be attributed to participants with limited skills in Spanish. In a later study, Karapetsas and Andreou (1999) found that fluent bilingual Greek–English adults outperformed their Greek monolingual counterparts on fluency in divergent thinking assessed by the Uses of Objects Test (Getzels & Jackson, 1962). In a recent study, the performance of monolingual and bilingual undergraduate colleague students was compared on insight spatial object-move problems (Cushen & Wiley, 2011). An example of insight problem-solving task in this study presents a triangle formed out of 10 coins arranged in such as way that it points toward the top of the page. The task is to move three coins to get the triangle to point to the bottom of the page while the coins still form a perfect triangle. This task probes an individual's ability to approach a problem in a nontraditional manner. An example of noninsight problem-solving task in this study encourages participants to find an exact number for a variable by selecting the smallest set of mathematical equations out of a larger set. Bilingual individuals who acquired two languages by the age of 6 demonstrated better rate of insight problem solving than noninsight problem solving, whereas their monolingual counterparts showed the opposite effect. Note, however, that bilinguals did not reveal better insight problem-solving abilities than monolinguals. These results could be due to inaccurate selection of bilingual sample, which included participants speaking English and a large variety of other languages, whose proficiency was not controlled for. Hommel et al. (2011) demonstrated a high-proficient bilingual advantage for convergent thinking and a low-proficient bilingual advantage for fluency in divergent thinking. These findings, however, should be taken with caution due to a number of methodological inconsistencies. Specifically, a monolingual sample included German University students who actually attained relatively high proficiency in English, which was indicated by their performance on the English proficiency test. Furthermore, English–Dutch bilinguals were claimed to be balanced bilinguals despite the fact that they were tested only in English and their proficiency in Dutch was not assessed. Last but not least, Mednick and Mednick's (1967) Remote Associates Test was considered as a convergent thinking test, whereas it is generally presented as a creativity test, which taps in ability to establish analogies.

In a series of studies initiated by the author in different geographic, linguistic and cultural locations, bilingual college students revealed advantages on various creativity and cognitive tests compared to their monolingual counterparts. Russian–English bilingual immigrants in the United States demonstrated greater capacity to generate multiple solutions to a problem (Kharkhurin, 2008). An additional analysis of the same samples revealed bilingual advantage in nonverbal creativity and a monolingual advantage in verbal creativity (Kharkhurin, 2010a). The United Arab Emirates resident Farsi–English bilinguals from the same educational group revealed advantages in originality in thinking (Kharkhurin, 2009). They also demonstrated greater ability to violate a standard set of category properties and better fluid intelligence. A follow-up study with multilingual college students in the United Arab Emirates revealed that more linguistically advanced participants demonstrated greater abilities to produce original and useful ideas and to think beyond standard categories in creative problem solving (Kharkhurin, 2011). This project is detailed in Chapter 4.

In sum, the advantages of bilingual children extrapolated from the early research in the field were supported by recent studies with adults. These studies not only show that bilingualism facilitates an individual's creative potential but also identify cognitive mechanisms potentially underlying creative thinking. A detailed discussion of these mechanisms and how they may be fostered by multilingual development is presented in Chapter 4. And meanwhile, similar to the discussion of multilingual cognitive advantages presented in the previous chapter, let us discuss theoretical premises for bilingual creative advantages.

Why Multilinguals Might have Advantages in Creative Performance?

The argument that multilingualism might contribute to an individual's creative abilities stems from two lines of research discussed in the previous chapters. First, although bilingualism researchers are still debating as to whether the ability to speak more than one language is beneficial or detrimental to an individual's cognitive development, a growing number of empirical studies show that speaking two languages extends rather than diminishes one's cognitive capacities. Second, following the creative cognition approach (see Chapter 1), creativity can be explained by enhanced normative cognition. As mentioned above, the differences in an individual's creative performance can be understood in terms of variations in the use of specifiable processes, and the richness and flexibility of stored cognitive structures to which the processes are applied. Chapter 2 presents evidence that multilingualism results in more elaborate cognitive structures and/or functioning. Therefore, the facilitatory effect of speaking more than one language on individuals' cognition may also manifest in their enhanced creative performance.

Thus, according to the creative cognition approach, creativity can be explained by enhanced normative cognitive functioning. One of the widely accepted mechanisms of normative creativity is divergent thinking. Holtzman (1980) argued that, if bilingualism results in better cognitive functioning, then it follows that it should facilitate divergent thinking as well. The studies reviewed above show that multilinguals' extensive cross-linguistic and cross-cultural experiences may enhance their performance on various cognitive tasks. This facilitatory effect is explained by specific processing in the bilingual mind: Experience with different linguistic and cultural settings may result in certain modifications of bilingual memory, which, in turn, may improve cognitive abilities. By analogy, the same experience may have an influence on multilinguals' divergent thinking. As was mentioned above, divergent thinking refers to the ability to simultaneously activate and process a large number of unrelated ideas and access the concepts from distant categories (Guilford, 1967). A key property of divergent thinking, therefore, is ability to establish a large pool of associations to link unrelated concepts from different categories. This property may benefit from a specific architecture of bilingual memory, which facilitates 'greater diversity of associations to the same concept because it is situated in two different linguistic conceptual networks' (Lubart, 1999: 344). The LMCA described in Chapter 4 may engage a larger set of simultaneously activated concepts and thereby ensure greater diversity of associations.

Furthermore, Lambert (1977) suggested that multilingualism often entails repeated switching from one language to another and constant dealing with several code systems (phonological, grammatical and lexical). Due to this experience, multilinguals may learn to encode and access knowledge in diverse ways. This may account for multilinguals' greater metalinguistic awareness (see discussion in the previous chapter), which presumably facilitates their cognitive flexibility. People speaking several languages learn that the same concept can have multiple referents in these languages. For example, an object can have a referent 'table' in English, 'der Tisch' in German or 'stol' in Russian. Individuals speaking these languages learn that this object can be referred to with all three words. They grasp an idea that there is no one-to-one match between an object and its referent, which in turn may encourage their abstract thinking. At the same time, multilingual cross-cultural experience opens 'two windows or corridors through which to view the world' (Okoh, 1980: 164). Multilinguals can see the same phenomenon in several different ways and have m perspectives on the same situation. Because different cultural commonalities may provide different perspectives on the same phenomena (Ricciardelli, 1992b), multilinguals 'may have a greater tolerance for ambiguity because they are comfortable with situations in which one basic idea may have different nuances' (Lubart, 1999: 344). Both cognitive flexibility and tolerance for ambiguity are considered as valuable traits of divergent thinking because unrelated, often contradicting, elements coexist during this process.

Altogether, this book proceeds from the assumption that multilingual development may facilitate an individual's divergent thinking. It is important to note, however, that although divergent thinking is identified as one of the major components of creativity (Guilford, 1967), other processes (such as synthesis, reorganization, analysis and evaluation) may be the essential contributors to eminent creative performance. Therefore, although multilingualism might facilitate an individual's creative abilities, its contribution could be limited to divergent thinking. This consideration introduces another issue that stems from an observation of a discrepancy between empirical findings showing bilingual creative advantages and the lack of those in the real life. This problem is discussed in the context of methodological issues in the field presented in the following section.

Methodological Issues

As mentioned earlier, despite some indirect evidence favoring multilingual creative advantages, real-life observations do not support empirical findings demonstrating greater creative performance of multilingual individuals. In particular, we do not witness exceptional creative accomplishments in the predominantly multilingual countries. One possible explanation for this discrepancy stems from a complexity of the creativity construct. Creativity is prompted by a large variety of factors such as education, expertise, motivation, personality traits, personal experience and socioeconomic and sociocultural conditions. Multilingualism may play here an insignificant role and its effect can be overridden by those factors. In other words, the specific economic, political, social, cultural and educational aspects of individuals' development may have impact on their creative performance above and beyond the effect of multilingualism. Nevertheless, we find a consistent pattern of multilingual advantages in empirical research. This suggests that these studies may overlook some important determinants of creative performance. To ensure a systematic evaluation of multilingual creativity research, this book identifies potential methodological problems related to procedures employed to assess creativity and language proficiency, assignment of participants to different language groups, confounding nature of multilingual and multicultural experiences and research design of these studies.

Most of the studies on the relationship between bilingualism and creativity used tests of divergent thinking, most frequently – one or more of the TTCT subtests or their variations (Cramond, 1994). The choice of this paradigm was supported by a large body of research, which provides evidence for the ability of these tests to predict certain aspects of creative problem solving. However, as Chapter 1 indicates, there is a meaningful argument that questions the validity of divergent thinking tests as a measure of creativity, because there is remarkably little evidence showing a strong correlation between highly creative people and high scores on these tests. Moreover, the divergent thinking tests were demonstrated to show little convergent validity. Thus, it is entirely possible that the mundane cognitive processing assessed by the divergent thinking tests cannot predict eminent creative performance. In the context of this book, due to limited convergent validity of the tests, bilinguals' greater divergent thinking performance in psychometric studies should not automatically imply their overall greater creative accomplishments in real life. At the same time, a multitude of other assessment techniques have been completely excluded from the multilingualism–creativity investigation. These methods include, but are not limited to, the Invented Alien Creature Task (Ward, 1994), the Consensual Assessment Technique (Amabile, 1982), the Lifetime Creativity Scales (Richards et al., 1988), the Creative Personality Scale (Gough, 1979) and the Barron–Welsh Art Scale (Barron & Welsh, 1952). Instead of assessing divergent thinking, these tests tap into imagination, openness to experience, creative personality, self-concept, hobbies and interests and other traits that seem to be more likely to express genuine creativity. It is feasible that these tests are more pertinent to uncovering multilingual creative advantages than those adopted in the psychometric research.

Furthermore, an obvious limitation of the language proficiency tests in the field is that they do not assess all four major language skills: speaking, writing, listening and reading (cf. Padilla & Ruiz, 1973). For example, in most of his studies the author employs a test of productive vocabulary to determine participants' linguistic skills. A picture-naming test assesses vocabulary knowledge by rating participants' responses to 120 drawings of simple objects (see description in Chapter 4). Clearly, it cannot assess the entire scope of linguistic aptitude and therefore should be limited to psychometric research assessing an individual's productive vocabulary knowledge. It is important to mention, though, that the use of this test could be justified by the prior use of similar tests in a number of studies of bilingual cognitive abilities (e.g. Bialystok *et al.*, 2004; Lemmon & Goggin, 1989). Moreover, the author (Kharkhurin, 2012) found that this test significantly ($p < 0.001$) correlated with Test of English as a Foreign Language ($r = 0.54$), DIALANG placement test (Chapelle, 2006; $r = 0.49$), Cloze procedure (Taylor, 1953; $r = 0.40$) and the fourth edition of Peabody Picture Vocabulary Test (Dunn & Dunn, 2007; $r = 0.57$).

Although the employed tests may have a limited scope of application, they provide at least some assessment of language skills, which helps to identify participants' linguistic background. However, many studies, especially early studies in the field did not use any of them and provided no assessment of participants' language proficiency at all. For example, Chorney (1978) found that Ukrainian–English 6- to 9-year-old bilinguals outperformed their English monolingual counterparts on the figural TTCT measures of fluency, flexibility and originality. However, the interpretation of these results in favor of bilingualism would be premature since participants' language proficiency was not assessed. Similarly, Torrance *et al.* (1970) did not specify what criteria they used to include Chinese–English and Malay–English speaking children in the bilingual group. No scores of children's proficiency in two languages were obtained to ensure a bilingual–monolingual dichotomy (Hakuta, 1984). In the same fashion, Landry (1974) selected bilinguals from an urban elementary school with a 'Foreign Language in the Elementary School' program and monolinguals from another urban elementary school without this program. His findings of bilingual superiority on the verbal and figural TTCT should be taken with caution for no assessment of participants' language proficiency was administered.

A related methodological issue arises from a procedure that assigns participants to bilingual and monolingual groups. Most of the early studies of bilingual creativity did not control for participants' comparative language proficiency when selecting them for one or another group. For example, Price-Williams and Ramirez (1977) based participants' selection solely on their ethnic background. Children attending Catholic parochial schools in Houston, Texas, were included in the bilingual group if they were Mexican- or African-American on the assumption that they speak languages other than English. In the same fashion, Carringer (1974) assigned to the bilingual group only those participants who scored high on the Word Association Test (used as a measure of language proficiency) in both languages, whereas all others were included in the monolingual group. The results of this study favored bilingual divergent thinking. However, they are likely to be misleading, because the participants in the monolingual group were not adequately controlled for their linguistic abilities (MacNab, 1979). Due to the selection strategy employed, the monolingual group consisted of participants speaking only one language (whose linguistic skills were not tested) and those who spoke more than one language, but with low proficiency in one of these languages. Therefore, it is entirely possible that divergent thinking performance differences between bilinguals and monolinguals were, in fact, the differences in individuals with high and low language proficiency. Moreover, a bias in favor of bilingual creative achievement could arise from disproportional linguistic skills of participants in different groups. If a bilingual group included individuals with high proficiency in both languages, and a monolingual group consisted of participants whose language skills were not controlled, the variation in the groups' creative performance could result from their linguistic rather than cognitive abilities.

As Hakuta and Diaz (1985: 329) pointed out, 'in the real world, there is no such thing as random assignment to a bilingual and monolingual group,' and it is almost impossible to control all variables that may have an impact on this distinction. Recent studies provided more careful assessment of participants' languages and considered the specific language skills of the individuals assigned to bilingual and monolingual groups. Despite this improvement, the problem of participants' selection cannot be resolved. On the one side, selection of monolingual participants presents an apparent challenge as there are virtually no individuals in certain geographic areas who were never exposed to other languages. For example, studies conducted in the New York City area (e.g. Kharkhurin, 2008; Konaka, 1997) assumed that monolingual participants spoke no other language but English. However, due to a highly mixed linguistic environment, these individuals were likely to experience languages other than English. The mere fact of the tacit presence of the foreign languages in their linguistic surrounding poses a challenge to integrity of the monolingual group. On the other side, some participants included in the bilingual group can speak more than two languages. For example, the majority of Russian–English bilingual participants in the author's study (Kharkhurin, 2008) were immigrants from different republics of the former Soviet Union who, in addition to Russian, were exposed to their ethnic languages (e.g. Ukrainian, Belarusian and Moldavian). Moreover, some of them reported that they took classes in foreign languages other than English. Although none of them indicated linguistic fluency, the mere fact of experience with these languages may defy homogeneity of the bilingual group. A similar problem was identified in the bilingual sample collected by the author in the United Arab Emirates (Kharkhurin, 2009). In addition to Farsi and English controlled in that study, participants selected for the bilingual group revealed knowledge of other languages acquired either in a classroom setting (e.g. French, Spanish) or from a natural multilingual environment of the country (e.g. Arabic, Urdu). Thus, these studies omit an important detail that most participants selected for a bilingual group are, in fact, multilingual. This nuance decreases the reliability of the findings due to methodological inconsistency: If the studies deal with multilingual samples, all participants' languages should be assessed and conclusions should be made about the multilingual (not bilingual) population.

Another concern raised by bilingualism–creativity research is related to cross-cultural experience of multilingual individuals as discussed in the previous chapter. In most of the studies of bilingual cognition, bilingual groups included immigrants who in addition to speaking two languages were also likely to experience and participate in two cultures. This cultural element has been virtually ignored in the investigation of the possible cognitive impact of bilingualism. However, it is likely that in addition to the virtue of speaking two languages, bilinguals who experience and participate in two cultures may benefit from the meta- and paralinguistic advantages of biculturalism, leading to an increase in their creative abilities. For example, the author found that L1 and L2 proficiency, the age of L2 acquisition and the length of exposure to L2 cultural settings correlated with the ATTA measures of fluency, flexibility and elaboration (Kharkhurin, 2008). He concluded that both bilingual and bicultural developmental factors may contribute to an individual's creative performance. In the same fashion, a positive effect of bilingualism on the innovative capacity in the author's other study (Kharkhurin, 2009) has been taken with caution as language groups were suspected to differ in a number of uncontrolled sociocultural factors that could potentially mediate the effect of bilingualism. In short, while this theme has been brought up in some theoretical considerations (e.g. Cummins & Gulutsan, 1974; Francis, 2000; Okoh, 1980), it has not received enough attention in the empirical research.

The confounding nature of the linguistic and cultural factors in creative development can also be illustrated with historiometric research on the creative contributions of European Jews. 'It is clearly evident that Jews have been more creative on a per capita basis than have members of the majority Christian community' (Simonton, 2008: 155; also see this article for a list of studies supporting this notion). At the same time, in addition to the official language of the host country, Jews spoke at least Yiddish at home and Hebrew during religious services. This indirect evidence of their multilingual practice can be related to their exceptional creative accomplishments to support a notion of a positive relationship between multilingualism and creativity. However, the fact that the Jewish population also suffered from economical, political, social or cultural deficits should be taken into account. As these obstacles were imposed on Jews to a greater extent than on the Christian population, an individual of Jewish heritage had to reveal greater cognitive and creative capacities to compete with a non-Jew. Therefore, a positive effect of multilingualism on creativity may be obscured and even reversed by the sociocultural factors.

Returning to the original question, another plausible explanation for the observation that the nationals of multilingual countries do not show exceptional creative performance can be traced to the fact that these individuals have acquired their languages in the primarily monocultural environment of their respective countries. Thus, they cannot benefit from the potential cognitive advantages of the cross-cultural experience. More generally, it is entirely possible that the inconsistency in the findings in research on cognitive impacts of bilingualism can be explained by a failure to have controlled for this factor.

In addition to creativity and language proficiency assessments, bilingual and monolingual group assignment, and confounding nature of linguistic and cultural factors, methodological complication in bilingual creativity research seems to be loaded with issues related to a study design. First, it is striking that majority of the studies in the field were conducted with children and young teenagers (see Ricciardelli, 1992b). The focus was on the effect of bilingual development on cognitive growth. These studies showed an apparent gain of bilingual children over their monolingual counterparts. However, they did not answer the question as to whether the benefits of bilingualism detected in childhood persist into adulthood when linguistic and conceptual systems are well established. This issue was addressed in more recent studies that compared creative performance of bilingual and monolingual adults. However, the focus in these studies was on college students, and none of them looked into creative behavior of older adults.

Second, these studies revealed a large dispersion of participants' linguistic and geographic backgrounds. The tested languages included Arabic, Chinese, Czech, English, Farsi, French, German, Greek, Italian, Kannada, Malayan, Polish, Russian, Spanish, Tamil, Ukrainian, Urdu, Welsh and Yoruba. The participants were sampled in Asia, Africa, Europe, the Middle East and North America. A large variety of language–location combinations could present a particular intricacy to convergent validity of these studies. Specifically, the contribution of bilingual development to creative potential may differ across linguistic and cultural groups. The author found that Russian–English bilinguals in the North American sample showed greater generative capacity, whereas Farsi–English bilinguals in the Middle Eastern sample revealed greater innovative capacity compared to their respective monolingual counterparts (Kharkhurin, 2010b). The concepts of generative and innovative capacities are detailed and discussed in Chapter 4. In brief, the former addresses the ability to activate a multitude of unrelated concepts and work through the concepts already activated, whereas the latter accounts for the ability to produce original and useful ideas. These findings were explained by different creative strategies employed by individuals speaking different languages and residing in different sociocultural contexts. Most of the studies in the field, however, ignored these factors and therefore supplied incoherent results. Moreover, due to variations in these factors, the comparison of these results seems to be unreliable.

Third, despite the fact that bilingual participants were tested in a large variety of languages, in most studies they spoke their native language and English. Virtually, no research was conducted with individuals speaking other language combinations. However, it is plausible to assume that the variation in lexical and conceptual characteristics of bilinguals' languages may determine their performance on linguistic, cognitive and creativity tests. For example, Chou (2008) found that English language learners in the United States perceived linguistic distance between languages as one of the important factors in language acquisition. Moreover, this factor could significantly predict students' language proficiency. Paradis (2004) claims that variations in combination of languages may influence the organization of bilingual memory. He notes: 'The greater the typological and/or cultural distance between the two languages, the greater the difference in the organization of mental representations corresponding to a word or utterance and its translation equivalent' (2004: 199).

Fourth, it is worth noting that the reviewed studies made no specific distinction between participants with different histories of language acquisition and cultural experience. However, it is important to differentiate bilinguals who acquired their L2 in a decontextualized environment (e.g. in a classroom setting) from those who acquired this language in environment where they used this language in everyday life and mapped it within culture-specific events (Pavlenko, 2000). Moreover, the latter ones also do not present a homogeneous group. These individuals could be immigrants, migrant workers, members of the minority groups or foreign students. Their socioeconomic status can stipulate not only the degree of linguistic involvement and acculturation but also their cognitive development (see discussion of the conceptual changes in bilingual memory in the previous chapter). For example, literature suggests that the experience of the immigrants varies depending on their isolation or participation both in a new culture and in a bilingual community (e.g. Birman & Trickett, 2001; Birman *et al.*, 2002; Szapocznik *et al.*, 1978). The process of immigration changes an individual's status and may result in a shift of social standards and values (Pavlenko, 1997). Sociological research on immigrant communities shows that immigrants often develop their own subculture that is distanced from their source culture and yet differs from the culture of the country of their current residence (Ervin-Tripp,

2000). In addition, the process of acculturation in immigrants was often found to be accompanied by a variety of negative experiences (see Birman & Trickett, 2001). These experiences may result in the attrition of the essential knowledge of the original country and at the same time inability to fully acquire the knowledge of a new culture. The limited knowledge acquisition may affect cognitive development and consequently creative performance (Kharkhurin, 2005).

Finally, most research investigating a relationship between bilingualism and creativity uses a cross-sectional design, which can be subsequently divided into between- and within-group designs. The former compares bilinguals with monolinguals, whereas the latter focuses on bilinguals with different histories of language acquisition and use. The early studies in the field employed a between-group design, which posed particular methodological problems. As discussed earlier, the criteria used to assign participants to bilingual and monolingual groups were often poorly specified and inconsistent from study to study. Moreover, individuals included in a bilingual group could have different levels of linguistic proficiency in each of their languages. The inconsistency in assigning participants to respective groups could cause biases in evaluation of groups' creative performance.

This bias was eliminated in a within-group design, which employed a continuous assessment of bilingualism. Instead of comparing bilingual and monolingual groups, these studies considered various factors in bilingual development (level of expertise in each language, age of acquisition of each language and sociocultural context in which each language was acquired). This approach seems to tap into more subtle differences between different types of bilinguals and provides a more sophisticated analysis of potential bilingual creative advantages. For example, Konaka (1997) determined bilingual type based on the score computed from bilinguals' self-rating and the Word Association Test, which was subsequently transformed into a five-point scale ranging from balanced bilingual to unbalanced bilingual. She found that the degree of bilingual balance significantly predicted divergent thinking abilities of Japanese sixth and seventh grade students living in the New York area. The within-group design allowed Lemmon and Goggin (1989) to determine that the negative effect of bilingualism could be attributed to participants with limited skills in Spanish. Similarly, based on the scores on the English and Russian picture-naming test, the author divided bilingual participants into high (high scores in both languages), unbalanced (high score in one language and low in the other) and low (low scores in both languages) proficiency groups (Kharkhurin, 2008). Only a high-proficiency group was found to outperform a monolingual group on the ATTA measure of elaboration. In the same study, the age of L2 acquisition was found to relate to the ATTA measures of fluency and flexibility and the length of exposure to new cultural environment to fluency, flexibility and elaboration.

Thus, the within-group cross-sectional design that employs group comparison of different types of bilinguals and monolinguals seems to provide a more plausible solution to studying the effect of multilingualism on human creativity. However, it is important to keep in mind that causal inferences in this design have low internal validity (Campbell & Stanley, 1963). The findings of bilingual creative advantages could be attributed to other factors not related to bilingualism per se. These include education, expertise, motivation, personality traits, personal experience and socioeconomic and sociocultural factors. The potential impact of these factors can be eliminated or at least reduced in a within-subject longitudinal design. In this paradigm, creative performance could be regularly assessed as a person proceeds through bilingual education. For example, a group of students can be administered a battery of creativity measures every semester as they advance through the full series of language courses. This design would help to determine whether a person's creative abilities improve with increase in his or her linguistic skills while controlling for other potentially confounding factors. Unfortunately, longitudinal studies are extremely rare in the field (Simonton, 2008).

Summary

The reviewed studies demonstrated a tendency of bilingual individuals to outperform their monolingual counterparts on the creativity tests. These findings were placed in a theoretical framework arguing that individuals' cross-linguistic and cross-cultural experiences may have impact on the structure and/or functioning of their memory. The modifications in bilingual memory may facilitate metalinguistic awareness and cognitive flexibility, which together promote bilinguals' creative functioning. However, it is important to note that the greater bilingual creative performance found in the empirical studies receives virtually no support either in historiometric research or in real-life observations. The methodological limitations discussed in this chapter hint to a possible explanation of the discrepancy in the laboratory findings and the observations outside the controlled settings. Due to methodological specificity of the research in the field, the empirical studies are likely to assess different aspects of creative performance than the ones resulting in eminent creativity. That is, multilingualism may encourage the use of certain cognitive processes in a more efficient way, which paves the way for more sophisticated cognitive processing. The latter may result in creative production in some individuals, but other factors in their development (such as intelligence, education, motivation and personal experience) may play a more dominant role. Therefore, it is plausible to refrain from pretentious statements about the effect of multilingualism on overall creativity. Rather, the emphasis should be placed on specific cognitive mechanisms facilitating creative performance, which may be encouraged by multilingual practice. This is the focus of the next chapter.

4 Multilingual Creative Cognition

Overview

The scientific enquiries into multilingualism and creativity delivered a sound argument concerning a relationship between these two human endeavors. The empirical studies demonstrated a predominant advantage to those individuals who speak more than one language over their monolingual counterparts in various creativity tests. However, the results of most of these studies were interpreted with caution for they revealed a number of methodological drawbacks. The author attempted to overcome these limitations and initiated a project, which investigated a relationship between multilingualism and creativity using improved scientific tactics. In a series of studies conducted in different geographic, linguistic and cultural locations, college students speaking various languages were compared with their respective monolingual counterparts. As a general tendency, bilinguals outperformed monolinguals on various tests of cognitive and creative abilities. However, the author went further and employed the within-group cross-sectional design to assess participants' cross-linguistic and cross-cultural experiences. This approach was used to investigate the effect of these factors on an individual's creative potential. In line with bilingual cognition research discussed in Chapter 2, the project revealed that language- and culture-related factors have an impact on the development of the specific cognitive mechanism underlying an individual's creative performance. One additional step was taken to elaborate on these findings and to identify those mechanisms that could benefit from one's multilingual and multicultural practices. This chapter presents a brief description of these studies and outlines possible cognitive mechanisms encouraged by an individual's cross-linguistics and cross-cultural experiences.

Participants and Procedures

The project includes studies conducted with three samples of college students in the United States and the Middle East. The US sample included Russian–English bilingual immigrants from the former Soviet Union to the United States and English monolingual residents of this country (Kharkhurin, 2008). The Iranian sample consisted of Farsi–English bilingual residents of the United Arab Emirates and Farsi monolinguals residing in Iran

(Kharkhurin, 2009). Finally, the data from the Emirati sample was collected from multilingual residents of the United Arab Emirates speaking various languages (Kharkhurin, 2011). In all these studies, participants' linguistic and cultural backgrounds were determined with a biographical questionnaire, their skills in respective languages were assessed by the picture-naming test (PNT), their creative performance was measured by the divergent thinking and structured imagination tests and their cognitive skills were assessed by the tests of fluid intelligence and selective attention. The description of these assessment tools is provided in the next section.

Assessment Techniques

Biographical questionnaire

The author developed the initial version of this questionnaire (Kharkhurin, 2005) that, among other issues, obtained data on participants' place of origin, age of migration, length of residence in different countries, languages they speak, age of acquisition of these languages, their assessment of linguistic skills in each of these languages, their language dominance, language use and language preference (see also Kharkhurin, 2008). The questionnaire has been made available to participants in their respective native language: English, Russian or Farsi.

In the later studies, this paper-based questionnaire was replaced by the internet-based multilingual and multicultural experience questionnaire (MMEQ). Appendix A presents a version of this questionnaire adopted for the book format. The functioning version of the questionnaire can be found at http://surveys.aus.edu/index.php?sid=87644. The MMEQ expands language-related questions to address participants' experience with more than two languages, their language preferences and use in various settings as well as the languages spoken by their parents. In addition, the questionnaire gathers information about participants' multicultural experience in terms of their cultural background, exposure, competence and preferences as well as the cultural background of their parents. An apparent advantage of the MMEQ constitutes an automatically generated file with all participants' responses that can be directly uploaded to statistical software for further processing.

Language proficiency assessment

Participants' linguistic skills were evaluated by a test of productive vocabulary, the PNT (Kharkhurin, 2005). Language proficiency was assessed by the accuracy of the participants' responses to 120 pictures of simple objects (see Appendix B), a technique similar to the Boston Naming Test (Kaplan *et al.*, 1983) and the one used by Lemmon and Goggin (1989). The pictures, randomly selected from those scaled by Rossion and Pourtois (2001), an improved version of Snodgrass and Vanderwart (1980), were arranged on four pages. The pages were then duplicated to make an eight-page booklet, with each picture appearing twice. Responses were recorded in booklets with numbered lines corresponding to the pictures. Each participant was given 4 minutes to label in one language as many as possible of the 60 pictures on the first 2 pages and was given additional 4 minutes to do the same task in the other language for the 60 pictures on the second 2 pages. The procedure was then repeated with the language order reversed. To prevent the emergence of a language priming effect, the order of languages was counterbalanced across participants. Each response was scored either 1 or 0, so that the maximum number of points for picture naming in either language was 120. A list of appropriate labels in English, Russian and Farsi was generated for each picture by two independent native speakers for each language. If the participant's label matched the corresponding item on the list, they scored 1 point; otherwise, 0 point. Spelling errors in the participants' responses were disregarded.

Later studies employed an internet-based version of this test (iPNT; Kharkhurin, 2012). This test can be administered online without involvement of any additional resources. The same 120 pictures as in the paper version are used in the iPNT. They are arranged in four groups each of which appears on a separate webpage; each picture is accompanied by a 50 character space provided for an answer. The presentation order of the pictures within each group is randomized. Participants are given 2 minutes to label as many as possible of the 30 pictures on each page. The timer in the top left corner of the page indicates the elapsed time. After the time is elapsed, an 'out of time' message appears on the screen and next page is loaded automatically. The iPNT score is calculated within the testing environment and test users are provided with a result immediately upon completion of the test. They also have an option to download a file with all responses that can be subsequently uploaded to statistical software for further processing. To utilize an automatic rating of the iPNT, only those responses that perfectly matched corresponding items from a list of correct responses were scored a point. To ensure convergent validity of this scoring, four rating strategies were applied to participants' responses: primary strict, primary lenient, secondary strict and secondary lenient. They were developed as the following.

A list of appropriate labels was generated for each picture. A list of primary labels was adopted from Snodgrass and Vanderwart (1980). The average name agreement coefficient[1] for these labels was 0.50 with 94.79% of participants giving the primary label, which according to Snodgrass and Vanderwart, suggests high name agreement for these labels. The word frequency for the primary list ranged from 1 to 431 (M = 35.01, SD = 70.40) per million according to Kučera and Francis (1967) and from 0.12 to 483.06 (M = 33.26, SD = 68.44) per million according to Brysbaert and New (2009). A list of secondary labels was formed based on the synonyms for the primary lables obtained by Snodgrass and Vanderwart. The word frequency for both primary and secondary lists ranged from 0.12 to 509.37 (M = 35.75, SD = 76.60) per milion according to Brysbaert and New. If the participants' response matched the corresponding item on the list, they scored 1 point; otherwise, 0 point. Two sets of rating strategies were used: the *primary* rating gave a point only if the label from a primary list was used; the *secondary* rating gave a point if the label from either primary or secondary list was used; the *strict* rating gave a point if the produced label was spelled correctly; the *lenient* rating disregarded the spelling errors. Thus, each response was scored according to four rating strategies: primary strict, primary lenient, secondary strict and secondary lenient. All four rating strategies obtained nearly perfectly correlated scores (r ranging from 0.95 to 1.00, p < 0.001), which justifies the iPNT rating based on the primary list of labels and strict spelling. According to this rating schema, only those responses that perfectly match correct labels score a point. Therefore, a simple algorithm was implemented in a computer that processes the responses and automatically provides a language proficiency score.

An important advantage of this test is its suitability for any language. The iPNT can be used in any language providing a list of correct labels in that language. The test interface prompts to select which language is tested. Its current version includes English and Russian and is available at http://www.harhur.com/research/ipnt.html.

Divergent thinking assessment

Divergent thinking abilities were assessed using the Abbreviated Torrance Test for Adults (Goff & Torrance, 2002). The standard ATTA has three paper and pencil activities preceded by a written instruction that explains general guidelines and encourages participants to use their imagination and thinking abilities. In Activity 1, participants are asked to suppose that they could walk on air or fly, and then to identify the troubles that they might encounter. This activity provides verbal fluency and originality scores. A Russian–English bilingual college student who resided in the United States provided the following response to this activity: 'People can cross borders without documents and visas.' This response reflects his migrant experience, which presumably refers to hardship that this person had to go through to immigrate to the United States. In Activity 2, participants are presented with two incomplete figures and are asked to draw pictures with these figures and to attempt to make these pictures as unusual as possible. This activity provides figural fluency, originality and elaboration scores. Figure 4.1a provides a response of another Russian–English bilingual college student residing in the United States. The original incomplete figures are depicted with bold lines and the responses produced by the participant are depicted with fine lines. The drawing on the left presents a culture-specific response: a female figure next to the Santa Claus is his granddaughter Snow Maiden, a necessary attribute of the New Year festivity in Russian folkloric tradition. Note that the picture is entitled not as a Christmas tree, but as a New Year tree, which also reflects the tradition in the former Soviet Union where the religious festivity of Christmas has been replaced by the celebration of the New Year Eve. In Activity 3, the participants are presented with a group of nine triangles arranged in a 3 × 3 matrix and are asked to draw as many pictures or objects as they could using those triangles. This activity provides figural fluency, originality, elaboration and flexibility scores. Figure 4.1b shows a response of another Russian–English bilingual college student residing in the United States, in which all nine triangles are combined in a single picture.

The standard ATTA assessment consists of four divergent thinking traits: fluency, flexibility, elaboration and originality. Fluency measures the ability to produce quantities of ideas, which were relevant to the task instructions. The sum of fluency scores in all three activities provides a fluency raw score. Flexibility measures the ability to process information or objects in different ways, given the same stimulus. A flexibility raw score is obtained from Activity 3. Elaboration measures the ability to embellish ideas with details. The sum of the elaboration scores in Activities 2 and 3 provides an elaboration raw score. Finally, originality measures the ability to produce uncommon ideas, or ideas that are totally new or unique. The sum of originality scores in all three activities provides an originality raw score. The raw scores for fluency, flexibility, elaboration and originality obtained in the test are subsequently transformed into scaled norm-referenced scores by the recommended procedure (Goff & Torrance, 2002) which takes age-related norms into account. The ATTA manual reports the Kuder–Richardson (KR21) reliability coefficient for the total raw score for the four traits measured by the ATTA as 0.84.

A factor analysis of four ATTA norm-referenced scores performed with data obtained in distinct geographic locations with different sociocultural samples (Kharkhurin, 2008, 2009, 2011; Kharkhurin & Samadpour Motalleebi, 2008) revealed that they can be grouped together as two types of creative functioning: fluency, flexibility and elaboration traits seem to represent the

(a)

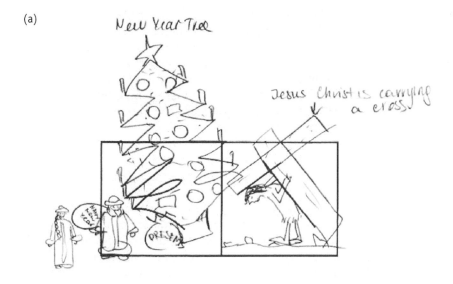

(b)

Figure 4.1 Sample responses to the ATTA activities 2 (a) and 3 (b). The original incomplete figures are depicted with bold lines and the responses produced by the participants are depicted with fine lines

ability to generate and to elaborate on various, often unrelated, ideas, while the originality trait is likely to represent the ability to extract novel and unique ideas. The first type is referred to as *generative* capacity; it addresses the ability to activate a multitude of unrelated concepts and work through the concepts already activated. The second type is referred to as *innovative* capacity; it accounts for the ability to produce original and useful ideas. The distinctions and parallels of these two types of creative functioning and other creativity traits are discussed in Chapter 6.

In addition, a verbal criterion-referenced creativity indicators score is computed as a sum of the five verbal responses in Activity 1 (e.g. humor and conceptual incongruity, future orientation and provocative questions); and a figural criterion-referenced creativity indicators score is computed as a sum of 10 figural responses in Activities 2 and 3 (e.g. resistance to premature closure, internal visual perspective and richness and colorfulness of imagery). Each of these 15 responses is given a rating of 0 if the indicator does not occur, 1 if the indicator appears once or 2 if the indicator appears more than once. Then, a creativity index is computed as a sum of four norm-referenced and two criterion-referenced creativity indicator scores. The index represents a composite measure of overall creativity. For each sample, two independent raters, highly proficient in the respective languages, assessed participants' divergent thinking abilities using the standard ATTA assessment procedure (Goff & Torrance, 2002).

Structured imagination assessment

Structured imagination was assessed using a modified version of the Invented Alien Creatures task (IAC, Kozbelt & Durmysheva, 2007; cf. Ward, 1994). It requires imagining, drawing and describing a creature living on a planet very different from Earth. Participants were encouraged to be as imaginative and creative as possible and not to worry about how well or poorly they drew. They had 12 minutes to complete the task.

Two independent raters used an invariant coding system (Kozbelt & Durmysheva, 2007) to categorize each drawing on three invariants: bilateral symmetry, two eyes, and four limbs (see discussion in Chapter 1). The chosen invariants were similar to the ones extracted in Ward's (1994) original study, in which he found that 'the majority of imagined creatures were structured by properties that are typical of animals on earth: bilateral symmetry, sensory receptors, and appendages' (Ward: 1). Each invariant had five categories each of which was assigned a value indicated in parentheses. For bilateral symmetry, the categories were clearly bilaterally symmetric (0), bilaterally symmetric if the creature was rotated (0), superficially violating bilateral symmetry (e.g.

an extra limb on one side; 1), clearly not bilaterally symmetric (2) and unclear (0). For eyes and limbs, the categories were clearly following the invariant (two eyes or four limbs; 0), drawing more features than the invariant (more than two eyes or four limbs; 2), drawing fewer features (one eye or one to three limbs; 2), drawing no relevant features (1) and unclear (0). So, each drawing received an invariant value ranging from 0 (not violated) to 2 (clearly violated). The total *invariants violation* score was calculated as a sum of three invariant scores averaged across both raters. A higher invariants violation score indicated more violation of the standard invariants in the drawings. Figure 4.2 presents responses of two Iranian college students, which illustrate the difference between high and low invariant violations. The 'hell boy' in Figure 4.2a resembles terrestrial creature and preserves all three invariants; therefore, it received low invariant violation score. In contrast, the creature in Figure 4.2b violates all three invariants: it is not bilaterally symmetric, it has only one eye and it has only three limbs. Therefore, this response received high invariant violation score.

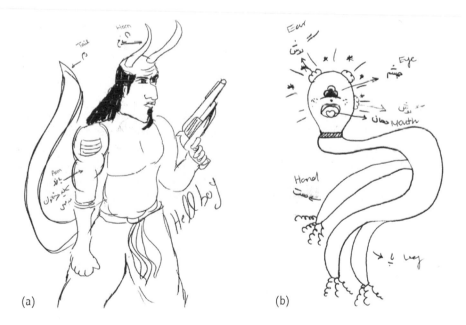

(a)   (b)

Figure 4.2 Sample responses to the IAC task that received low (a) and high (b) invariant violation scores, respectively

Selective attention assessment

One of the most widely used tests, which implicates selective attention and response inhibition, is the Stroop task (Stroop, 1935). This test exploits the conflict between an automatic behavior (i.e. reading) and a decision rule that requires this behavior to be inhibited. This task taps into the ability to inhibit inappropriate responses and resist interference. To evaluate bilinguals' selective attention, the present project used a version of the standard Stroop color-naming task similar to Bialystok et al. (2008a). The stimuli were the color names *red, green* and *blue*, printed in capital letters in 100-point Arial font, and presented in the center of the screen. Each trial began with a fixation cross presented for 550 ms immediately followed by the stimulus. Participants responded into a voice key, and their response onset time was recorded by the E-Prime 2.0 software. The interval between the trials was 200 ms. The response accuracy was determined at the end of the session by playing the E-Prime-generated sound files against a checklist of correct responses.

Four conditions were presented in random order. In three color-naming conditions, the task was to name the font color, and in the word-reading condition, the task was to read the word. The first condition was a color-naming control, in which an XXXX string was presented in one of the target colors. The second condition was the word-reading control, in which the target color word was presented in black font. The third was a congruent color-naming condition, in which the target color word was presented in the same font color. Finally, the incongruent Stroop color-naming condition presented the color names in conflicting font colors. The experiment included 8 blocks of 24 trials each, consisting of 2 blocks for each of the 4 conditions. The order of blocks presenting each condition was randomized across participants.

Following Bialystok and her colleagues' (2008a) analysis, the author introduced three variables describing the processes assessed by the Stroop test (Kharkhurin, 2011). The *Stroop* effect was calculated as the percentage increase in response time from congruent to incongruent trials. This effect shows the rate of resistance to the interference of the automatic behavior (i.e. reading) during decision making (i.e. color naming); the greater Stroop effect value indicated lower resistance to the interference. Furthermore, the Stroop effect was assumed to arise from two processes working in opposite directions. The assessment of these processes provided a more detailed description of the attentional control: facilitation taps into ability to focus on the word when it is helpful (congruent condition), and inhibition taps into ability to ignore the word when it is misleading (incongruent condition). Therefore, the *facilitation* effect was calculated as the percentage decrease in response time from the control color-naming condition to the congruent condition. This effect shows the rate of the facilitation associated with the word printed in its own color relative to the neutral color-naming condition when no word is present; the greater effect value indicated more facilitation. The *inhibition* effect was calculated as an inverted percentage increase in response time from the control color-naming condition to the incongruent condition. This effect shows the rate of inhibition associated with the word printed in another color relative to the neutral color-naming condition; the greater effect value indicated stronger inhibition. Subsequently, all effects were transformed into standardized scores. The Stroop effect revealed a negative correlation with the inhibition effect and a positive correlation with the facilitation effect.

Fluid intelligence assessment

Participants' fluid intelligence was assessed by the standard Culture Fair Intelligence Test (Cattell, 1973). The employed Scale 3 Form A of the CFIT contains four subtests involving different perceptual tasks, so that the composite intelligence measure does not rely on a single skill. Each subtest was preceded by the standard instructions orally presented by the experimenter and followed by examples to ensure participants' understanding of the task requirements. In the Series subtest, participants were presented with incomplete progressive series. Their task was to select, from among the choices provided, figure which best continues the series. In the Classification subtest, participants were presented with five figures, among which they had to correctly identify two figures, which are in some way different from the other three. In the Matrices subtest, the task was to correctly complete the design of a matrix presented at the left of each row. The last, Conditions subtest, required participants to select from the five choices provided the one which duplicates the conditions given in the far left box.

The raw scores obtained from all four subtests were summarized and subsequently transformed into a normalized fluid intelligence score by the recommended procedure (Cattell, 1973) which took age-related norms into account. The CFIT manual reports the reliability coefficients for consistency over items as 0.74, and test–retest consistency as 0.69. It also reports the concept validity as 0.85, and concrete validity calculated as a direct correlation with other tests of intelligence as 0.66. In addition, the manual reports a number of studies demonstrating insignificant effects of sociocultural environment on test scores.

The Findings of the Project

The first study of the project was conducted in Brooklyn College (USA). Russian–English bilingual college students demonstrated greater generative capacity by scoring higher than their English monolingual counterparts on the ATTA measures of fluency, flexibility and elaboration (Kharkhurin, 2008). The comparison of these samples on the ATTA verbal and nonverbal creativity indicators demonstrated a bilingual advantage in nonverbal creativity and a monolingual advantage in verbal creativity (Kharkhurin, 2010a). This last finding is discussed later in terms of domain specificity of bilingual creative thinking. Bilinguals' greater generative capacity was found to relate to their proficiency in two languages, the age of acquisition of these languages and the length of exposure to the new cultural settings that accompanies the acquisition of a new language. This bilingual advantage was explained by the efficient LMCA. As follows from the discussion in this section, this mechanism produces a large pattern of activation over unrelated conceptual representations. It could encourage bilinguals to simultaneously process a large number of unrelated concepts from different categories. As previously explained, generative capacity addresses the ability to activate a multitude of unrelated concepts and work through the concepts already activated. Thus, the LMCA facilitates processes underlying generative capacity. Moreover, the discussion of the results of this study proposed that the cognitive processes underlying bilinguals' greater generative capacity could assist them in overcoming the limitations of structured imagination. Recall from Chapter 1 that one's imagination tends to be limited by a set of standard properties of a category. When participants were asked to draw an alien creature, they tended to produce a picture that resembled a terrestrial creature such as the one in Figure 4.2a. The simultaneous activation of unrelated concepts could result in considering a mental set formed by the conceptual representations from different categories. This mental set extends beyond the standard category boundaries, which in turn may facilitate generation of more uncommon solutions. That is, individuals with greater generative capacity can easier avoid common solutions to a problem, which is obviously beneficial to their creative thinking.

The follow-up study with Farsi–English bilinguals and Farsi monolinguals (Kharkhurin, 2009) investigated these propositions. It was based on the following premises: if (1) greater generative capacity may result in greater invariant violation and (2) bilinguals reveal superior generative capacity, then (3) bilinguals should violate invariants more often than monolinguals. It was found that the first condition was not satisfied: there was no relation between invariant violation (assessed by the IAC task) and generative capacity either in the whole sample or in the separate language groups. The second condition was also not satisfied as bilingual generative capacity was not significantly different from the monolingual one; rather bilinguals demonstrated greater innovative capacity compared to their monolingual counterparts. Although both conditions were not satisfied, the consequent premise was met: bilinguals showed a tendency to violate invariants more often than monolinguals. These findings indicate an apparent contradiction between the US and Iranian samples. The former revealed greater generative but not innovative capacity in bilinguals, whereas the latter revealed the opposite pattern. This contradiction raised important questions, which brought the project to a discovery of an additional cognitive mechanism underlying bilingual creative potential.

Why did bilinguals reveal a greater ability to violate the standard set of characteristics of a category if it is not due to their greater generative capacity? A possible answer to this question was inferred from two additional findings of Iranian study (Kharkhurin, 2009). First, bilinguals demonstrated better fluid intelligence than monolinguals. Second, participants' performance on the CFIT was found to relate to their ability to violate invariants, and this relation was more evident in the bilingual group. These findings suggest that bilinguals' tendency to more readily violate invariants may be facilitated by the cognitive processes underlying their fluid intelligence. To shed light on the nature of these processes, two subsequent questions need to be answered.

First, why did bilinguals score higher than monolinguals on the CFIT? A closer look into the nature of the intelligence test used in that study provides a possible answer to this question. As discussed in Chapter 1, the CFIT assesses the ability to focus attention on the common features of the figures in the series and to extract the correct relationships between these features. Individuals with greater ability to focus on relevant information in the series' elements should be more efficient at extracting the regulations and therefore should show greater test performance. Therefore, selective attention could be the cognitive function underlying fluid intelligence. At the same time, Chapter 2 presents an argument that selective attention is enhanced by bilingualism. Thus, bilinguals' advanced mechanisms of selective attention could explain their greater performance on intelligence test in Iranian study.

Second, how did bilinguals' ability to focus attention on the relevant aspects of a problem facilitate their capacity to violate the standard set of characteristics of a category? The answer to this question is rather speculative as it considers one of the possible strategies participants could employ to solve the problem of the IAC test. The task was to draw, as imaginatively and creatively as possible, an alien creature living on a planet very different from

Earth. Suppose that participants mentally select a category of a creature living on Earth, extract its typical characteristics and modify them in order to draw a creature that differs from a prototype. If this process is conscious, it requires the focus of attention on the characteristics of a category and the ability to manipulate them. The mere instruction to be 'as creative as possible' could encourage participants to employ a conscious, attention-demanding strategy. Studies using a creature invention task support this idea by providing evidence that this kind of instruction boosts creativity (e.g. Niu & Sternberg, 2001). Thus, selective attention mechanisms could enhance bilinguals' ability to violate a standard set of category properties, which could have led to their greater performance on the test of structured imagination in Kharkhurin's (2009) study. The fact that the correlation between the rate of invariant violation and the CFIT score was found only in a bilingual group suggests that bilinguals and monolinguals could use these cognitive mechanisms differently. Moreover, the efficient selective attention could also support creative problem solving at the stage where a conscious attention demanding process assists in narrowing a multitude of possible alternatives down to a single original solution; that is, it may have also facilitated bilinguals' greater innovative capacity found in that study.

To test these assumptions, the author hypothesized that the cognitive mechanisms of selective attention underlie performance on both creativity and intelligence tasks, and that these processes are facilitated by multilingualism. The study conducted with multilingual college students in the United Arab Emirates (Kharkhurin, 2011) revealed an advantage of more linguistically proficient individuals on both creative and cognitive tasks. Specifically, participants with high proficiency in English revealed greater innovative capacity and greater ability to violate invariants in creative problem solving. Furthermore, highly proficient individuals were found to moderately outperform their less proficient counterparts on the fluid intelligence. However, this effect turned out to be mediated by selective attention. Selective attention (but not fluid intelligence) was also found to have a moderate effect on the difference in creative performance of the language proficiency groups. The intrusive role of selective attention in multilingual intelligence and creativity could be attributed to a variation in its functioning in two language proficiency groups. Participants with different levels of linguistic skills seemed to utilize the inhibition and facilitation mechanisms of selective attention differently. The highly proficient participants showed greater inhibition effect, whereas the moderately proficient bilinguals showed greater facilitation effect (these effects are described in the previous section). The two groups also revealed different relationships between creative and cognitive measures. In the high-proficiency group, the inhibition mechanism was found to contribute to the innovative capacity, whereas the facilitation mechanism was found to contribute to the generative capacity. In the moderate proficiency group, the generative capacity was found to stipulate the ability to violate invariants.

Altogether, the project identified three cognitive mechanisms that can be related to three aspects of an individual's creative potential. The LMCA and the facilitation of relevant information relate to generative capacity, and the inhibition of irrelevant information relates to both the innovative capacity and the violation of structured imagination. Multilinguals with different levels of linguistic skills utilize these mechanisms differently and therefore employ different strategies in creative problem solving. Subsequent discussion elaborates on these mechanisms in the context of multilingual creative cognition.

The Cognitive Mechanisms Underlying Multilingual Creative Potential

Bilingual advanced generative capacity was explained by the efficient LMCA (Kharkhurin, 2008). The LMCA is based on the previously discussed assumptions that translation equivalents activate each other through shared conceptual representations, and some of these representations are not identical. Due to this mechanism, distant concepts can be activated through shared lexical units. Recall the distributed lexical/conceptual feature model discussed in Chapter 2. The activation can take place on two levels of processing: the lexical-semantic (lemma) level, on which conceptual representations sharing the same lemmas can be activated (e.g. the figurative meaning of the word 'cat' as in 'cat burglar' in English, or the figurative meaning of the word '*die Katze*' as in '*die Katze im Sack kaufen,*' to buy a pig in a poke, in German), and the lexical features level, on which conceptual representations sharing the same word forms can be activated (e.g. 'marker' in English and '*marka*' /stamp/ in Russian).

The lemma-mediated concept activation is believed to work as follows. A word in L1 activates corresponding lemmas in the L1 lexicon, which in turn, activate the corresponding conceptual features. The conceptual features send partial activation back to the L2 lexicon, which activates the corresponding L2 lemmas. These lemmas, once activated, may send partial activation to the conceptual features representing concepts that share this lemma with the target word. In the cat/*die Katze* example, the presentation of the English word 'cat' to English–German bilingual activates a lemma {cat} in the English lexicon (see Figure 4.3a). This lemma in turn sends activation to conceptual features that represent the literal meaning of a cat; in addition, it may send a partial activation to the conceptual representation of the alternative meaning of the lemma {cat} such as the one in the 'cat burglar.' Thus, the conceptual representation of a BURGLAR is activated. At the same time, the conceptual representation of a CAT sends partial activation back to the lemmas level in the German lexicon, thereby activating the lemma *{die Katze}*. This lemma, once activated, may in turn send partial activation to the conceptual representation of the additional meaning of the lemmas *{die Katze}* such as

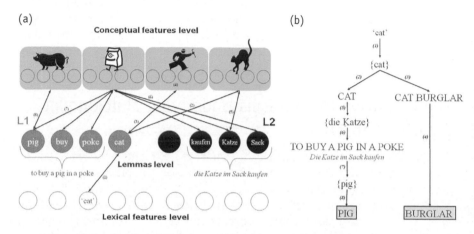

Figure 4.3 Illustration of a lemma-mediated spreading activation underlying the Language–Mediated Concept Activation. Schematic representation of (a) a fragment of bilingual memory structure and (b) the information flow in bilingual memory. The bilingual memory consists of the distributed lexical features level, language-specific lemmas level and distributed conceptual features level. The presentation of the English word 'cat' activates a lemma {cat} in English lexicon (1). This lemma, in turn, activates conceptual features that represent the literal meaning of a cat (2) as well as the conceptual representation of the additional meaning of the lemma {cat} such as the one in the 'cat burglar' (3). Thereby the conceptual representation of BURGLAR is activated (4). At the same time, the conceptual representation of a cat sends partial activation back to the lemma level in German lexicon thereby activating a lemma {die Katze} (5). This lemma sends partial activation to the conceptual representation of the additional meaning of the lemma {die Katze} such as the one in 'die Katze im Sack kaufen' (6). Accordingly, the latter sends partial activation back to the lemma level in English lexicon thereby activating a set of lemmas corresponding to the idiom 'to buy a pig in a poke.' Therefore, among the others, a lemma {pig} is activated (7) and, in turn, triggers its corresponding conceptual features (8). Thus, the LMCA results in a simultaneous activation of two unrelated conceptual representations of a pig and a burglar.

the one in *'die Katze im Sack kaufen.'* Accordingly, the latter may send partial activation back to the lemma level in the English lexicon, thereby activating a set of lemmas corresponding to the idiom 'to buy a pig in a poke,' an English translation equivalent to the German expression. Therefore, among the others, the lemmas {pig} is activated and, in turn, triggers its corresponding conceptual features. As a result, a large pattern of conceptual representations is activated that allows simultaneous exploration of unrelated concepts (such as BURGLAR and PIG) from distant categories (such as 'crime' and 'animal'). Figure 4.3b presents an activation flow between lemms and conceptual features level. It is important to note, however, that this algorithm is rather speculative and requires empirical investigation.

In addition, the lemma-mediated concept activation is facilitated by lexical features level activation. Words that share the same word forms (e.g. orthographic, phonological) may activate each other in the same way as the words with similar lexical properties activate each other in the monolingual memory (e.g. Allopenna *et al.*, 1998). This assumption was inspired by the findings of eye-tracking studies showing that cross-linguistic homophones tend to activate each other in bilingual memory. Marian and Spivey (2003) recorded the eye movements of Russian–English bilinguals while giving them instructions in target language (e.g. *'Podnimi marku'* /Pick up the stamp/). The recording showed that while participants' eyes focused on the stamp, they also looked briefly at the objects with a phonologically similar name in nontarget language (e.g. a marker, *flomaster* in Russian). Similar results were obtained in research on cross-linguistic orthographic priming with French–English bilinguals (Bijeljac-Babic *et al.*, 1997). In the lexical decision task, orthographically related words in French and English tended to inhibit each other, indicating that printed strings of letters can simultaneously activate lexical representations in each of the bilinguals' languages. Thus, semantically unrelated words in bilingual lexicons can activate each other if they share similar lexical features. A set of distributed lexical features shared by both lexicons can send the activation to the lemmas in different languages, thereby initiating the lemma-mediated concept activation. For example, the oral presentation of the English word 'marker' to English–Russian bilinguals may activate a set of phonological features that are present in both 'marker' and *'marka.'* These features therefore activate the lemma {marker} in the English lexicon and the lemma {stamp} in the Russian lexicon. These lemmas in turn activate the conceptual representations of the marker and the stamp, which appear to be unrelated in a monolingual lexicon.

The proposed LMCA mechanism seems to offer a plausible explanation for the spreading activation in bilingual memory that promotes generative capacity. Activation flow on the conceptual features level mediated by the lemmas and lexical features levels establishes the links between various, often unrelated, concepts. In this manner, the LMCA encourages conceptual representations from distant categories to be activated simultaneously. This, in turn, may enhance generative capacity in more advanced bilinguals to a greater extent than in their less advanced and monolingual counterparts. The factors of multilingual development that could increase the efficiency of the LMCA are discussed in the next chapter.

In addition to the efficient LMCA, facilitation mechanism of selective attention seems to encourage multilingual generative capacity. The author found a relationship between the facilitation mechanism and the generative capacity in participants with moderate proficiency in their L2 (Kharkhurin, 2011). As discussed earlier, the generative capacity refers to the ability to activate a multitude of unrelated concepts and work through the concepts already activated. It plays an important role during the preparation stage of the creative process when a large pool of possible solutions is generated. It is essential to keep active all possible solutions to a problem during this stage. The facilitation mechanism of selective attention keeps relevant information in focus. According to the discussion in Chapter 2, this mechanism is readily employed by less advanced L2 learners to maintain the link between both languages. Although, it was argued that, with progress in L2 acquisition, the role of the facilitation mechanism decreases, one can still assume that its function appears to be essential in multilingual language processing. Thus, multilinguals (especially those with moderate language proficiency) may employ the facilitation mechanism of selective attention to enhance the activation of a larger number of possible solutions to a problem.

The same study revealed that bilingual innovative capacity was predicted by the inhibition effect of selective attention (Kharkhurin, 2011). The innovative capacity accounts for the ability to extract innovative and useful ideas from the pool of already generated ones. This capacity is useful during the later stage of the creative process when the generated ideas should be evaluated and implemented. It is prudent to suppress irrelevant and/or nonoptimal solutions to a creative problem during this stage. The inhibition mechanism of selective attention (or interference suppression) ignores misleading information. According to the discussion in Chapter 2, more advanced L2 learners readily employ the inhibition mechanism to suppress the interference of one language during the processing of the other. Therefore, multilinguals with high language skills may utilize the inhibition mechanism of selective attention to enhance the extraction of innovative and useful ideas by suppressing the interference of the ideas that fail to satisfy task requirements.

It was also demonstrated that inhibition mechanism of selective attention had a moderate effect on the greater ability of more advanced bilinguals to violate the invariants in the test of structured imagination (Kharkhurin, 2011). How does bilinguals' interference suppression enhance their capacity to violate a standard set of category properties? The answer to this question is rooted in a proposed earlier speculative strategy that participants could have employed to solve the IAC problem. According to this proposition, they could mentally manipulate typical features of a category of a terrestrial creature to produce an atypical response. Highly proficient bilinguals, who according to the previous discussion benefit from greater interference suppression, could be more efficient in extracting relevant characteristics of a category. As a result, these individuals construct a well-organized set of category features relevant to the problem in question. These features can be easily manipulated to meet the task requirements; in this case it implies a violation of the category boundaries. Thus, highly proficient individuals could demonstrate greater violation of the invariants compared to their less proficient counterparts.

In sum, a relatively consistent pattern of multilingual creative problem-solving strategies can be traced down from the findings of this project. A specific architecture of multilingual memory provides an opportunity for the language-mediated concept activation. This mechanism facilitates the activation flow among unrelated conceptual representations in the multilingual brain to a greater extent than in monolingual one. More intense information flow could boost multilingual generative capacity. As discussed in the next chapter, various factors in multilingual development may stipulate the lexical–conceptual structure of multilingual memory. Therefore, various types of multilinguals may employ this mechanism with different efficiency, which could be manifested in diversity of their performances.

In addition, individuals with different levels of language proficiency seem to employ different strategies of creative problem solving based on what cognitive mechanisms they utilize. Highly proficient multilinguals are likely to have well-developed inhibition mechanisms of selective attention. On the one side, the suppression of rudimentary solutions in creative problem solving may facilitate the extraction of an original solution (innovative capacity). On the other side, the inhibition of typical characteristics of a category may result in focusing attention on the unconventional, atypical solutions to creative problems (nonstructured imagination). Multilinguals with moderate language proficiency are likely to employ facilitation mechanisms of selective attention more readily. This mechanism may encourage greater activation of unrelated concepts (generative capacity), which spreads the activation to the conceptual representations lying beyond a standard set of category properties. This allows multilinguals to simultaneously consider a large number of properties from different categories and therefore overcome the limitations of structured imagination. As a result, original solutions to creative problems can be harvested. Which of these problem-solving strategies is more successful? As the results of Kharkhurin's (2011) study demonstrate, linguistically advanced bilinguals outperformed their moderately proficient counterparts on both creativity measures, and therefore, the strategy inspired by more developed interference suppression seems to be more efficient.

Finally, the finding that the generative capacity contributes to the violation of standard invariants only in bilinguals with moderate language proficiency (Kharkhurin, 2011) shed some light on the discrepancy found in the previous study (Kharkhurin, 2009). As previously stated, the hypothesis that the generative capacity stipulates the invariants violation did not obtain any empirical support. Rather, it was found that the ability to violate the standard invariants – which was more evident in bilinguals – was not related to their generative capacity. As Kharkhurin's (2011) study revealed, the generative capacity predicted the violation of the invariants only in bilingual individuals with moderate linguistic skills. Those with more advanced language abilities could not benefit from the generative capacity possibly due to the restrictions imposed by the inhibition mechanism on the spreading activation in their conceptual network. Since Kharkhurin's (2009) study did not distinguish between bilinguals with different levels of language proficiency, the effect of the generative capacity may have been masked.

Domain Specificity of Multilingual Creative Performance

Chapter 2 reviewed empirical evidence that bilingualism tends to hamper verbal and to facilitate nonverbal cognitive performance. Does this tendency extrapolate to bilingual creative performance? That is, if bilinguals suffer from a limited access to their languages, their performance on verbal creativity tasks should also be poorer than for monolinguals. At the same time, if they benefit from the functioning of certain mechanisms that facilitate their performance on nonverbal cognitive tasks, their performance on the nonverbal creativity tasks should also be better.

The aforementioned studies (Gollan et al., 2002; Rosselli et al., 2000) employing a verbal fluency task (generation of as many exemplars of a given category as possible) hint to the possibility that divergent thinking performance in the verbal domain is poorer in bilinguals than in monolinguals. These studies provide evidence that monolinguals obtained greater verbal fluency scores than bilinguals. Recall that fluency constitutes an important characteristic of divergent thinking and bilinguals' poorer performance on this task suggests the limitations in their verbal creative abilities. However, the studies reviewed by Ricciardelli (1992b) reported highly mixed results with respect to bilinguals' and monolinguals' performance on verbal and nonverbal divergent thinking tests. Specifically, 2 studies demonstrated monolinguals' superiority on nonverbal divergent thinking tasks, 14 bilinguals' superiority on verbal and 12 on nonverbal divergent thinking tasks, and 1 study showed no performance differences. These studies tend to show greater creative abilities of bilinguals in both verbal and nonverbal domains and therefore contradict the findings in noncreative cognition domains. A possible explanation for this discrepancy could be grounded in the nature of the processes assessed in the studies employing verbal and nonverbal fluency tasks and those reviewed by Ricciardelli. The fluency tasks seem to assess an individual's conscious processes, whereas divergent thinking tasks are likely to assess unconscious processes. Moreover, most of the studies reported by Ricciardelli were conducted with children and suffered from the lack of control over various factors in bilingual development (see discussion in the previous chapter).

The author investigated the influence of bilingualism on the ATTA verbal and nonverbal criterion-referenced creativity indicators in college students, providing a careful control over their linguistic skills and their language dominance (Kharkhurin, 2010a). The results obtained from the creativity test revealed a consistent pattern of performance differences between language groups. Bilinguals performed better on nonverbal creativity, whereas monolinguals showed better performance in verbal creativity. These results are consistent with the studies in language production showing monolingual advantages in the fluency tasks. For example, Bialystok et al. (2008a) showed monolingual advantages on both letter (produce as many words as possible that started with a given letter in 1 minute) and category (name as many animals as possible in 1 minute) fluency tasks. These tasks tap into the ability to rapidly produce a large number of solutions to a problem, which is considered an important trait of divergent thinking (Guilford, 1967). Monolinguals' creative performance in the verbal domain may benefit from their greater linguistic skills. Creative problem solving that takes place in the linguistic context might be enriched by the greater ability to manipulate the linguistic units. On the other hand, as discussed earlier, bilinguals' limited linguistic skills may cause a deficiency in their creative problem solving if a task is framed in a verbal context (Bialystok, 2005).

At the same time, as the results of the author's study (Kharkhurin, 2010a) show, when the problem was presented in a nonverbal context, bilinguals demonstrated greater creative performance. Specifically, they outperformed their monolingual counterparts on an important indicator of creativity such as resistance to premature closure. Goff and Torrance (2002: 16) specify this trait as follows: 'The creative person is able to keep open and delay closure long enough to make the mental leap that makes possible original ideas. Less creative persons tend to leap to conclusions prematurely.' This may arise from routine ambiguity inherent to multilingual practice, in which the same basic idea may have different nuances in different languages (Lubart, 1999). This tolerance for ambiguity, in turn, may facilitate their ability to keep a pool of possible solutions open long enough to generate a creative idea. On the other hand, an argument presented in the next chapter claims that inability to evaluate multiple solutions simultaneously and a tendency to leap to the most obvious solution hampers an individual's creative performance (Kharkhurin & Samadpour Motalleebi, 2008).

A remarkable difference in the performance of bilinguals and monolinguals was obtained on the richness and colorfulness of imagery. Monolinguals scored higher on this indicator in the verbal domain, whereas bilinguals obtained higher scores in the nonverbal domain. This trait is considered an important indicator of creativity (Goff & Torrance, 2002), with richness addressing variety, vividness, liveliness and intensity of imagery, and colorfulness addressing the appeal to the senses of touch, smell and sight. Again, a monolingual advantage on the verbal indicator could result from a larger lexicon available to express possible solutions to a problem. However, when the constraints of the linguistic context were removed, bilinguals obtained better results. A speculative explanation of this finding is rooted in bilinguals' experience with different linguistic and cultural frameworks. As discussed in Chapter 3, this experience allows them to perceive the world through the amalgam of different conceptual prisms and view events with a wider range of enriched experiences. In turn, nonstandard perspectives may promote novel and creative ways of problem solving.

In this manner, the answer to the question about the domain specificity of multilingual creative potential can be answered positively. Speaking more than one language increases creativity in the nonverbal domain and decreases it in the verbal one. However, since the reviewed study is just an initiation into the realm of domain specificity of multilingual creative potential, no definite conclusion can be made and further research is required to provide more elaborate control of the multilingual and multicultural factors in an individual's development. The next chapter sketches initial steps in elaborating on these factors.

Summary

The project described in this chapter constitutes a series of studies conducted by the author in different geographic, linguistic and cultural locations. Multilingual college students speaking various languages were found to outperform their respective monolingual counterparts on various tests of cognitive and creative abilities. Furthermore, the project revealed that multilingual practice may have an impact on the development of the specific cognitive mechanism underlying an individual's creative performance. Moreover, these mechanisms seem to facilitate the performance of multilingual individuals on the nonverbal creativity tasks.

The language-mediated concept activation that takes place due to specific organization of multilingual memory facilitates the activation flow among unrelated conceptual representations and thereby could boost multilingual generative capacity. The inhibition of irrelevant information that is more efficient in individuals with great command of their languages seems to facilitate the extraction of an original solution and assist in focusing attention on the unconventional, atypical solutions to creative problem. The facilitation of relevant information that is more typical in individuals with moderate command of their languages seems to encourage greater activation of unrelated concepts and to overcome the limitations of structured imagination. These findings suggest that individuals with different levels of language proficiency may employ different cognitive mechanisms, each of which has certain benefits for creative performance. However, the mechanism of interference suppression seems to be more efficient for creative thinking.

Notes

(1) Snodgrass and Vanderwart (1980) defined a name agreement coefficient as a distribution of names given to a picture across participants. A picture that obtained the same name from every participant had a name agreement coefficient equal to 0.00 (perfect name agreement). A picture that obtained exactly two different names with equal frequency had a name agreement coefficient equal to 1.00. Increasing name agreement value indicated decreasing name agreement.

5 Multilingual Creative Development

Overview

So far, we have discussed multilingual creative potential in comparison with the monolingual one. The reviewed studies demonstrated a clear pattern of creative advantages in participants speaking more than one language compared to those speaking only one language. The previous chapter identified several cognitive mechanisms facilitated by multilingual practice that could underlie an individual's creative functioning. The purpose of this chapter is to elaborate on these findings and to specify what factors in multilingual development may encourage the functioning of these mechanisms.

Chapter 2 specified several factors in multilingual development that may enhance an individual's cognitive capacities. According to creative cognition approach discussed in Chapter 1, increase in certain cognitive functioning may result in greater creative performance. Therefore, it is prudent to investigate the impact of multilingual developmental factors on one's creativity. The studies utilizing the within-group cross-sectional design pinned those factors down. In contrast to the between-group design comparing multilingual creative performance with the monolingual one, this method distinguishes between different types of multilinguals that reflect the specificities of their cross-linguistic and cross-cultural development. The performance differences found between different types of multilinguals might indicate what developmental factors influence their creative abilities. In line with bilingualism research reviewed in Chapter 2, bilinguals' proficiency in two languages and their age of acquisition of these languages (both assumed as cross-linguistic experience) as well as their participation in and experience with sociocultural settings of the countries in which these languages were acquired (assumed as cross-cultural experience) are proposed as potential contributors to increase in their creative functioning. In addition to identifying the cognitive mechanisms underlying multilingual creative potential, the research project reviewed in the previous chapter looked into the relationship of the developmental factors and multilingual creative capacities. These findings and the ones of the earlier studies in the field pertinent to this relationship are presented in this chapter.

Developmental Factors Related to Cross-Linguistic Experience

The first factor in cross-linguistic development reflects bilinguals' proficiency in both languages. As previously expressed, Cummins's (1976) threshold theory argued that bilinguals need to achieve high levels of proficiency in both of their languages before bilingualism can promote cognitive advantages. By analogy, one anticipates that the degree of language proficiency would stipulate an individual's creative abilities. Indeed, previously reported studies with bilingual children and college students showed greater divergent thinking performance of participants with high proficiency in both languages compared to their linguistically unbalanced counterparts. Ricciardelli's (1992a) study with Italian–English bilingual and English monolingual children revealed that only bilinguals with high proficiency in both languages showed greater fluency and imagination compared to their monolingual counterparts. Similarly, Lemmon and Goggin's (1989) study with Spanish–English bilingual college students found that the tendency of monolinguals to outperform their bilingual counterparts on fluency and flexibility – assessed by Guilford's (1967) Utility and Object Naming tests – was ascribed to those participants classified as a low-proficiency group. In the same fashion, Konaka (1997) found that the degree of bilingual balance (based on the score computed from Japanese–English bilingual children's self-rating and their performance on the Word Association Test) significantly predicted the TTCT performance on fluency, flexibility and originality. It is important to note, however, that the procedure used in her study to distinguish between bilingual groups seems to have a methodological flaw. As discussed in Chapter 3, the Word Association Test employed to determine participants' linguistic abilities seems to tap into one's fluency in divergent thinking (ability to generate associations). This seems to explain why the degree of bilingual balance could predict creative performance assessed by the TTCT.

A study described in the previous chapter revealed that bilinguals with high proficiency in both English and Russian performed better on the ATTA measure of elaboration than their less proficient counterparts (Kharkhurin, 2008). Similarly, Farsi–English bilinguals highly proficient in both languages outperformed their unbalanced and moderately proficient counterparts on the ATTA measure of fluency (Kharkhurin, 2011). As previously stated, both elaboration and fluency serve as the constituents of the generative capacity. The findings that language proficiency has an impact on the generative capacity of creative thinking were complemented by the findings of another study conducted with multilinguals with different proficiency levels in English (Kharkhurin, 2011). This study revealed that more linguistically proficient multilinguals tended to have greater innovative capacity and greater ability to violate a standard set of category properties. The influence of language proficiency on multilingual creative performance was explained by the functioning of cognitive mechanisms specified in the previous chapter.

Recall that individuals' multilingual practice was suggested to encourage the LMCA, which in turn may facilitate their generative capacity. The latter addresses the ability to simultaneously activate a multitude of unrelated concepts and work through the concepts already activated. This ability is facilitated by establishing multiple links in a conceptual system. The proficiency in multilinguals' languages determines the strength of the connections between the lexical and the conceptual systems in their memory. The degree of linguistic skills may influence the intensity of the lexical access: greater language proficiency may result in establishing stronger and more elaborate links to the conceptual system. As a result, more concepts become readily available for the LMCA. Therefore, multilinguals who attained a high expertise in their languages would have stronger and more efficient links between lexical and conceptual levels than those who were not able to develop any of their languages to a high degree. Thus, individuals highly proficient in their languages would employ the LMCA mechanism more effectively and therefore show greater generative capacity compared to their less proficient counterparts.

At the same time, multilinguals' inhibition mechanism of selective attention promotes their innovative capacity and nonstructured imagination by suppressing the interference from the irrelevant information. An extensive practice with multiple languages calls for a more efficient inhibition mechanism to suppress the interference of one language during the processing of the other. That is to say, individuals with higher proficiency in their languages would develop this mechanism to a greater extent than their less proficient counterparts. In turn, greater interference suppression ability may increase their innovative capacity and nonstructured imagination.

Another factor in cross-linguistic development influencing multilinguals' creative potential refers to the age at which their languages were acquired. There is evidence that the age at which L2 was acquired related to fluency and flexibility in divergent thinking, which serve as the constituents of the generative capacity (Kharkhurin, 2008). The individuals who acquired L2 at a younger age showed greater abilities in these traits. To the author's knowledge, no other study has reported the effect of the age of L2 acquisition on bilingual creative performance. This finding can be explained by a possible effect of the age of L2 acquisition on the structure and/or functioning in the bilingual memory system as suggested in Chapter 2. The differences in the memory systems of early and late bilinguals could be manifested in the variation in the functioning of the LMCA. The latter could relate the age of bilinguals' language acquisition to their generative capacity. Individuals who acquired both languages early in life may develop a greater sensitivity to underlying concepts and more refined connections between lexical and conceptual representations for both languages. As Chapter 2 suggests, the memory system in early bilinguals might foster the LMCA by providing fast routing of information exchange between both lexicons and conceptual representations. On the other hand, late bilinguals may develop an asymmetry in lexical access, with fewer shared conceptual features having direct links from both lexicons. The asymmetrical routing in the lexical–conceptual network may result in a less efficient LMCA. Thus, the age of language acquisition might have an influence on bilinguals' LMCA. Specifically, due to a more symmetrical distribution of lexical–conceptual routes, more conceptual representations become readily available for the LMCA in early bilinguals. A larger span of available conceptual representations encourages greater generative capacity in these bilinguals compared to those who acquired L2 later in life.

Developmental Factors Related to Cross-Cultural Experience

In addition to the developmental factors resulting from the cross-linguistic experience, multilinguals may benefit from experience within various sociocultural settings. A significant contribution of this factor can be inferred from a twofold argument: First, recall the discussion in Chapter 2 that language acquisition is often accompanied by adoption of the cultural values of the country in which this language is acquired. Bilingual individuals who participated in the creativity studies were primarily immigrants, migrant workers, members of the minority groups or foreign students. They acquired each of their languages in the respective cultural environments where different cultural cues are available. Second, creativity research demonstrates that the specific economic, political, social and cultural aspects of the environment can have a considerable influence both on levels of creative potential and on how creativity is evaluated. In particular, Lubart (1999) identifies four ways that cultural influence might affect creativity: (1) people from different cultures may have different concepts of creativity, (2) people from different cultures may use different psychological processes when they engage in creative endeavors, (3) language may influence the development of creativity and (4) environment can either promote or reduce people's creativity. These directions suggest that sociocultural values and norms determine and shape the concept of creativity, which in turn may influence the manner in which creative potential is apprehended and incarnated. These two sets of findings suggest the following logical chain of reasoning. If multilinguals acquire their languages in different countries, they are most likely to have been exposed to different sociocultural environments. This multicultural experience encourages a variation in the development of creative potential. Therefore, multilingual individuals' experience with multiple sociocultural settings may increase their creative abilities.

This argument found support in the historiometric research discussed in Chapter 3. It provides evidence that people who resided in ethnically diverse and politically fragmented geographic areas and in the countries exposed to outside influences tended to exhibit exceptional creative abilities. Immigrants and ethnically diverse or marginalized individuals revealed relatively high rates of creativity. In addition, research in an organizational setting provides evidence that collaborative groups containing diverse members tended to show greater creative potential (Guimerà *et al.*, 2005). The psychometric cross-cultural research complements this evidence by demonstrating that multilingual experience is often confounded with multiculturalism and sociocultural factors may modulate the influence of multilingualism on creativity (e.g. Kharkhurin, 2010b; Leung *et al.*, 2008). The confounding nature of cross-linguistic and cross-cultural effects on multilingual cognition was discussed in Chapter 2. The same principle can be applied to multilingual creative potential. There is evidence that multicultural experience can enhance cognitive processes underlying creative performance beyond the effect of bilingualism (e.g. Kharkhurin, 2008; Leung & Chiu, 2010; Maddux & Galinsky, 2007). Unfortunately, empirical studies examining the cultural effects on bilingual creative potential are few in number and highly inconsistent. Exposure to cultural settings, although recognized as an important factor in bilingual development (e.g. Cummins & Gulutsan, 1974; Lopez, 2003; Okoh, 1980), has been virtually ignored in psychometric research, possibly due to the fact that it is difficult to measure and relate to an individual's cognitive functioning (Francis, 2000).

Several attempts were made to overcome this problem by introducing quantitative measures of cross-cultural experience. Research on cultural adaptation emphasizes that the rate of exposure to new cultural settings should be assessed by the participants' age of arrival in a new country and their length of residence in that country. These two factors are argued to be conceptually different and to have different implications for immigrants of different ages (e.g. Birman & Trickett, 2001; Marin *et al.*, 1987). In particular, Tsai *et al.* (2000) claim that individuals who were exposed to both cultures early or late in life would exhibit variations in cognitive functioning, which might result in a different perception of the L1 and L2 cultural values. They reported that Chinese immigrants, who came to the United States early and late in life, responded differently to identity-related questions. The early immigrants were barely exposed to their L1 culture and perceived their L2 culture as dominant. In contrast, the late immigrants were already preformed by the experience with L1 culture and therefore perceived their L2 culture through the prism of the former. The researchers proposed that the frequency and recency of exposure to different cultural settings may have an impact on the cognitive system. The variations in the cognitive functioning in turn may influence an individual's perception of the L1 and L2 cultural values. Therefore, it is prudent to measure the length and the age of individuals' exposure to their L1 and L2 cultures. The author adopted this view and took the age of arrival in a new country and the length of residence in the country as the measures of Russian–English bilinguals' cross-cultural experience. One study (Kharkhurin, 2007) combined both factors into one variable – the cultural exposure coefficient (similar to Marin *et al.*, 1987; Tropp *et al.*, 1999) – which was computed by dividing the absolute value of the difference between the length of residence in Russia (an indicator of the age of arrival in a new country) and that in the United States (an indicator of the length of residence in the new country) by a participant's age. That study revealed that the cultural exposure coefficient had no significant effect on divergent thinking performance. The other study (Kharkhurin, 2008) considered these factors separately and revealed that the length of residence in the new cultural environment related to bilinguals' performance on fluency, flexibility and elaboration in divergent thinking (which together form the generative capacity) above and beyond the effect of bilingualism.

Similar findings were obtained by Maddux and Galinsky (2007) who had MBA students from 40 different nations solve the Duncker's (1945) candle-mounting problem. The problem is to fix a lighted candle on a wall using a matchbook and a box of thumbtacks so that the candle wax will not drip onto the table below. The creative solution is to empty the box of thumbtacks, put the candle into the box and use the thumbtacks to nail the box (with the lit-up candle in it) to the wall. The task measures the ability to think outside of the box or to overcome functional fixedness manifested in using an object only in the way it is traditionally used (cf. IAC described above). The study showed that people who had lived abroad had a significantly greater probability to provide a creative solution to the problem than those who had not. More pertinent to the present discussion, the amount of time participants had lived abroad was found to significantly predict creative solutions when the effect of bilingualism was controlled.

Despite the temptation to interpret these findings in favor of cross-cultural effect in creative performance, it is important to acknowledge that using these factors degrades the psychological effects of acculturation. This effect cannot and should not be reduced to measures of the exposure to a cultural environment, for the mere cultural exposure does not necessarily reflect the psychological ramifications of that experience (Tropp et al., 1999). For example, some individuals may live in the United States throughout their lives without developing a strong connection to the country and may, in turn, be less likely to embrace North American cultural norms and expectations. Conversely, some recent immigrants may identify strongly with prevailing North American norms and standards and may therefore attempt to integrate aspects of North American culture into their daily lives. Certainly, further research is required to provide a more sophisticated assessment of cultural experience, which allows one to disentangle both cross-linguistic and cross-cultural effects and to relate them to an individual's creative performance.

The research reviewed so far suggests that both language- and culture-related factors may influence multilingual creative performance. Another line of research proposes that, in addition to direct contribution to this performance, the specific settings of the sociocultural environment to which an individual was exposed may modulate the impact of multilingualism on creativity. This idea stems from the cross-cultural research in creativity demonstrating variation in performance on creativity tests among the representatives of different cultures. For example, Torrance and his colleagues (e.g. Ball & Torrance, 1978; Torrance & Sato, 1979) revealed cultural differences in participants' performance on divergent thinking tests. Aviram and Milgram (1977) compared the performance of 12–14-year-old children on Wallach and Kogan's creativity battery. At the time of testing, all children lived in Israel, but they were educated in the United States, Israel or the Soviet Union. The findings that American and Israeli children scored higher on divergent thinking than Soviet children were interpreted in terms of differences in socialization within Soviet and Western societies. Similarly, Niu and Sternberg (2001) provide an overview of empirical evidence showing that the representatives of the Western and Eastern cultures obtained significantly different divergent thinking scores. They argue that the differences in creative performance were determined by the specific cultural characteristics, namely, independent-self culture in the West and interdependent culture in the East. These differences are grounded in the self-perception of an individual in the community with the focus on self-expression in the West and subordination to the interests of the community in the East. A more recent study (Zha et al., 2006) showed that American doctoral students obtained significantly higher divergent thinking scores compared to their Chinese counterparts. These findings were explained by the differences in the respective societies: individualistic (citizens serving themselves) in the United States and collectivistic (citizens serving society) in China (see the next chapter for a detailed account of the individualistic/collectivistic dichotomy). Finally, the author and his student compared monolingual college students in the United States, Russia and Iran (Kharkhurin & Samadpour Motalleebi, 2008). They found that the US and Russian participants scored significantly higher on fluency (one of the constituents of the generative capacity) and originality (the constituent of the innovative capacity) in divergent thinking compared to their Iranian counterparts. These findings were explained by the differences in sociocultural environment in these countries. Specifically, they argued that Iranians scored lower on fluency because they tended to fail on the task requiring finding multiple solutions to a problem, which has no single solution. This failure was attributed to limitations inherent in the Iranian educational system.[1] At the same time, Iranians' lower originality scores were explained by their tendency to present the most common traditional answers instead of looking for original solutions to the problems presented in the task. The lower capacity for original thinking could result from the prescribed ritualistic patterns of behavior reinforced by a low tolerance for deviant groups in Iran.

On this basis, historiometric research with eminent people suggests that the effects of the environment on creativity could vary depending on the situation in which these people are integrated. Cross-cultural psychometric research points out that the variations in the manners of socialization, degrees of self-perception and self-expression and education and social conduct may modulate the differences in creative performance of the representatives of different cultures. If individuals' creative potential may be influenced by their experience with different cultures, the variations in multilinguals' cultural settings may have an impact on different aspects of their creative thinking.

The author explored this thesis by systematically comparing the performance of bilinguals and monolinguals in different sociocultural environments (Kharkhurin, 2010b). He found that the latter had a measurable impact on bilingual creative potential. Specifically, the ATTA performance of Farsi–English bilingual and Farsi monolingual college students residing in the Middle East was compared with the performance on this test by their Russian–English bilingual and English monolingual counterparts residing in the United States. The study demonstrated that the interaction between bilingualism and the sociocultural environment had a significant influence on creative performance. This effect was found for both the generative and the innovative capacities. Bilinguals and monolinguals in the Middle Eastern sample demonstrated no significant difference in the generative capacity, whereas the US bilinguals significantly outperformed their monolingual counterparts on this measure. In contrast, there was no innovative capacity difference between bilinguals and monolinguals in the US sample, whereas the Middle Eastern bilinguals obtained higher scores on this measure than their monolingual compatriots. As shown in the previous chapter, the greater generative capacity of the US bilinguals could be explained by their LMCA. The efficiency of this mechanism could be partially supported by the availability of the cultural cues in the environment where both languages were acquired. The greater innovative capacity of the Middle Eastern bilinguals could be explained by their ability to produce original ideas different from those listed among common ATTA responses. This ability could be attributed to a freedom of expression (see below) in the United Arab Emirates environment in which this bilingual group resided. Overall, these findings indicate a variation in bilingual creative behavior in different sociocultural environments.

Another interesting finding of this study hints to a specific nuance of cross-cultural experience that may also play a role in an individual's creative behavior. The bilingual participants in the Middle Eastern sample demonstrated greater innovative capacity than their monolingual counterparts, whereas this effect was not found in the US sample. A possible explanation for this discrepancy is based on the notion of cross-cultural distances in those samples. The Middle Eastern bilinguals were exposed to two distinct sociocultural systems. Iran is perceived as a highly collectivist country with a fairly typical set of restrictions imposed on its residents which limit freedom of expression and nontraditional thinking (Hofstede, 2001; Zandpour & Sadri, 1996), whereas the United Arab Emirates, although officially advocating a traditional, Islamic lifestyle, has rapidly developed toward the Western community and has eagerly (if unofficially) adopted individualistic values and norms. Thus, Iran is assumed to be a highly collectivist country, whereas the United Arab Emirates has a more individualistic way of life. The experience with two distinct cultural systems may result in an expansion of the conceptual system as new connotations, even entirely new meanings, may develop through acculturation. In turn, newly developed conceptual representations may promote novel and creative ways of encoding experience, and subsequently increase the innovative capacity. In contrast, although the US bilinguals were also exposed to different environments, the patterns of sociocultural behavior in these countries (the United States and Russia) could not be as radically distinct as those of Iran and the United Arab Emirates. As cross-cultural literature indicates, modern Russia is rapidly growing toward an individualistic and democratic society (e.g. Naumov & Puffer, 2000; Triandis, 1995), and the educational system in the country is more Western-oriented (Hudson & Hoffman, 1993). Thus, due to the lesser differences in the US bilinguals' sociocultural environments, their conceptual system could have undergone less conceptual changes. The bilinguals in this group, therefore, could not show significantly greater innovative capacity compared to their monolingual counterparts. Therefore, the contradiction in innovative capacity patterns between the US and the Middle Eastern samples could be attributed to the cultural distance between the environments to which bilingual groups were exposed in the respective countries. However, to test this hypothesis, a reliable measure of cultural distance should be provided and related to an individual's creative potential.

In conclusion of this discussion, it is important to acknowledge that the cross-cultural experience may also have a negative effect on an individual's creative potential. Recall the argument in Chapter 2 that bilinguals undergo conceptual changes due to experiences within different cultural and linguistic environments. These changes were hypothesized to increase cognitive flexibility and creative abilities due to, for example, the internalization of new concepts and convergence and restructuring of the concepts. This hypothesis was based on the assumption that bicultural individuals combine the values and norms of both the new and the original culture. In the 'turkey' example presented in Chapter 2, the conceptual representation of a turkey may expand as it includes additional features related to the experience of North American festivity. The expanded conceptual system was supposed to facilitate individuals' perception of a variety of events from different culture-specific perspectives, and therefore to increase their cognitive flexibility and creative abilities. However, it is entirely possible that the specific nuances of the immigration experience of participants in many studies in the field may have hindered the conceptual changes. Namely, instead of multicultural experience, they could have, in fact, acquired a 'subcultural' one. For example, the majority of participants in Kharkhurin's (2008) study were immigrants from the former Soviet Union residing in Brooklyn (USA), and therefore they might have been influenced by the pervasive Russian immigrant community of Brooklyn. This community is notoriously famous for its explicit isolation from the mainstream North American lifestyle. Birman and Tyler (1994) explain this by the nature of the relationship between the North American and the Russian cultures that may be particularly antilogous for the Soviet refugees. They came from a country that for many years was seen as an enemy of the United States and in many respects was defined as its 'mirror opposite.' At the same time, this community fails to maintain traditional Russian lifestyle due to geographic isolation from the source country and its presence on the territory of the United States. As a result, the US and Russian cultural values and norms are likely to suppress or cancel each other. A limited experience with Russian cultural settings could cause the attrition of the Russia-related knowledge, and a limited experience with the North American cultural settings could be a reason for inability to fully acquire the knowledge related to North American culture. That is to say, these participants might have developed perspectives that were distanced from the source culture and yet differed from the culture of the country of their present residence (Ervin-Tripp, 2000). Due to a variety of negative effects that were found to accompany the process of acculturation (see Birman & Trickett, 2001), the subcultural experience could have resulted in the attrition of the essential knowledge of the original country and, at the same time, in the inability to fully acquire the knowledge of the new culture. In other words, one can speculate that due to the subcultural experience, participants in such studies underwent those conceptual changes that resulted in a poorly developed conceptual system. This notion is supported by Pavlenko's (2000) model of conceptual development, in which the interaction of two languages and cultures may result in conceptual changes that may include the internalization of new concepts, convergence of the concepts and restructuring, but at the same time, attrition and/or substitution of previously learned concepts by new ones and a shift from one conceptual domain to another. The conceptual changes of the latter types could entail the inability of multilingual participants to develop their conceptual system to a greater extent. This, in turn, may result in no significant (or even negative) influence of their cross-cultural experience on divergent thinking performance. Therefore, it is prudent for future research to control the history of acculturation of multilingual individuals, namely, for the sociocultural environment in which they are resided.

Another typical characteristic of immigrant experience is related to code-switching practice. This observation hints at the inability of some multilingual individuals to demonstrate advantages in their creative performance. Code-switching refers to concurrent use of more than one language in the same sentence, constituent or word (Poplack, 2004). For example, a German–English bilingual can switch whole clauses in a sentence: 'Papa, wenn du das Licht ausmachst, then I'll be so lonely' (Daddy, if you put out the light, I'll be so lonely). Or Russian–French bilingual can switch a single word in a clause: 'Imela une femme de chamber' (She had a chambermaid). Code-switching may result in underdevelopment of one's languages due to insufficient intrinsic motivation to acquire translation equivalents in both languages. For example, code-switching individuals can use L1 word for a referent in L2, which discourages them from acquiring L2 translation equivalent, and vice versa. Limited vocabularies in both languages may deteriorate their LMCA and consequently their creative abilities. Code-switching may also weaken multilinguals' interference suppression. When using the first language that comes to their mind, people end up having little exercise for focusing on the target language and suppressing the interference from another language. This in turn may handicap their selective attention mechanism and consequently their creative performance.

Other Factors Unrelated to Cross-Linguistic and Cross-Cultural Experiences

The discussion of multilinguals' developmental factors influencing creativity would be incomplete without mentioning other factors not directly related to their cross-linguistic and cross-cultural experiences. Chapter 3 mentions that the within-group cross-sectional design employed in most of the recent studies in the field provides low causal inferences. The irony of the relationship between multilingualism and creativity constitutes a possibility for a myriad of other factors to influence an individual's creative potential. These include education, expertise, motivation, personality traits, personal experience as well as political, socioeconomic and sociocultural factors. This section speculates about some of them using the findings of the empirical studies.

Let us recall the study of Farsi–English bilinguals and Farsi monolinguals conducted in the Middle East (Kharkhurin, 2009). An alternative explanation of a significant difference in their innovative capacity could stem from how political situations in Iran and the United Arab Emirates are reflected by the creativity assessment. The innovative capacity addresses the ability to produce original ideas different from those produced by most people in the same situation. All three ATTA activities consider the response original if it is not listed among common responses provided by the ATTA manual (Goff & Torrance, 2002). Thus, to reveal high innovative capacity, participants had to produce responses different from those obtained from the others. A number of uncommon responses provided by Iranian monolingual participants were considerably lower than those provided by their bilingual counterparts. According to Kharkhurin and Samadpour Motalleebi (2008), the prescribed ritualistic patterns of behavior reinforced by a low tolerance for deviant groups in Iran could encourage Middle Eastern monolingual participants (residing in Iran) to provide rather traditional responses. Instead of looking for original solutions to the problems presented in the ATTA, they tended to provide the most common traditional ones, which were not considered as original by the ATTA procedure. On the other hand, by the mere fact of leaving Iran and residing in a more individualistic environment of the United Arab Emirates, bilingual participants may benefit from more freedom of expression compared to their monolingual compatriots residing in Iran. The experience with the more liberal social environment of the United Arab Emirates could facilitate their innovative capacity and encourage them to find less traditional solutions to the ATTA problems. This line of reasoning was confirmed by Kharkhurin and Samadpour Motalleebi's study, in which the cultural differences, specifically those related to individualist/collectivist settings, were found to have an impact on an individual's attitude toward originality in thinking. They found that Iranian college students scored lower on the ATTA measure of originality compared to both their American and Russian counterparts.

Furthermore, a detailed analysis of the history of Farsi–English bilinguals revealed that only those who presumably emigrated to the United Arab Emirates for educational purposes, showed significantly greater innovative capacity compared to their monolingual counterparts (Kharkhurin, 2010b). This finding suggests that they could be intrinsically motivated to move to a new country in search for alternative education. Current theories considering the role of motivation in creativity (see Collins & Amabile, 1999, for an overview) emphasize the necessity of intrinsic motivation in the creative process. Intrinsic motivation refers to motivation that is based on taking pleasure in an activity rather than on acquiring an external reward. It is driven by an individual's interest in the task itself rather than by external pressure. It is contrasted with extrinsic motivation that refers to the performance of an activity in order to attain an outcome that is externally rewarded by money, grades, coercion and so on. Intrinsic motivation exists within the individual, whereas extrinsic motivation comes from outside of the individual. Sternberg and Lubart (1991) include motivation as one of the six required resources in their investment theory of creativity. The interactive models of the development of an individual's creative potential within the society emphasize intrinsic motivation as a personal characteristic contributing to creative abilities (e.g. Csíkszentmihályi, 1990; Gardner, 1993b). The empirical studies also provide extensive support to the assertion that motivation is beneficial for creativity. Heinzen *et al.* (1993) found that youths talented in math and science revealed higher levels of intrinsic motivation than their less gifted peers. Collins and Amabile reported Carney's longitudinal study of art students showing that prevalence of intrinsic imagery in their Thematic Apperception Test pictures (emphasizing the pleasure of producing art) predicted their persistence in the field and achievement of eventual success. Since motivation plays an important role in creativity, those Farsi–English bilinguals who were intrinsically motivated to change their country of residence could have shown greater innovative capacity. In contrast, one could assume that those individuals who resided in the United Arab Emirates for an extensive period of time were not intrinsically motivated. They were likely to have emigrated from their respective countries of origin with their parents at a relatively early age, presumably for economical and/or political reasons. In the proposed framework, those individuals showed no significant differences in the innovative capacity with their monolingual counterparts because they were not intrinsically motivated.

Thus, the reviewed findings suggest that it is entirely possible that the freedom of expression and intrinsic motivation may play an important role in the stimulation of one's creative potential. Although these factors are not related to multilingual experience per se, their presence in multilinguals' development may facilitate their creative performance.

Summary

This chapter focuses on various developmental factors that may facilitate multilingual creative capacity. In addition to the linguistic context of multilingual development, other factors not related to multilingualism per se were identified as potential contributors to one's enhanced creativity. These factors hint at a possibility that although cognitive advantages of multilinguals are traditionally associated with the virtue of developing two linguistic systems, there is an alternative view that states that this effect can be attributed not to the cross-linguistic variations, but to the cross-cultural values adopted in parallel with language acquisition. Moreover, other factors in individual development such as intrinsic motivation and freedom of expression, not accounted for by multilingualism/multiculturalism dichotomy, may be necessary contributors to the ultimate creative production. The inability to develop these factors to a greater extent may prevent multilingual individuals from showing superior creative performance.

Notes

(1) After the establishment of the Islamic Republic in Iran, the clerical rulers enforced a puritanical set of religious rules on society that significantly limited individual freedom (Moaddel, 2004). The political situation in the country influences the structure and the goals of educational systems. The Iranian educational institution is fully dominated by the ethics and moral stance of Shi'ism, which disregards personal social development and puts a great emphasis on gender segregation (Bahador & Somerville, 1969; Moaddel, 2004). An individual educated in such institution tends to avoid 'what if' questions and to pursue a route that leads more directly to concrete answers (Zandpour & Sadri, 1996). The anecdotal evidences obtained in the author's personal communication with Iranian students suggest that the Iranian education system puts more emphasis on the manipulating of existent knowledge that results in finding a single correct solution. The idea that there is always a right solution that needs to be found encourages people to memorize the answers provided by others instead of finding their own. Reciprocally, this tradition often discourages people from exploring the problem and generating new solutions.

6 Implications of Multilingual Creative Cognition for Creativity Domains

Overview

The focus of this book is on the relationship between multilingualism and creativity. In line with this objective, we discussed the findings in the fields of creative cognition research, multilingual cognition research and the research in multilingual creativity. We have identified specific cognitive mechanisms facilitating an individual's creative functioning and the factors in multilingual and multicultural development that presumably make the use of these mechanisms more efficient. Now, it seems to be appropriate to change the focus of our attention from the empirical findings of multilingual creative cognition project to its more theoretical and speculative implications. While developing this project, several interesting considerations pertinent to creativity research have appeared to the author's attention.

First of them is concerned with the assessment of creative capacities largely employed in contemporary research. The author has noticed that across all samples being tested in various geographic, sociocultural and linguistic locations, the scores obtained by the ATTA procedure were consistently divided into two groups. The first one taps into an individual's ability to generate and elaborate on a multitude of ideas, and was labeled with the term generative capacity. The second one addresses the ability to extract original and useful ideas from the previously generated pool of ideas, and was labeled with the term innovative capacity. Both generative and innovative capacities are considered to encourage creative thinking. What is more appealing is that they seem to characterize divergent and convergent thinking, respectively; the latter traditionally assumed as two major processes involved in creative processing. And now, we come up with an interesting contradiction. The ATTA, which is traditionally regarded as a test of divergent thinking, assesses generative and innovative capacities, which characterize both divergent and convergent thinking. In other words, the divergent thinking test seems to assess both divergent and convergent thinking. This observation may account for some inconsistencies in creativity research.

The inconsistency in the findings of creativity research paved the way for another consideration. It was observed that the empirical research in creativity utilizes different definitions of this construct, which seem to tap into overlapping but still distinct traits. Indeed, as Chapter 1 mentioned, the creativity construct is highly ambiguous and fuzzy and there are a lot of debates about what should be considered as creativity. Most current scientific research utilizes a definition of 'creativity' that emphasizes the novelty and utility functions of this process. However, these traits seem to be prominent only in the Western perspective on creativity. In contrast, the Eastern view on this construct emphasizes aesthetic and authentic values of this phenomenon. Therefore, is seems to be prudent to unite both Western and Eastern perspectives and introduce a four-criterion construct of creativity, in which novelty and utility are complemented with aesthetics and authenticity.

Once a new construct is provided, it requires a new model of creativity that accounts for all four criteria. These four generic creativity features are perceived to be inherent to all areas of creative endeavor, and therefore serve as the conceptual domains for a new model of creative thinking. This model is composed of four creative spheres and three force axes. Each force axis penetrates creative spheres and establishes a creativity unit in the place of infiltration. Therefore, the proposed model consists of 12 creativity units, each of which presents a separate phase of creative processing.

Generative and Innovative Capacities of Creative Thinking

The studies conducted in several distinct geographic locations (the United States, Russia, the United Arab Emirates and Iran) used the ATTA procedure as an assessment of creative performance. Recall that the norm-referenced creativity scores of this test were grouped together as two factors that represent generative and innovative capacities. The former reflects the ability to generate and elaborate on a multitude of ideas, whereas the latter addresses the ability to extract original and useful ideas from the previously generated pool of ideas. A difference between generative and innovative capacities resembles Mumford's (2000) distinction between early and late cycle capacities that are argued to play equally important roles in creative thinking. Early cycle capacities in this framework refer to the cognitive processes involved in the initial generation of new ideas, whereas late cycle capacities are the ones involved in the evaluation and implementation of new ideas. The generative/innovative capacity model also coincides with Guilford's (1967) divergent/convergent thinking model. The generative capacity seems to describe the processes constituting divergent thinking during which one establishes a new plane of thought with a multitude of possible solutions to a problem. The innovative capacity in turn, is likely to characterize the processes, which manipulate and evaluate a pool of solutions on the plane constructed during divergent thinking and extract and/or generate an original and novel solution. This capacity therefore might at least partially characterize processes underlying convergent thinking.

Similar to classical Mumford's (2000) and Guilford's (1967) models of creativity, the generative/innovative capacity model relies on two-phase processing. This approach was utilized by other researchers as well. In Campbell's (1960) blind variation and selective retention model, the production of ideas is followed by judgment of those ideas. Simonton's (1988) chance configuration theory of creative thinking, which is rooted in Campbell's model, assumes similar two-step processing. The major difference between proposed and other reviewed models constitutes the manner of application of the respective capacities. In the reviewed models, the two steps are performed in consecutive order: early cycle capacity is applied before the late cycle one; convergent thinking occurs after divergent thinking. The solutions generated during earlier stage of creative problem solving are judged or evaluated during the later stage. This approach assumes that the solution to creative problem has been already generated during the earlier stage, and it merely needs to be identified and selected during the later stage. At this stage, all possible solutions are explored, criticized and evaluated in order to recognize the solution that satisfies conditions of a creative problem. The generative/innovative capacity model, however, assumes that both capacities may be applied in parallel and that the order of occurrence is not stipulated. They differ in the nature of the underlying processes rather than in the chronological order. Generative capacity encourages an individual to produce a multitude of solutions to a problem. They could be more or less creative, but it is not guaranteed that the desired creative solution should be found among them. Moreover, it is entirely possible that during the application of the generative capacity, the problem has not been sufficiently conceptualized to identify a solution. This may occur during the application of the innovative capacity. The latter encourages one not only to explore, criticize and evaluate obtained solutions but also to manipulate and revise them to produce novel creative solutions. Therefore, only interrelated application of both creative capacities might lead to successful creative functioning.

The intertwined nature of these capacities resembles the extension made by Cropley (2006) to Wallas's (1926) classical model. In addition to the four stages discussed in Chapter 1, this model proposes that the creative process starts with the information stage and ends with the communication and validation stages. The information stage involves activation of information that was perceived, learned and stored in one's memory. This stage relies on general and special knowledge and skills obtained over the life span prior to the process of creation. The last two stages involve effective presentation of the creative product so that it gains acclaim by relevant judges. The new seven-phase model assumes that each stage involves either divergent or convergent thinking, or both. An important characteristic of this model pertinent to this discussion is that both types of creative thinking may take place simultaneously. Thus, previous metaphors of creative functioning (e.g. divergent/convergent thinking) appear too rigid and provide a limited description of the nature of the underlying processes (Baer, 2003). The proposed generative/innovative capacity approach may compensate for at least some of these limitations. However, in line with psychometric tradition, this model requires empirical investigation.

Divergent Thinking Tests Measure Convergent Thinking

The generative/innovative capacity approach also questions the integrity of the divergent thinking measure widely used in contemporary creativity research. Recall from the discussion in Chapter 1 that the ATTA was built on the basis of the TTCT, which is traditionally employed as a measure of divergent thinking. The new version is argued to utilize the same rationale as activities in the original TTCT. The four norm-referenced creativity scores obtained by the ATTA procedure (Goff & Torrance, 2002) in several distinct geographic and sociocultural environments were factor analyzed in the author's studies described earlier. The principal component factor analysis with varimax rotation used in those studies extracted two factors (whose eigenvalues exceeded 1), which accounted for a consistent pattern of the variance ranging from 70.30 to 72.83%. That is, these factors (interpreted as generative and innovative capacities) accounted for a substantial variation in the ATTA assessment of divergent thinking. However, as the previous discussion suggests, conceptually these factors measure distinct capacities. Recall that the generative capacity accounts for the ability to generate and to elaborate on various, often unrelated, ideas. Therefore, it seems to overlap with Guilford's (1967) characteristics of divergent thinking, namely, ability to generate a numerous alternative answers or solutions to a problem. It is represented by the ATTA scores of fluency, flexibility and elaboration. On the other side, the innovative capacity is built on the ATTA score of originality and accounts for the ability to extract novel and unique ideas. Guilford assumes originality as a trait of divergent thinking, whereas the reviewed studies suggest that originality could have its source in a different process, which results from the mental activity defined by Guilford as convergent thinking. This consideration is supported by the findings of the author's project described in Chapter 4. The innovative capacity was found to relate to fluid intelligence, and both processes were proposed to benefit from the inhibition mechanism of selective attention. Convergent thinking was also argued to relate to intelligence to the extent that the test of the latter was assumed as a measure of the former (Runco et al., 2006). Moreover, selective attention was also proposed as a mechanism underlying successful convergent thinking when a conscious, attention-demanding process is needed to narrow a multitude of possible alternatives down to a single original solution.

In other words, generative capacity parallels divergent thinking in that both phenomena account for the ability to generate and process multiple ideas. On the other side, innovative capacity seems to coincide with convergent thinking as they both refer to the ability to extract a single original solution. Although, according to the discussion in the previous section, these approaches reveal important conceptual differences, one can identify substantial overlaps in the processes that constitute both models. Now, the ATTA presented as a test of divergent thinking seems to measure both generative and innovative capacities and therefore could be assumed to assess at least some of the processes underlying both divergent and convergent thinking. That is, the test of divergent thinking could measure convergent thinking as well.

This conclusion may shed some light on a debate in creativity research concerning whether divergent thinking tests measure intelligence rather than creativity (see Chapter 1). For example, in their overview of the research on creativity and intelligence, Sternberg and O'Hara (1999) report Guilford and Hoepfner's findings of mean correlations of 0.37 and 0.22 between the California Test of Mental Maturity (a measure of intelligence) and the semantic and visual-figural divergent production tests, respectively. They also reported Mednick and Andrews' finding of a correlation of 0.55 between the Remote Associates Test and the Wechsler Intelligence Scale for Children. At the same time, they presented substantial research data demonstrating that divergent thinking tests seem only weakly to relate to other assessments of creativity. In line with our discussion, divergent thinking tests such as the ATTA may provide an ambiguous assessment of the creative processes. The originality trait traditionally presented as characteristic of divergent processing was interpreted as innovative capacity, which seems to characterize convergent processing. Therefore, one can conclude that the ATTA assesses cognitive functions that contribute to both divergent and convergent thinking. As was discussed earlier, the literature often relates convergent thinking to intelligence (cf. Runco et al., 2006), and both processes may be supported by the selective attention capacity. Thus, it is entirely possible that divergent thinking tests may include the assessment of the processes related to intelligence. A similar idea was expressed by Runco *et al.* (2006: 270), who argued that divergent thinking tests 'are assessing more than generative ideational processes.' Therefore, it is not surprising that some studies found a relationship between creativity (assessed by divergent thinking tests) and intelligence.

Ambiguous Definitions of the Creativity Construct in Scientific Research

The previous section presents an argument that divergent thinking tests provide an ambiguous assessment of an individual's creative potential. Are there other tests in the field that supply more reliable evaluation of this construct? Yes, there are, but, as Chapter 1 indicates, the tests employed in creativity research have a low convergent validity because they provided mixed assessments with no strong correlation among each other. One of the reasons for this discrepancy stems from the definition of the construct itself. Most current scientific research utilizes a definition of 'creativity' that emphasizes the novelty of what is being created. What emerges should be original and unexpected, and in many instances these products were, in fact, creative, at least by this definition. However, there may be an array of other factors that play an important role in creative enterprise and that are largely disregarded by most existing scientific endeavors. This section reviews the empirical findings and theoretical considerations that present a counterargument to the validity of the generally accepted definition of creativity construct.

The results of the IAC test demonstrated that the capacity for invariant violation predicted the creativity rating of independent judges (Kharkhurin, 2009). The drawings in which the invariant characteristics (bilateral symmetry, eyes and limbs) were different from more ordinary terrestrial creatures were given higher creativity scores by the raters. The latter were instructed to look at each drawing and decide how creative they think the creature is and judge the creativity by placing it on one of the six folders in front of them. Each folder was marked 1 through 6: '1' corresponds to a very low creativity rating, '6' corresponds to a very high creativity rating, and '3' or '4' correspond to medium creativity ratings. The raters were encouraged to define creativity any way they liked. This finding suggests that people perceive the lack of the standard characteristics of a category as more creative. Similar results were obtained by Kozbelt and Durmysheva (2007), although the effect they found was rather small. They also reported other findings demonstrating similar effect: Ward, Patterson and Sifonis, for example, found that novelty ratings of the creatures were correlated with the scores based in part on the absence of senses, appendages and symmetry.

What does make people perceive atypical exemplars of a category as more creative? As was mentioned earlier, the focal feature of most standard definitions of creativity traditionally refers to originality in thinking and its closely related property of novelty. Researchers perceive creativity as something 'contrasting with conformity,' 'that breaks out of a mould and is surprising in light of what was known at the time of the discovery' (Niu & Sternberg, 2001: 226). Some of them take a more radical position and claim that in order to consider an act as creative, novelty should be complemented by a modification or rejection of previously accepted ideas (Kaufmann, 2003). The philosophical roots of creativity relate this concept to invention (the ancient Greek word corresponding to creation is *poiein*, 'invention,' Niu & Sternberg, 2006), which means bringing something new into being. Empirical research assumes originality as an important trait of creative behavior (e.g. Sternberg & Lubart, 1995). Originality constitutes one of the four Guilford's (1967) divergent thinking traits. Goff and Torrance's (2002: 6) divergent thinking procedure identifies originality as 'the ability to produce ideas that are generally not produced, or ideas that are totally new and unique.' We consider people as creative if they produce ideas that are different from those of others. Solutions that deviate from a standard set of possible answers are regarded as creative. In the invented alien creature studies mentioned above, a creature that is constructed using fewer standard categories (invariants) was perceived by the independent raters as more creative. In the same fashion, the nonacademic community regards a person or a product as creative if they violate traditional rules or introduce a new paradigm deviating from a norm. For example, an artist or a musician is proclaimed creative when their style reveals novel and unique elements that were never encountered before. However, equating creativity with originality seems to simplify the former and present a limited view on this construct. Specifically, there is an argument in the literature that novelty or originality in thinking as a characteristic of creative process can be culture specific. It is entirely possible that these traits appear as defining features only of the Western concept of creativity.

The worldview theory distinguishes between the West and the East with respect to individualism and collectivism (Triandis, 1975, 1977) or with respect to an independent and interdependent perspective (Markus & Kitayama, 1991).[1] This dichotomy can influence not only people's belief systems, languages and social cognitive systems but also how they perceive and think (Nisbett, 2003). The distinction between Western and Eastern social systems is grounded upon the degree of subordination of an individual's personal goals to the goals of some collective (Triandis *et al.*, 1985). Western societal values comprise a person's unique qualities, initiative and achievement, whereas Eastern values place more emphasis on consensus with the community, on being in line with the others. Niu and Sternberg (2001) argue that people in Western cultures are independent and focus on internal thoughts. The existential problem of the Westerner revolves around expressing oneself and becoming different from the others. In contrast, people in Eastern cultures are interdependent and focus on fitting themselves in with the others. Their life credo is linked with subordination to the needs and requirements of the community. For example, the studies of the Iranian social system demonstrated that independent nontraditional ways of thinking do not earn a high opinion (e.g. Zandpour & Sadri, 1996). Individuals with very divergent views and behaviors are observed in Iran as unusual or strange, as opposed to interesting. Moreover, humility is very characteristic of the communicational patterns of most Iranians. They seldom feel comfortable in taking credit for their achievements, good taste or choice and tend to become embarrassed as a result of excessive praise.

The worldview dichotomy between the West and the East manifests itself in different perceptions of creativity. The Western individualistic ideology considers nonstandard ways of thinking as a virtue of creative behavior, whereas creative endeavor in the Eastern, more collectivist cultures would constitute an adherence to sociocultural norms and traditions. The Western view of creativity emphasizes individual characteristics, which facilitate the unique, creative endeavor of a person. In contrast, the Eastern perspective considers the social and moral values of creative engagement, often in relation to society. For example, according to the Book of Changes, *Yin* and *Yang* – female and male complementary principles – are an ultimate origin of everything. The endless change and interaction of *Yin* and *Yang* represent *dao*, which creates the world (Chan, 1967). The nature of *dao* is goodness, including moral goodness (Lao-tzu, 1992). According to Confucian philosophy, since *dao* is good, the created universe is inherently good, and hence, a person born to this universe is also inherently good. Then, it follows that creative activity always embraces goodness, and this rather than novelty should be the emphasis of creative achievement (Lao, 1983). In Confucian classics, creative act that simply brings forth something new was not considered as a valued example of creativity if it lacks goodness. In the Chinese mind, such goodness also directs toward a collective being or contribution to the whole society. Confucianism prescribes to creative individuals not only to satisfy their own needs as human beings but also to devote themselves to other people and the interests of society as a whole (Niu & Sternberg, 2006). The historical and philosophical emphases on collective interest encourage the Chinese to follow the crowd rather than to defy the crowd (cf. Sternberg & Lubart, 1995). In general, the latter element is missing from the Eastern notion of creativity. As was mentioned earlier in the context of Iranian society, defying the crowd may be seen as less valuable than making contributions to the society and sometimes defying the crowd may even be seen as strange rather than as creative (Kharkhurin & Samadpour Motalleebi, 2008). These considerations bring us to an important conclusion: a defining feature of the Western concept of creativity – novelty – is not necessarily embraced by the Eastern one.

These observations suggest that originality in thinking is largely adopted within Western ideals and less pervasive in the Eastern frame of thought. No doubt creative activity is inherent to human nature and therefore it earns recognition in all areas of human enterprise across all cultures. However, the manifestation of creative potential might differ in various cultural groups. Li (1997) distinguishes between horizontal and vertical traditions in the production of art. According to the former (typical for Western cultures), the symbols, methods and aims of art are subject to modification and even radical change. In contrast, the latter tradition (more characteristic of Eastern cultures) constrains both the content and the techniques of the artistic work, and places more emphasis on the aesthetic values of the product. For example, traditional Western poetics encourages innovation in the poetic technique, verse meter and word use, whereas traditional Eastern poetics prescribes a set of strict regulations regarding the form and even the theme. Western poetics delivered a range of rhythmic structures of a verse and a number of lines in verse starting from the Classical Greek meter (such as dactylic that uses verses of 6 feet), through Classical French meter (such as alexandrine, composed of two hemistiches of six syllables each), to contemporary free verse poetry, and even further to visual poetry that abandons any canons of poetics and integrates nonverbal elements into a poetic text. A traditional Japanese haiku, by contrast, retained its form and theme through the history: three lines containing five, seven and five syllables, respectively, and a seasonal reference. In both cases, the product is considered to be creative, but if the former encourages novelty and originality, the latter assumes the conformity to the standard. In the same fashion, one may think about exemplars in contemporary Western art, which focuses solely on novelty and radical rejection of existing paradigm (see discussion of this approach in the next section). The modification and rejection of existing ideas is contrasted in Confucian aesthetics of creativity by breathing in a new essence into existing ideas to reflect an individual's own values and beliefs (Tu, 1985). In traditional Arabic calligraphy or Chinese brush painting, the old ideas are to be smoothly modified to fit new circumstances. Here, an artist's authentic perception becomes a creative tool that captures the 'spirit' of the object portrayed. Instead of trying to establish a unique phenomenon by breaking up with old traditions, a person cultivates one's authentic approach, which can be applied to both old and new (Averill *et al.*, 2001).

Thus, the Western creative tradition places more emphasis on novelty and originality in thinking. In contrast, in a manifestation of creative abilities in the Eastern tradition, aesthetics, goodness and authenticity rather than originality play a pervasive role. These considerations suggest that creativity should be perceived as a multidimensional construct. Reducing this construct to one trait drives creativity research into an epistemological cul-de-sac, which has no way out. Trapped in this dead end, a growing number of studies showing the superior creative performance of the Western participants compared to their Eastern counterparts (e.g. Jaquish & Ripple, 1985; Niu & Sternberg, 2001; but see Niu & Sternberg, 2002, for a literature review showing opposite effect) could fall a victim to a conceptual flaw. These performance differences could be attributed to the distinction in the perception of the very concept of creativity in these two cultural groups. A related issue is concerned with assessment techniques developed in creativity research. Most of the creativity tests adopted a Western, culture-specific definition of creativity, which emphasizes originality in thinking. Therefore, they are biased toward typical Western creative behavior and disregard creative principles inherent to non-Western cultural groups. A logical conclusion of this discussion calls for a careful definition of creativity that includes different culture-specific perspectives on the goals, tasks and aesthetic values of creative endeavor.

Four-Criterion Construct of Creativity

As was mentioned earlier, creativity is a complex and versatile construct that can be evaluated from different perspectives. Various areas of creativity research provide domain-specific operational definitions, which often reveal low convergent validity. The purpose of this section is to introduce a unified construct of creativity that addresses philosophical, epistemological and empirical aspects of this construct. This task requires identification of generic creativity features that are inherent to all areas of creative endeavor. These features could serve as the conceptual domains for the model. One of the widely used definitions of creativity presented in Chapter 1 indicates that this is an ability to produce work that is novel and appropriate. However, reducing creativity to the features of novelty and utility seem to devalue the rich constellation of meanings to which this construct refers. Moreover, these two properties may also refer to intelligence. As Kaufmann (2003: 247) radically asserts, 'The lax definition of creativity as "novel" and "useful" is, indeed, revealed to be a quick and dirty approach that leaves the door open for all sorts of differing approaches to the scientific study of the field.' He presented a convincing argument that these two properties could define intellectual capacity as well as creative capacity. Cross-cultural research cited in the previous section also provides substantial evidence that novelty is pervasive in the Western tradition, whereas aesthetics and authenticity are typical for the Eastern perception of creativity. To provide a comprehensive definition of creativity, the present work combines the typical Western and Eastern properties of creative product. Creativity, therefore, is presented as a four-criterion construct that includes novelty, utility, aesthetics and authenticity.

Contemporary creativity research considers novelty and utility as two defining features of the construct. Both terms were adopted in English from old French *novelté* (newness) and *utelite* (from Latin *ūtilitās*, usefulness) circa late 14th century. According to the Collins dictionary, novelty is 'the quality of being new and interesting,' this is a property of 'a new or unusual experience or thing'; utility is 'the quality of practical use; usefulness; serviceability', this is a property of 'something useful.' Martindale (1989: 2011) characterizes a creative idea with three attributes: 'It must be original, it must be useful or appropriate to the situation in which it occurs, and it must actually be put to some use.' Sternberg and Lubart (1995: 6) assert that 'to be creative, one needs to generate ideas that are relatively novel, appropriate, and of high quality.' Mayer (1999a) summarizes the definitions of creativity provided by contemporary researchers in the *Handbook of Creativity* (Sternberg, 1999). He reveals that most of them identify novelty and utility as key creativity features. Gruber and Wallace (1999: 94) state, 'What do we mean by creative work? Like most definitions of creativity, ours involves novelty and value: The creative product must be new and must be given value according to some external criteria.' Martindale (1999: 137) defines a creative idea as 'one that is both original and appropriate for the situation in which it occurs.' Feist (1999: 274) asserts that 'psychologists and philosophers who study the "creative" process, person, and product are in consensus about what is "creative": novel and adaptive solutions to problems.' Boden (1999: 351) has a similar view: 'Creativity is a generation of ideas that are both novel and valuable.' Lubart (1999: 339) defines creativity as 'the ability to produce work that is novel and appropriate,' but only from a Western perspective, which refers to a previous argument about cultural specificity of this term. Nickerson (1999: 392) also presents a definition of creativity with a slight touch of caution: 'Although not everyone considers it possible to articulate clear objective criteria identifying creative products, novelty is often cited as one of their distinctive characteristic, and some form of utility – usefulness, appropriateness, or social value – as another.' Finally, Lumsden (1999: 151) summarizing the creativity literature defines the construct as 'a kind of capacity to think up something new that people find significant.' The creative process therefore refers to 'those mental events by which an organism intentionally goes beyond its prior experience to a novel and appropriate outcome' (ibid.).

The term novelty is pervasive in most of the definitions of creativity, sometimes being synonymous with originality, innovation and uniqueness. This property implies that creative acts should involve the production of something new, both ideas and concrete objects. Kaufmann (2003) takes an even more radical position, asserting that in order to consider an act as creative, novelty should be complimented by a modification or rejection of previously accepted ideas. In this regard, one may think about exemplars in contemporary Western art, which focuses solely on novelty and on a radical rejection of existing paradigms. Many 20th century artists purposely moved away from the 'artiness' in their work and utilized mundane materials from everyday life. Their intent was to establish an antithesis to traditional perception of art. For example, Dadaists concentrated their program on a rejection of the prevailing standards in art through antiart works in visual arts, literature, theatre and graphic design (Richter, 1965). Marcel Duchamp – a French artist whose work is most often associated with the Dadaist and Surrealist movements – submitted a urinal (entitled *Fountain*) to the Society of Independent Artists exhibit in 1917. This was an exemplar of what he called *readymade* or *found art*, a technique in which an existing object or objects are exhibited in their normative appearance with the least involvement of an artist. The show committee insisted that *Fountain* was not art, and rejected it from the exhibition (Tomkins, 1998). The idea of removing mundane objects from their context and installing them in the museum was further elaborated by Pablo Picasso, in the *Fluxus* movement and *Pop Art*, and by surrealists who defined readymades as 'manufactured objects promoted to the dignity of works of art through the choice of the artist' (Breton, 2002: 88). German artist Joseph Beuys exhibited modified found objects, such as rocks with a hole in them stuffed with fur and fat, a van with sledges trailing behind it and a rusty girder. In 1986, the state of North Rhine-Westphalia (Germany) had to pay 40,000 German Marks in damages as a result of notorious lawsuit. This case was filed because a superintendent of the Düsseldorf Arts Academy removed a 5 kg piece of rancid fat from a corner of Beuys's studio space (Am Ende, 1987). This was an art work *die Fettecke* (the Fat Corner), which became one of the best-known works by the artist. The purpose of the work was to initiate a controversy over what should be considered as art. These examples illustrate the aspect of creative performance, which values rejection of an existing paradigm in order to establish a new framework, thereby securing the novelty.

The utility attribute of creativity is less clearly articulated in scientific literature. The citations presented above describe a creative work as valuable, appropriate, useful, significant and adaptive (meeting task constrains); that is, this work can be put to some use. The utilitarian characteristic of creative work can be easily identified in scientific and business context when a product of creative endeavor makes a measurable theoretical or practical contribution. For example, Einstein's (1920) Theory of Relativity advanced science on the notion of gravitation and the structure of space–time. An obvious utility of this discovery was that it superseded a 200-year-old theory of mechanics elucidated by Isaac Newton and laid the foundations for a new research paradigm in physics and astronomy. In the same fashion, the utility of Google, Inc. established by Brin and Page is obvious to every internet user at the turn of the 21st century. Identifying the utility of a creative work in humanities seems to be more intricate. Note that this work cannot be put to some practical use for its primary value is not utilitarian per se. The utility function of a creative work in the humanities can be viewed from three mutually complementing standpoints, from the individual, sociocultural and temporal perspectives, respectively.

First, a creative work is what an author considers as creative. Recall Breton's (2002) claim that a work of art gains its status when the artist perceives it as such; that is, its significance is in the eye of the creator. This seems to be a rather subject perspective, which annihilates any objective evaluation criteria of the relevance of the creative work. It ascribes the evaluative power to individuals whose objectivity should be questioned, given their emotional attachment to the product of their own creative endeavor. On the other side, an individual's intrinsic creative effort could be the only valuable criterion of a creative work. This relates the utility attribute to another property of creativity described below, namely, authenticity. The authentic engagement in a creative process makes the outcome creative. This consideration reduces to a common denominator the creative enterprise of, for instance, the eminent Russian artist Kazimir Malevich – the author of famous *Black Square* – and someone enthused to cook brownies for dinner. Both of them – by means of their commitment to the activity, which each of them considers creative – can be said to produce creative work that satisfies the criteria of utility. As an ironic remark, the latter work would be considered of greater value to the majority of lay people who have little understanding of art.

Second, a creative work is what others consider as creative. Schärer (2009) suggests that art is all that is understood as such regardless of the professional preparedness of the beholder. He refers to the *Brockhaus Encyclopedia*'s definition of art, which emphasizes that this is a work that is perceived by a viewer for its aesthetic value. Two important considerations regarding the utility of creative work can be inferred from this definition. An appropriate creative work is the one considered by others as creative.

As soon as the piece of fat discussed above is perceived not as a blunder of negligent cleaner but as a creative effort, it becomes *die Fettecke*, a famous piece of art. In this regard, the context plays an important role in suggesting the appropriateness of the creative work. An object placed in the context of the museum is tacitly perceived as a piece of art. A poem published in literary magazine is considered as creative, even if it is a computer generated poem (unless of course, its authorship is explicitly stated). In this respect, social recognition represents a viable aspect of creativity (Csíkszentmihályi, 1988). The capricious opinion of public judgment claims many victims in arts and science (Koestler, 1964). The case of Italian astronomer Giordano Bruno serves as the most striking example: not only was his theory of the infinity of the universe rejected by society but he was also accused of heresy and burned at the stake. Another dramatic example of rejection and condemnation by society is the Russian poet and Nobel Prize winner Joseph Brodsky, who was sentenced to exile and expelled from the Soviet Union. The Eastern tradition considers goodness a defining attribute of creativity (Niu & Sternberg, 2006). It comprises not only moral values but also social values, a contribution to collective being. The utility function of creative work therefore stipulates usefulness to a collective and the recognition of this virtue by the collective. Another consideration stemming from the Brockhous's definition relates the appropriateness of creative work to its aesthetic value. The utility of creative work is stipulated by the aesthetic reaction of the beholder, which places this work in an appropriate context. The aesthetic aspects of creative work are discussed below.

Third, as the artistic director of the 53rd Venice Biennale noted, a work of art is an expression of a world or a worldview (Birnbaum, 2009). According to this perspective, a creative work should reflect spiritual, cultural, social and political atmosphere of the time period in which an artist works. The adaptive aspect of creative utility refers to the ability of a creative work to meet the task constrains. These constrains can be relatively clearly defined in a scientific and business context. Using the previous examples, the task constraints for Einstein's discovery were set up by the laws of physics; Google's task was to streamline a rapidly growing vast amount of data presented on the internet. The rules and regulations in artistic creativity that can potentially serve as the task constraints seem to be rather vague. What constrains do Rembrandt's *Night Watch*, Malevich's *Black Square* and Warhol's *Campbell's Soup Cans* have in common besides the fact that all of them were oil painted? Nevertheless, all three works were recognized as masterpieces of artistic creativity. Can we identify a common task that these works have accomplished? In spite of great controversies that erupted around the value of these works, all of them met a task constraint identified by Birnbaum: The artists reflected the political, social and/or cultural perspectives on the environment in which they resided, each in their respective time period. *Night Watch* (or *The Company of Frans Banning Cocq and Willem van Ruytenburch*) depicts a militia unit marching off to guard the streets of Amsterdam. Citizen militia (or civic guard, *schutterij* in Dutch) in the medieval and early modern Netherlands were formed to protect towns or cities from attack and to act in case of revolt or fire. The civic guards were respectable community members providing defensive military support for the local civic authority. The painting was completed in 1642, during the last years of the Eighty Years War (1568–1648), which resulted in Dutch independence. Rembrandt therefore portrayed an important symbol of that epoch: civic guards protecting citizens of the independent Netherlands. *Black Square* (1915) reflected the essence of the *Suprematism* movement originated by Malevich, which represented an important transformation in the artistic consciousness at the beginning of the 20th century. The modern art as well as literature and music of that period realized that the established traditions were unviable and had led to a developmental cul-de-sac. To overcome the limitations of the existing forms, *Suprematism* proposed an extreme reduction of meaning. The purpose was to construct images that had no reference to reality, no connection with the real world. The depiction of real objects yielded to abstract paintings that combined fundamental geometric forms, in particular, a square and a circle. Thereby, a traditional perception of a work of art by the conscious mind has been annihilated and substituted by expression of intrinsic experience of both an artist and a beholder. Malevich (1926/2003: 67) expressed this idea in the *Suprematism* manifesto:

> Under Suprematism I understand the supremacy of pure feeling in creative art. To the Suprematist the visual phenomena of the objective world are, in themselves, meaningless; the significant thing is feeling, as such, quite apart from the environment in which it is called forth.

This development in artistic expression came about when Russia was in a revolutionary state: new ideas were fermented and the old order was being swept away. Therefore, the *Black Square* along with other suprematist works by the artist manifested a new era in both the artistic mind and the social and political environment of the country. Warhol exhibited his *Campbell's Soup Cans* in 1962 when the US art scene was dominated by the abstract expressionist art movement with its 'fine art' values and aesthetics. This work ushered in *pop art* as a major art movement in the United States. The combination of the semimechanized process in art production, the nonpainterly style and the commercial subject of *pop art* presented a direct affront to the technique and philosophy of existing expressionistic paradigm.

In his work, Warhol expressed his view of modern culture as being dominated by blatantly mundane commercialism. By presenting eminently recognizable pop culture items, he ridiculed the modern era of commercialization and indiscriminate 'sameness.' Therefore, his work was perceived by many as a satire on capitalism and a critique of pop culture (Bourdon, 1995; Livingstone & Cameron, 1992).

So far, we identified two defining features of creativity. The novelty function constitutes the production of original work that may or may not include rejection of existing paradigm. A creative work can be said to have a utility function if it is regarded by a producer or a recipient as creative or if it represents an important landmark in spiritual, cultural, social and/or political environment. An interesting observation can be extracted from the analysis of multiplying exemplars of contemporary Western art. Recall the earlier discussion of *die Fettecke*: this work is regarded as creative for it satisfies the criteria of novelty and utility.[2] It also clearly demonstrates that aesthetics – at least in its traditional definition – should not be considered as an integral component of a creative work. In general, there is a tendency in the modern world to shift a focus of creative work from aesthetic value to the novelty and utility.

At the same time, increasing empirical evidence supports the notion that individuals' aesthetic development facilitates their achievements in various areas of creative endeavors (Kay, 1996). Aesthetic reaction commonly refers to the ability to appreciate and respond to beauty. Due to this reaction highly creative people recognize ingenious problems in their field and proceed to finding creative solutions (Zuo, 1998). The mathematician Hardy (1940: 25) wrote: 'Beauty is the first test; there is no permanent place in the world for ugly mathematics.' The novelist and journalist Koestler (1964) expressed the same attitude toward the role of aesthetics in the work of many artists and physicists. The psychologist MacKinnon (1962: 490) asserted: 'For the truly creative person it is not sufficient that problems be solved, there is the further demand that the solutions be elegant. He seeks both truth and beauty.'

Indeed, aesthetics is perceived as a twofold construct. On one side, it refers to the perception of beauty, a pleasure gained by a beholder of an object. On the other side, it is bounded to the conceptions of good and truth. Ancient Greek philosophers provided a speculative perspective that aesthetical objects were beautiful in and of themselves. Plato (1991) insisted that these objects should incorporate proportion, harmony and unity among their parts. Similar to Plato, in his treaties on poetry and rhetoric, Aristotle (1998) defined the universal elements of aesthetics as order, symmetry and determinateness. He distinctly recognized that the aim of aesthetics is immediate pleasure. At the same time, these philosophers seemed to be reluctant to reduce beauty to merely sensuous pleasure. Plato perceived absolute beauty in light of Socrates' ideals: beauty is a reflection of the ideal of beauty. Aristotle determined the beautiful as the absence of all lust or desire in the pleasure it bestows. Both Plato and Aristotle believed that the concept of beauty reveals itself in relation to the concepts of truth and goodness. In his attempt to distinguish between these two phenomena, Aristotle claimed that the goodness is a characteristic of a deed, whereas the beauty may exist in motionless objects. He also asserted that although these two elements are different, the goodness might under certain conditions be called beautiful. This idea is reflected in Keats's (1819/2000: 34) poetic line 'Beauty is truth, truth beauty,' which presents the core of aesthetical sense in creation.

The aesthetic value of creative work is related to an ability to reflect ultimate truth. According to different mystical, philosophical and religious traditions, the latter may refer to the primordial infinity (*Ein-Sof* in Kabbalah, Scholem, 1974), the creative principle (God the Creator in monotheistic religions) or nature (*yin-yang* in the *Book of Changes*, Chan, 1967). It represents the essence of all things and is pervasive in all manifestations of phenomenal reality. The manifestation itself cannot be judged from an aesthetical perspective for it is the truth in and of itself. For example, we cannot evaluate the aesthetic qualities of a sunset for it embodies the truth of nature. However, we may assess the aesthetic qualities of a photograph, a painting, or a poem presenting the sunset. In this case, we talk about ability of creative work to reflect the truth of natural phenomenon. The beauty of this work can be measured by a degree of approximation to the aesthetical reaction elicited by the original. Beauty and truth were argued to be nearly synonymous (Stewart, 2007). Reber *et al.* (2004: 366) provide empirical evidence that judgments of beauty and judgments of truth both rely on 'the ease of identifying the physical identity of the stimulus' and 'the ease of mental operations concerned with stimulus meaning and its relation to semantic knowledge structures.' In other words, the judgment of both constructs is influenced by perceptual and semantic fluency. Recent research complements these findings by demonstrating that people use beauty as an indication for truth in mathematical pattern tasks (Reber *et al.*, 2008). This finding suggests that beauty in an aesthetic sense is not necessarily a characteristic of an object that provides a perceptual experience of pleasure or delights the senses. The criteria of sensual beauty seem to be subjective and contingent on time, geographic location and sociocultural environment. Peter Paul Rubens's ideal of a beautiful woman would not sustain today, especially in the Western frame of mind, the criteria of which shifted from curvaceous women to a slim model. An African tribal woman mounting large clay jewelry into her under lip may not be considered particularly beautiful by Europeans. Moreover, although beauty is semantically contrasted with ugliness, these two constructs seem to exist in one conceptual plane (Eco, 2007). Can we assert that *Las Meninas* (Maids of Honor) by Diego Velázquez is beautiful, whereas its replication by Pablo Picasso is ugly? Do we admire Sandro Botticelli's *Nascita di Venere* (The Birth of Venus) and detest Vincent van Gogh's *De Aardappeleters* (The Potato Eaters)? In both cases, these masterpieces are judged for their aesthetic value. Thus, aesthetics unites both beauty and ugliness. Rosenkranz (1853) regarded ugliness as a drawback of beauty, which became autonomous of a prototype and developed into self-standing aesthetic principle. He argued that any scientific study of aesthetics should take in consideration both beauty and ugliness. Intuitively speaking, ugly objects cannot be considered aesthetic: excrement or decayed wombs and breasts should not elicit any other reaction but disgust. However, they can find aesthetic realization in, for example, poetry concerned with the physical decay of the flesh as in Gottfried Benn's (1912) *Morgue and Other Poems*. Beauty and ugliness are characteristics of phenomenal reality, whereas their depiction is an attempt to imitate this reality. Successful imitation elicits an aesthetic reaction if it succeeds to express the truth. The image of a decomposed human body is aversive, whereas its artistic depictions such as ones in the right panel of Hieronymus Bosch's triptych *The Garden of Earthly Delights* illustrating Inferno may have great aesthetic value. Thus, aesthetics refers to sensitivity to ultimate truth.

What is beautiful about a creative solution that reveals the truth? In line with the Greek philosophical tradition discussed above, beauty is more than simple pleasure of the beholder. Rather, following Kant (1790/2007), beauty reflects perfect order in phenomenal reality, which manifests the truth. When we see a man with an edentulous mouth, we feel awkward not only because of the shape of his lips and few remaining teeth, but rather because next to those teeth should be ones that are not there (Eco, 2007). We have an unaesthetic reaction when we cannot observe the wholeness of the pattern, when we perceive a distorted order of things. Rudolf Arnheim was a great proponent of the primacy of order and balance in aesthetic judgment of creative work. He systematically applied the principles of Gestalt psychology to the study of visual perception and the arts (Arnheim, 1974). His aesthetics is based on the validation of structured order in perceptual experience. Arnheim (1992: 238) asserted: 'Great painting and sculpture as well as great architecture offered the perfection of harmony and order.' In his early writings on film, he believed that the introduction of sound into film would break the structural unity of the visual image and therefore create a 'radical artistic impoverishment' (Arnheim, 1957: 230). Then, he concluded: 'When the eyes and ears are prevented from perceiving meaningful order, they can only react to the brutal signals of immediate satisfaction' (Arnheim,

1957: 7). The aesthetic sense therefore constitutes understanding and appreciation of the fundamental truth presented in a perfect order. Moreover, as Arnheim (1971: 55–56) claimed, the latter should reflect the former: 'A high level of structural order is a necessary but not sufficient prerequisite of art. What is ultimately required is that this order reflect a genuine, true profound view of life.' This aesthetic sensitivity may lead to a realization of the absence of order and harmony and thus create an unbearable tension, and this constitutes a creative problem finding (Zuo, 1998). Arnheim believed that the fundamental goal of an organism is striving toward a balance that minimizes tension in the phenomenal field (Levine, 2002). Thus, having an aesthetic sensitivity could lead eminent individuals to the discovery of important problems in their domains. An intrinsic desire to find a perfect order could lead creative individuals to formulate a solution in the most efficient way, thereby conveying the essence of the phenomenal reality.

Indeed, the aesthetic value of creative product was argued to relate to the efficient presentation of its essence. Schmidhuber (1997) formulated an algorithmic theory of beauty, which postulates that the greatest aesthetic value is assigned to a work with the lowest complexity. The term low complexity was adopted from a theory of Kolmogorov (or algorithmic) complexity (Kolmogorov, 1965), which refers to the length (measured in number of bits) of the shortest algorithm that can be used to compute a given computable object. Schmidhuber (1997: 98) applied this term to art to identify low-complexity art objects with shortest possible description, which potentially 'capture "the essence" of what is being depicted.' Note that this theory largely relies on a beholder's particular knowledge and a specific method of information processing, for the beholder should be able to identify that a creative work has a low complexity in order to appreciate its aesthetic value. Scientific creativity provides numerous illustrations of this theory. Mathematicians respect simple proofs with a short description in their formal language. Charles Darwin summarized the entire history of natural evolution in just three words: generation, selection and preservation (Perkins, 1988). Albert Einstein brought a complex theory of relativity to a concise mathematical equation, $E = mc^2$ (Zuo, 1998). These examples demonstrate the elegance of a creative solution, which reflects the simplicity of the laws of nature. The same principles can be applied to the artistic creativity. The climax of poetic ingenuity appears in an elegant metaphor that constructs an intelligible analogy transcending conventional thinking. Italian figurative artist Amadeo Modigliani drew a pencil portrait of Russian modernist poet Anna Akhmatova using just few lines depicting Akhmatova's most prominent features and thereby revealing her essence. Schmidhuber proposed low-complexity art, which accentuates the essence of creative work with minimum description length. This genre presents 'the computer-age equivalent of minimal art' (Schmidhuber, 1997: 97), with the latter exploring the reductionist idea pervasive in the artistic mind over the entire 20th century. Kandinsky (1912/1994) identified three elementary forms (triangle, square and circle) and three primary colors (yellow, red and blue), and produced paintings using these basic visual elements. As mentioned earlier, Malevich (1926/2003) and other suprematists used abstract paintings based on fundamental geometric forms. In a similar fashion, Levine (2002) claims that Arnheim's 'law of simplicity' postulates that any perceived structure should express itself in the simplest form possible. In this theoretical framework, simplicity refers not to the expressive capacity of the work of art, but to 'its ability to encompass the highest levels of tension and complexity within the simplest possible form' (Levine, 2002: 269). Following the law of simplicity, the creative forces in a work of art should find equilibrium presented in 'the simplest structure capable of containing its complexity' (Levine, 2002). The minimalism movement in art and design presents an illustration of this perspective by utilizing the minimum facilities to reach the maximal impression. The aforementioned Malevich's *Black Square* is an example of minimalism in art. The ideal of a minimalist literary work is a blank page as in Vasilisk Gnedov's *Poem of the End*, which consists of its title alone on a blank page, and which the poet performed on stage using a silent gesture, and its ultimate realization is an empty book. The most striking example of minimalist music is John Cage's silent composition 4'33''. However, complexity for Arnheim (1977: 163) should not entail the contradiction, which he believed is 'an offense against order.' This argument contradicts Vygotsky's (1971) theory of aesthetical reaction. In his approach, the aesthetical reaction increases as a result of a complication of creative work. He asserts that additional (parallel) interpretations complicate the plot, elicit curiosity, arouse conjectures and divide attention. This encourages greater psychic energy consumption and thereby an increase in the aesthetical reaction: 'The greater the expenditure of nervous energy, the more intense is the effect produced by the work of art.'(Vygotsky: 205). Any work of art – if it claims to elicit a strong aesthetical reaction – should include several psychic planes with opposite force. The contradiction between conflicting psychological aspects of creative work creates an 'explosion' of psychic energy, elicits cathartic experience, which in turn reinforces the aesthetical reaction. For Vygotsky, 'Aesthetic response, above all, is a response that annihilates our nervous energy; it is an explosion' (ibid.). He explains a multifaceted nature of creative work in the following passage:

> In order to be really alive, the tragic character must be composed of contradictory traits and must carry us from one emotion to another.

The physiognomic incongruency among the various details of the facial expression in a portrait is the basis for our emotional reaction; and the psychological non-coincidence of the various factors expressing the character in a tragedy is the basis for our tragic sympathy. By forcing our feelings to alternate continuously to the opposite extremes of the emotional range, by deceiving them, splitting them and piling obstacles in their way, the tragedy can obtain powerful emotional effect. (Vygotsky: 194)

As one can see, there is an apparent disagreement between Vygotsky's emphasis of the essential role of contradiction in the aesthetical reaction and Arnheim's declaim against this. Arnheim, however, changed his opinion in his later works and recognized that 'because meaning is often complex, the work of art must admit tension and complexity as intrinsic to its structural wholeness' (Levine, 2002: 272). Nevertheless, complexity and even intrinsic contradictions should not lead to disorder, because if there is disorder the work of art loses its expressive capacity.

Thus, the aesthetic value of creative work reflects its ability to address its essence in a most intelligible and elegant way. Aesthetic sense therefore refers to 'both perfect understanding and appreciation of the truth' (Zuo, 1998: 309). The ideals of aesthetic experience discussed by Plato, Aristotle and Kant were concerned with the fundamental truth of nature, which is reflected in a perfect order. The beauty of creative work constitutes the resemblance of the perfect order inherent to the ultimate truth. At the same time, this work should be satisfactorily complex, expressing both tension and intrinsic contradiction. Together, they elicit an aesthetical reaction in the beholder. Therefore, the following keywords might describe aesthetics: truth, order, essence and complexity.

In the beginning of this section, a claim was made that novelty in thinking is a prerogative of the Western creative tradition. However, a unique approach in creative production is not completely rejected from the horizon of the Eastern thought. Rather, following Confucian aesthetics, creativity is a process of breathing in a new essence into existing ideas to reflect an individual's own values and beliefs (Tu, 1985). That is, the old ideas are to be smoothly modified to fit new circumstances. In this tradition, a person's authentic perception becomes a creativity transporter. Instead of trying to establish a unique phenomenon by breaking up with old traditions, a person cultivates one's authentic approach, which can be applied to both old and new. Therefore, self-cultivation of an individual's authenticity becomes a fourth criterion of creative process. Averill *et al.* (2001) illustrate the relelvance of this criterion with an example of a computer-generated fractal image. The outcome of computer-generated work can satisfy the criterion of novelty; it can meet task constraints thereby satisfying the criterion of utility; it can even have aesthetic value considering the order and complexity begotten by a simple design of the fractal. However, it misses an important component, which questions its overall creative value, namely, authenticity. Averill and coworkers cite Arnheim's assertion that creativity involves 'the pregnant sight of reality' (Averill *et al.*: 299). Then they continue: 'Computers are lifeless: they have no inner vision, pregnant or otherwise. In a word, they lack authenticity' (Averill *et al.*: 172).

What is the role of authenticity in creative production? This component seems to refer to ability to express one's inner self and to relate an individual's own values and beliefs to the world. A perfect copy of Velázquez's *Las Meninas* is not considered a creative work when each detail is replicated with ideal precision, whereas a variation produced by Picasso is regarded as a masterpiece. The difference between these two appears in the degree of self-expression that is minimal in the former work and striking in the latter one. Picasso's work is authentic whereas the copy is not. Authenticity imparts meaning to a creative act by providing an opportunity for realization and manifestation of the self. It enables individuals to explore their own nature and to relate events in phenomenal reality to their own values and beliefs. In Buddhist tradition, the self is identified with the universe: 'My mind is exactly the universe and the universe is exactly my mind' (Lu Hsuang Shan's complete book, cited in Niu & Sternberg, 2006: 30). In this framework, comprehension of the self endows an individual with the knowledge of ultimate truth and imparts meaning to one's existence. In words of great Confucian master Mencius:

> There is no greater joy for me than to find, on self-examination, that I am true to myself. […] For a man to give full realization to his heart is for him to understand his own nature; and a man who knows his own nature will know Heaven. (cited in Niu & Sternberg, 2006: 30)

Moreover, according to the earlier discussion, an ability to reflect the ultimate truth is related to the aesthetic value of creative work. Therefore, authentic involvement in a creative act increases the aesthetic value of the product. The realization of the self in the authentic act provides meaning to human life. Death eradicates this meaning. Sartre considered death 'the most unexpected event occurring in human existence, eliminating all its meaningfulness and transforming it into a useless passion' (Thomas, 1998: 322). Authenticity in creative performance allows the mortal self to embody in the immortal product, which gives a gratification to individuals in their combat with death.

We remember the names of Velázquez and Picasso, and disregard the names of countless art forgers copying the works of eminent artists.

The impetus of an authentically creative act should stem from inner urge rather than from outer request. This doctrine is known to psychologists as a humanistic model of self-actualization. Maslow (1943: 382) explicitly defines an individual's self-actualization as 'the tendency for him to become actualized in what he is potentially. This tendency might be phrased as the desire to become more and more what one is, to become everything that one is capable of becoming.' The creative acts of self-actualized people are inspired by their authentic perception. At the same time, Rogers (1961) believes that we can achieve the actualization of our intrinsic potential only if society allows it. This introduces an inherent controversy about authenticity that was largely discussed by Sartre (1943/1992). On the one side, an individual's self is unique and different from the world; on the other hand, this self is situated in a world that contains the authentic selves of other individuals. Therefore, the authentic realization seeks some compromise with external ideologies, which allows it to coexist in a manner acceptable by the others. In other words, the inner urges of authentic expression are limited by public ethics and morality. This consideration presents another aspect of creativity, moral goodness. Eastern ideology considers social and moral values as important criteria of creative behavior. Niu and Sternberg (2006: 24) argue that moral goodness was pervasive in the ancient Western tradition as well: 'Ancient Westerners were more likely to believe that moral goodness is necessary in creativity, because all God's creations are good.' If authenticity stems from realization of the inner potential, which is akin to the source of creation, and if the nature of the latter is creating all goodness, including moral goodness, the autheniticity principle requires high moral standards. In the Eastern mind, however, these standards imply collective being and refer to contribution to the whole society. Thereby, it points to the utility function of creative endeavor, which was discussed earlier.

A four-criterion construct proposed in this section expands the traditional perspective on creativity assumed as an endeavor that delivers an original product that can be put to some use. In addition to novelty and utility, creativity should have aesthetic and authentic merits. These criteria seem to represent the universal principles of creativity as they can be applied to different areas of human endeavor including arts, sciences and business. Only the presence of all four virtues ensures the ultimate creative outcome. This notion seems to be quite controversial as there is an opinion that 'Creativity is not something that products either have or do not have, but, there are both *levels* and *kinds* of creativity' (Cropley & Cropley, 2008: 157). Different products can express different kinds of creativity and express creativity to a greater or lesser extent (Sternberg *et al.*, 2001). According to this perspective, the creativity construct has a hierarchical structure comprising four levels: novelty, effectiveness, genesis and elegance (see Table 1 in Cropley & Cropley: 157). Routine product has only the value of effectiveness, the original product has an additional value of novelty, the elegant product an additional value of elegance and only the innovative product has all four values. Note, however, that even this hierarchical construct assumes that a product satisfying all four criteria is considered as most creative: 'Innovative is more creative than elegant, whereas elegant is more creative than original' (Cropley & Cropley: 157).

Another interesting observation is concerned with the authentic value of the proposed creativity construct. Previously mentioned Cropley and Cropley's (2008) creativity has four characteristics: novelty, effectiveness, genesis and elegance. The first one overlaps with the novelty dimension of the proposed construct, the second and third ones with utility and the fourth one with aesthetics. The authenticity criteria proposed in the present construct is omitted from that model. Similarly, the definition adopted in Creative Product Semantic Scale (Besemer & O'Quin, 1987) assumes creativity as a three-dimensional construct: novelty (the product is original, surprising and germinal), resolution (the product is valuable, logical, useful and understandable) and elaboration and synthesis (the product is organic, elegant, complex and well crafted). These three dimensions overlap with novelty, utility and aesthetics of the proposed four-criterion construct, respectively, and authenticity is omitted again. Cropley and Cropley's and Besemer and O'Quin's models approximate the proposed model the most, and nevertheless they disregard the authentic value of creative endeavor. This observation confirms an argument made earlier that this criterion is more pervasive in the Eastern frame of thought and not yet elaborated in the Western perspective of creativity.

Summarizing this discussion, it seems to be prudent to expand a theoretical framework of creativity and consider it as a four-criterion construct that includes novelty, utility, aesthetics and authenticity. An enriched definition of creativity requires a new model of creative thinking that accounts for all four criteria. This model is proposed in the following section.

An Alternative Model of Creativity

Although this model differs from most creativity models, it adopts their crucial characteristics. First, most creativity models assume that there is a sequential character to creative processes; this model, in contrast, presumes that parallel processing underlies creative thought. Second, the reviewed models converge on a fundamental distinction between two types of processing: Guilford's (1967) divergent/convergent thinking, Mumford's (2000) early/late cycle capacity, Kharkhurin's (2009) generative/innovative capacity and conscious/unconscious creative thinking. This dichotomy suggests an integration of two oppositely directed forces in creative processing. The proposed model adopts this dichotomy and introduces three force axes reflecting the nature of underlying creative processes: (a) *expansive* force characterized by the processes of expanding, revealing and generating; (b) *restrictive* force characterized by the processes of constraining, concealing and shaping; and (c) *integrative* force that combines, merges elements into a qualitatively new entity. These three forces correspond to a Hegelian-like dialectical triad: thesis stipulating its reaction, antithesis contradicting or negating the thesis and synthesis resolving the tension between the two (Kaufmann, 1965). Third, the model embraces the four-dimensional nature of the creativity construct discussed in the previous section. It reflects this multidimensional characteristic in the form of creativity spheres, each of which corresponds to a specific aspect of creativity: a superconscious sphere which corresponds to authenticity, an intellectual sphere to novelty, an emotive sphere to aesthetics and an active sphere to utility. Finally, creativity literature distinguishes between divinely inspired and individual creativity (see Niu & Sternberg, 2006, for a discussion). The former type of creativity ascribes the source of inspiration to supernatural forces, whereas the latter type attributes a particular inspiration to human cognition. The four sphere structure of the present model combines both traditions by differentiating between divine (superconscious) and mundane (conscious) layers. The former includes the superconscious sphere, consisting of superconscious pleasures and will, whereas the latter includes three other spheres: intellectual, emotive and active. The latter layer is divided into two stages of idea processing. The intellectual sphere is involved in idea conception, whereas the spheres of emotion and action are involved in idea realization and production. Thus, according to the proposed model, the construct of creativity is composed of four spheres and three force axes. The first sphere is grounded in superconscious layer and the other three in conscious layer. Each force axis springs from the superconscious layer and penetrates each conscious sphere, thereby establishing a creativity unit in the place of infiltration. Therefore, the proposed model consists of three superconscious and nine conscious creativity units (see Figure 6.1), each of which presents a separate phase of creative processing.

The first sphere reflects the tradition of divinely inspired creativity. It represents an authentic impulse to create. This sphere consists of two types of pleasure and will. The former is represented by supreme and creative pleasures. The *supreme pleasure* of creation reflects an individual's sense of

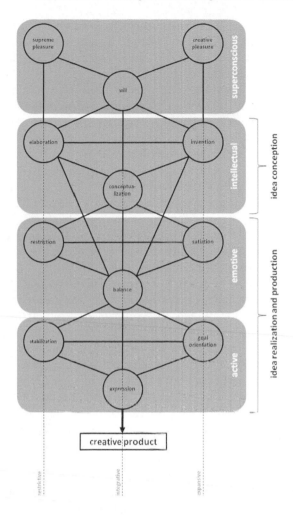

Figure 6.1 Schematic representation of the creativity model. It consists of superconscious sphere and three conscious spheres (intellectual, emotive and active) penetrated by three force axes (expansive, restrictive and integrative). Each force axis springs from the superconscious layer and penetrates each conscious sphere, thereby establishing a creativity unit in the place of infiltration. Each of these units presents a separate phase of creative processing. Thus, according to this model, creativity consists of three superconscious (creative pleasure, supreme pleasure and will), three intellectual (invention, elaboration and conceptualization), three emotive (satiation, restriction and balance) and three active (goal orientation, stabilization and expression) processes, the collaborative work of which results in creative product.

creative capacity and relates this capacity to a divine source of creation. This pleasure links one's ability to create to its divine prototype and thereby ensures the authenticity of creative process. The supreme pleasure facilitates an individual's anticipation of the creative process; that is, it serves as a precursor to creative pleasure. The *creative pleasure* represents a potential to gain gratification in the process of creation and signifies the initiation of creative process. The *will* represents a creative force that seeks outlets for creative capacity and ensures the gratification gained from a creative act. The creative pleasure reinforces the will by gaining gratification for intellect, emotions and actions. In contrast, the supreme pleasure restricts this creative force by identifying a pace of creativity that provides a closest approximation to the supreme source of inspiration. The combination of reinforcing and restrictive aspects of the will results in an individual's ability to suspend gratification of creative process to ensure a better outcome. Therefore, the supreme pleasure serves as a source of restrictive force, the creative pleasure expansive force and the will integrative force.

The second sphere represents the *intellectual* creative principle. This sphere ensures the originality of creative idea. The expansive force of intellect results in idea conception, which is accompanied by problem identification. This is a phase of *invention*, in which the intellect receives creative energy from creative pleasure, resulting in spontaneous insights characterized by an individual's realization of his/her creative potential. At the same time, the restrictive force of intellect facilitates the development of ideas, accompanied by problem formulation. This is a phase of *elaboration*, in which intellect, fed by supreme pleasure, ensures the transformation of invented ideas into full-bodied constructions of mature thoughts and ideas. In this phase, an individual experiences satisfaction through feelings of creative accomplishment. The integrative force synthesizes the inventive and elaborative efforts and finalizes the formulation of a problem so that it can be transferred to the other spheres for further processing. This is a phase of *conceptualization*, in which the unification of innovative and elaborative principles facilitates the free and uninterrupted flow of new insights into the cognitive realm while at the same time allowing those insights to constantly mature and develop. The conceptualization process serves as a relay station that binds together the scattered thoughts conceived and elaborated during other phases of the intellectual sphere into a well-defined creative idea and forwards this idea to the emotive sphere for further realization and production. It bridges the intellectual and emotive spheres and thereby brings the creative idea to reality. In this phase, the idea is converted into a force that vitalizes and inspires the creative composition as well as achieves expression through action and deed. This force enables creative individuals to bring their productive capacities to the enlightening power of their intellect. If the idea has not been sufficiently conceptualized, the intellectual and productive capacities resist the mediation and persist in operating independent of each other. The incongruence between intellectual conception of the idea and its realization might result in faulty creative processing and eventually in premature creative outcome. The conceptualization phase is a center of the creative process (and the center of the proposed model). On the one side, it connects emotions to the superconscious by submitting the formulated idea to the conclusions of reasoned analysis so that it can be refined and rectified. On the other side, conceptualization assists in finding equilibrium between contradicting elements of the emotive sphere (satiation and restriction) by applying structure to them. Finally, successful intellectual processing is contingent on the richness of both one's knowledge base and one's ability to manipulate its elements.

The third sphere represents the *emotional* component of creative production. Its function is to establish a composition of creative work that manifests its aesthetic principles. A creative problem formulated during the conceptualization phase seeks its solution in the emotive sphere. The expansive force of emotion enables an initial creative idea to propagate and flourish, to accumulate additional nuances. This is a phase of *satiation*, which elaborates on a problem and promotes maturation of the creative solution. During this phase, a creative individual endorses the total development of a creative idea. The opposite restrictive force of emotion limits creative space to prevent oversaturation with details (as in the works of art) or to express oneself in a circumlocutory manner (as in scientific work). This is a phase of *restriction*, which subtracts the unnecessary details and reduces the creative process to the expression of its essence, thereby preserving the integrality of creative work. The restriction phase facilitates a stylistic completeness that prevents eclecticism and chaos in the creative process. This phase encourages an increasing order that promotes the aesthetical reaction to creative work. The joint work of satiation and restriction phases ensures a high aesthetical value of the creative work, which is formalized in the harmonious blend of two opposites in the phase of *balance*. This phase represents equilibrium, a perfect solution to a creative problem. Note that when compromise between restriction and satiation is necessary, this phase favors the latter. The balance phase represents the central point of creative production in both emotive and active spheres, and therefore connects to the phases in both spheres. The focal point of this phase underlines the crucial virtue of creative product – its aesthetic value.

The fourth sphere represents *action*, the physical processing of creative ideas. Its function is to implement a creative idea in a presentable form: text, visual object, music, scientific presentation and so on. The outcome of this sphere is creative product. The expansive force of action mobilizes an individual's innate resources to design a realistic plan to achieve success in creative production. This is a phase of *goal orientation* reinforced by personality traits such as self-confidence and motivation. This phase is a response to the enlightened need aroused through the influence of intellect upon the emotions. Therefore, an individual's initiative and persistence in this phase plays a crucial role in overcoming the inertial opposition preventing one from translating thoughts and feelings into positive action. The restrictive force of action provides stability to creative production by ensuring an unshakeable commitment to a chosen path. This is a phase of *stabilization*, which provides a complementary anchor to goal orientation. This phase allows the process of creation to overcome obstacles and to hold its proper course even at its active momentum advancing toward creative fulfillment. This phase is reinforced by personality traits such as sincerity, constancy of vision and persevering optimism. Thus, these two phases stabilize creative production while moving it forward. Goal orientation serves to advance an individual toward the ultimate creative product and helps to overcome setbacks along the way. Stabilization provides the steadying force that bolsters one against spiritual fatigue by fixing one's consciousness on the ultimate goal. At the same time, the expansive and restrictive forces maintain a connection of these phases with the superconscious source of creation. The third phase of action provides the essential logistical input that helps to relate the ground plan of superconscious will to outer reality. This is a phase of *expression*, which constitutes concrete and active involvement of creative idea with the real world. During this phase, an individual seeks a balance between the abstraction of the initial creative idea and the expressiveness of creative product. Thereby, it reenacts the balance maintained during the conceptualization phase between intellectual and emotive spheres. During the expression phase, an individual deals with the moral aspect of creation (moral goodness) as well, thereby manifesting the utility function of creativity. This phase is a conclusion of creative process, which provides a means for the formulation and verification of the creative process. The outcome is the perfection of the material realization of a *creative product* and its unification with superconscious purpose to create.

Summary

This chapter presents speculative theoretical considerations in creativity inspired by the author's research in multilingual creative cognition. Two major frameworks for further investigation are proposed. First, generative/

innovative capacity model is introduced as an alternative to traditional creativity models. In contrast to the latter, which assume consequent order of application of the constituting processes, the proposed model assumes that both capacities may be applied in parallel. They differ in the nature of the underlying processes rather than in the chronological order. Generative capacity encourages an individual to produce and elaborate on a multitude of solutions to a problem. Innovative capacity encourages one to explore, criticize, evaluate, manipulate and revise obtained solutions to produce novel creative solutions. Only interrelated application of both creative capacities might lead to successful creative functioning.

Second, this chapter provides a new perspective on creativity construct and introduces a unified model of creativity that addresses philosophical, epistemological and empirical aspects of this construct. This perspective unites Western and Eastern traditions and proposes a four-criterion approach to creativity, which includes novelty, utility, aesthetics and authenticity. These creativity features serve as the conceptual domains for a new model of creative thinking. This model is composed of four creative spheres (superconscious, intellectual, emotive and active) and three force axes (expansive, restrictive and integrative). The superconscious sphere consists of two types of pleasure and will, each of which serves as a source of a respective force axis. The intellectual sphere is involved in idea conception. The emotive and active spheres are involved in idea realization and production. Each force axis penetrates intellectual, emotive and active spheres and establishes a creativity unit in the place of infiltration. Therefore, the proposed model consists of 12 creativity units, each of which presents a separate phase of creative processing: supreme pleasure, creative pleasure, will, invention, elaboration, conceptualization, satiation, restriction, balance, goal orientation, stabilization and expression.

The proposed model presents a speculative account for creative endeavor. It goes beyond the traditional definitions of creativity and expands an inventory of creative processes generally adopted in scientific literature. It is evident that its complexity requires substantial elaboration and empirical investigation to formalize it as a functional framework for creativity research. However, the author anticipates that this model may receive a substantial criticism in academic community for the infeasibility of empirical investigation of some of its component. This understanding comes from the fact that this model incorporates elements that address divine sources of inspiration, which are not readily appreciated by contemporary scientific research. Nevertheless, the author trusts that a combined effort of empirical and mystical investigations may provide evidence for this model and facilitate its further development.

Notes

(1) This distinction, although widely used in scientific literature, presents unsubtle, if not reductive, perspective on a rich variety of sociocultural values and norms found in these geographic locations. Actually, Western and Eastern worlds appear to be heterogeneous with respect to available social and cultural constructs. For example, the United States, which is typically considered as embracing Western ideology, comprises of communities such as Amish, which do not share traditional Western views. The geographic terms applied to sociocultural systems create confusion, and therefore should be taken with caution. Generally speaking, the Western thought refers to the European–American tradition since the Renaissance, and the Eastern refers to traditional cultures found in certain portions of Asia and Africa. Although, for the lack of a better distinction, the present discussion continues using these terms, it utilizes the differentiation between the West and the East along philosophical and sociocultural rather than geographic and racial/national dimensions.

(2) Fat and felt played a central role in formation of Beuys's artistic identity. In 1944, his combat plane was shot down and crashed on the Crimean Front. In a subsequent recount of this event, Beuys claimed having been rescued from the crash by nomadic Tatar tribesmen, who had wrapped his broken body in animal fat and felt and nursed him back to health. 'They covered my body in fat to help it regenerate warmth, and wrapped it in felt as an insulator to keep warmth in' (Tisdall, 1979: 16–17). From the perspective of the artist, fat presents an important symbol in the formation of his artistic persona, and therefore satisfies the utility function of creativity.

7 Implications of Multilingual Creative Cognition for Education

Overview

Modern people devote a vast period of their youth to education to acquire basic knowledge, skills and competencies. This baggage serves as a foundation for development throughout their life and to a large extent determines their career progress. This consideration emphasizes the essential role of education in human enterprise. In line with the content of this book, the present chapter focuses on multilingual and creative aspects of education. The objective of the chapter is to present an outline of a new educational program that combines the methods and teaching techniques of both bilingual and creative education. Naturally, before introducing a new concept, one needs to provide theoretical premises therefore.

The chapter starts off with discussing the importance of introducing bilingual and creative education to a school curriculum. In the era of massive migration and international cooperation, people with different native languages and cultural backgrounds form new social groups, in which multilingual practices appear to be prevalent. This tendency needs to be reflected in the educational context by means of focusing more attention on learning of foreign languages. It is also important to recognize a distinction between migrants learning a dominant language of the country of migration and autochthons learning a foreign language. The goal of the former is to both facilitate their autochthonal language learning and to improve their cultural adaptation. The goal of the latter is to improve foreign language skills and multicultural awareness. These two groups of language learners have somewhat distinct and at the same time overlapping goals. Thereby, the importance of combining bilingual programs targeting both migrant and local student populations is emphasized. Furthermore, the chapter criticizes existing school curriculum for discouraging students' creative abilities. What we observe is a steady decline of school children's creative behavior. A potential reason for this decline appears to be teachers' attitudes and methods generally adopted in standard education that provide little opportunity for the flourishing of creative potential in school context. The discussion pinpoints particular teaching methods hindering development of creative potentials. At the same time, the demands of contemporary world claim a growing need to nurture individuals with high standards of creative involvement. The contradictions between the current state of educational system and the increasing demands for creative enterprise emphasize the importance of creative education as never before.

A growing understanding of the importance of multilingual and creative factors in the educational system has been reflected in the policies implemented by a number of government institutions. They recognize creative education as a potential investment in students' and country's future. They also acknowledge challenges presented to the school system by increased migration. Specifically, they identify substantial differences in the quality of education available to children from migrant backgrounds and their native peers. A response to these policies was government-funded projects targeting bilingual and creative education. As a result of these initiatives, a number of bilingual and creative education programs have been developed. However, it is evident that programs are received with caution due to limited body of scientific support. Public opinion also casts doubts on the efficiency of these forms of education. The chapter presents these concerns and reveals their erroneous nature.

Altogether, a discussion of potential advantages and disadvantages of both bilingual and creative education models establishes a solid theoretical foundation on which a new program is being introduced. The Bilingual Creative Education (BCE) program combines the methods and teaching techniques adopted from both bilingual and creative education systems. The last section of the chapter provides empirical evidence for this form of education and sketches the essential attributes of the proposed program.

The Importance of Bilingual and Creative Education

The multilingual and creative aspects of education receive a growing interest as they were identified among the key directions in educational policies in many developed countries. For example, in a recent report to European parliaments the European Commission stressed 'the key role of education and training for the future growth, long-term competitiveness and social cohesion of the Union' in the 21st century (Comission of the European Communities, 2008: 3). The commission identified certain 'key competences,' which were defined as the 'combination of knowledge, skills and attitudes [...] all individuals need for personal fulfillment and development, active citizenship, social inclusion and employment' (Borrell Fontelles & Enestam, 2006: 13). Among these competencies were the learning of foreign languages and development of innovation and creativity.

A new era of massive migration and post-World War II international cooperation raised a need to accommodate people with different native languages and cultural backgrounds. In those decades, a substantial body of research on multilingual cognitive development (overviewed in Chapter 2) has delivered a sound argument that speaking more than one language has particular cognitive advantages for children and adults. In spite of some opposition (see discussion in the following section), professional and public opinions as well as government policies recognize the effectiveness of multilingual education. This recognition encourages a rapid expansion of a wide variety of programs fostering bilingual education.

In the United States, bilingual education receives considerable governmental attention already in the past 50 years. In 1968, the US Congress introduced the Bilingual Education Act, which was targeted directly at minority students, and has revisited that legislation on seven separate occasions. In that period, US Federal District Courts and the US Supreme Court have rendered judgments protecting the rights of language minority students. However, despite this consistent federal recognition, bilingual education has had a controversial history, particularly in recent years. Garcia (2008: 335) notes this ambivalence:

> Through state legislation, 12 states mandate Bilingual Education services for language minority students, 12 states permit these services, and one state prohibits them. Twenty-six states have no legislation that directly addresses language minority students. [...] states like California (2000), Arizona (2001), and Massachusetts (2003) have passed voter initiated propositions to limit the use of Bilingual Education. Colorado (2003) rejected a similar effort.

As one can see, the issues with bilingual education in the United States are primarily related to the migrant population. The students in bilingual programs are usually ethnic minorities (primarily of Latino origins), and the discourse of bilingual education here is concerned with the successful acquisition of English. The intention is to facilitate the learning process of students who come to school speaking a language different from the predominant language of instruction. This form of bilingual education therefore ensures a successful transition for nonnative speaking students so that they can follow their school's curriculum at an age-appropriate level in the language of instruction. These transitional programs can be categorized in two groups according to the methods of instructions and the content of the curriculum. The first group uses the umbrella term 'autochthonal language' as L2 (e.g. English for Speakers of other Languages, English as a Foreign Language and English as L2). Here, speakers of different native languages learn L2 through a set of standard language learning instructions. Mainly, these programs are organized by the host government or private organizations to help newcomers settle into their adopted country. The goal of these programs is to advance individuals' command of the autochthonal language so that they can perform the necessities of daily life and help their professional development. The second group is generally referred to as sheltered immersion programs (e.g. Sheltered English Immersion, Echevarria *et al.*, 2000). These programs provide language instructions in specific content areas (e.g. arts, natural sciences). The principal difference between, for example, the English for Speakers of other Languages and Sheltered English Immersion programs is that the latter facilitates students' academic development while improving their proficiency in English: students acquire the curriculum comparable at the same rate as the native English speakers. Thus, the sheltered instructions do not focus entirely on language development; rather L2 proficiency is achieved through a variety of curricular methods (e.g. classroom discussion, reading, writing and extramural activities). These methods allow students to attach content to newly acquired language by placing it in a natural linguistic context. Academic achievements are often accompanied by socialization practices, which make the content more accessible.

The major characteristic of both types of programs constitutes the detachment from the native language of the students. The absence of native language instructions presents a limitation to these programs, because the focus on L2 learning often comes at the cost of the native language skills. Even bilingual transitional education programs, which seem to emphasize both languages (Ovando *et al.*, 2006), start with native language instructions in early grades, continue L2 instruction with increasing consistency in later grades and eventually eliminate native language instruction completely toward the end of the program. The tendency to eliminate the native language from school curriculums in the United States seems to be stipulated by the urge of early immigrants to assimilate into mainstream American society. As Chavez (1992: 2) suggests:

> Every previous group – Germans, Irish, Italians, Greeks, Jews, Poles – struggled to be accepted fully into the social, political, and economic mainstream, sometimes against the opposition of a hostile majority. They

learned the language, acquired education and skills, and adapted their own customs and traditions to fit into an American context. Assimilation proved an effective model for members of these ethnic groups, who now rank among the most successful Americans, as measured by earnings and education.

Ironically, the social and professional success in the country of immigrants turns out to be contingent on an individual's ability to minimize the link to one's ethnic, cultural and linguistic origins and to assimilate into mainstream English speaking society. This tendency developed to the extent of forced assimilation like in a story described by Rodriguez (1985) when his Spanish was literally beaten out of him by the English-speaking nuns. The result of this kind of assimilation could be the substantial or complete rejection of both native tongue and tradition, forcing people with a natural predisposition to multilingualism and multiculturalism to become 'normalized' into a nation of anecdotal monolinguals and monoculturals.

Fortunately, this tendency was changed in the 1960s, when an increasing number of scientific studies came to conclusion similar to Garcia's (2008: 324) assertion that 'bilingualism is positive linguistic, social, and educational characteristic that should be developed in those children who come to school not speaking English.' Bilingual education therefore would encourage students to maintain their specific identity based on the language and traditions of their parents (Chavez, 1992). The rationale for combining both L1 and L2 training in bilingual programs finds its roots in Cummins's (1979: 222) argument that 'a cognitively and academically beneficial form of bilingualism can be achieved only on the basis of adequately developed first language [...] skills.' This argument is rooted in a combination of threshold and developmental interdependence hypotheses. The threshold hypothesis (Cummins, 1976) states that bilinguals need to achieve a minimum (age-appropriate) proficiency threshold in both of their languages to avoid possible cognitive disadvantages and to promote potential cognitive and academic advantages. According to this hypothesis, a student learning L2 should also ensure the appropriate acquisition of L1. The developmental interdependence hypothesis (Cummins, 1978b) proposes that the development of competence in L2 is partially stipulated by the mastery of already acquired L1. This hypothesis implies that linguistic and cognitive skills acquired through L1 can be transferred to L2. Together, these hypotheses suggest that students' successful linguistic and cognitive development and educational progress are contingent on a parallel acquisition of both languages. Cummins (1984: 40) argues that 'bilingual instruction appears to offer students a potentially enriching educational environment. For language minority students, this potential appears to be realized only when their L1 continues to develop as they are acquiring L2.' Thus, educational programs emphasizing acquisition of both languages should deliver the most beneficial outcome for both language acquisition and school progress.[1]

If the United States has a prolonged history of massive migration, many European countries are facing this phenomenon for the first time. In light of an increased migration to the European states, the debate on multilingual education in Europe has evolved around the support of the mother tongue of migrant children. The majority of the responses to the EU's study of the education of children from a migrant background emphasized that 'supporting the heritage language is an important contribution to the effort of promoting multilingualism in schools.' (Commission of the European Communities, 2009: 13). Supporting the mother tongue, it is argued, builds 'the necessary bridge towards learning the host country language; it contributes decisively to early socialization, and to emotional and cognitive development' (ibid.). Results of the consultation identified some member states that have already adopted policies supporting maintenance of migrants' native languages. Sweden ensures a right of foreign students to learn their mother tongue throughout compulsory education. The United Kingdom developed methods for teaching and certifying the knowledge of heritage languages. The Irish school leaving certificate may include heritage language grades. The Rucksack language development program in Nordrhein-Westfalen (Germany) provides materials for both students and parents supporting the heritage languages.

The government of the EU proposed a number of initiatives dealing with challenges presented to the school system by increased migration. Analysis of migration and education initiated by the European Commission (*Council of the European Communities* 2009) revealed substantial differences in the quality of education available to children from migrant backgrounds and their native peers. These differences increase segregation between migrant and native children on cultural and socioeconomic grounds. As a result, there is a considerable gap in achievement between migrants and autochthons. This difference is also manifested in the finding that early school drop-out among migrant students is twice as much as the one among their native counterparts, and in some countries second-generation migrant students show lower educational achievement than the first generation. These observations raise an important concern regarding limited opportunities for children from a migrant background for social integration, employment and active citizenship. As a result, the European Commission acknowledged that the presence of significant numbers of migrant children has far-reaching implications on the educational system and undertook a consultation on this issue in 2008. One of the foremost outcomes of the consultation (Commission of the European

Communities, 2009) accentuated the strengthening of language acquisition policies.

However, retention of the migrants' mother tongue appears to be not a dominant factor in bilingual education discourse in the Union. One can see that migrants comprise here only a small portion of the student body. Considering the tendency of multilingualism to promote linguistic and cognitive development, the acquisition of foreign languages by the native speakers of the European countries becomes primary concern of the educational programs. The EU provides substantial financial support for foreign language learning. For example, today it spends more than 30 million a year for the *Socrates* and *Leonardo da Vinci* programs, which promote language learning and linguistic diversity. Beginning in 1989, the EU Council issued the *Common European Framework of Reference for Languages* (broadened in 1996) as part of a larger project, *Language Learning for European Citizenship*. The Framework provides tools to assess foreign language learners' performance across Europe. In 2001, a Council Resolution recommended using this system of assessment and teaching for all language instruction in Europe.

Furthermore, to support multilingual practices, the EU Commission for Multilingualism has been established in 2007. Its purpose was to promote multilingualism by formulating language policies with a specific focus on foreign language learning. Moreover, *Presidency Conclusions* (European Council, 2002: 19) emphasized that the target of the European Council should be to promote multilingualism 'by teaching at least two foreign languages from a very early age.' This practice, though, has a long tradition in the schools in which the instructions are given in both native and foreign languages. For example, Peques bilingual Anglo-Spanish nursery in London (United Kingdom) provides education in Spanish and English to toddlers and preschool children. The French Gymnasium in Berlin (Germany) offers a certificate of secondary education (*das Abitur*) in both French and German. The students in this gymnasium are native speakers of either French or German and they study together in the same classrooms. The school management emphasizes the cultural and educational traditions of both France and Germany and operates according to the legal and official requirements of both countries.

The prudence of introducing creative education has also gradually gained support in some governments' policies. Policy makers recognize creative education as a potential investment in their students' and country's future. Craft (2007) reports that starting in the 1990s legislators from around the globe (Australia, Canada, China, Europe, Hong Kong, the Middle East and Singapore) began to endorse initiatives facilitating the development of students' creative potential. For example, the United Kingdom witnessed a revival of a discourse on the role of creativity in society and economy (Craft,

2005). In the late 1990s, the National Endowment for Science, Technology and the Arts and the National Advisory Committee on Creative and Cultural Education were established. Their goals are to identify and fund creativity and innovation in different areas of human endeavor, and to carry out research and evaluation focusing on these skills. The Qualification and Curriculum Authority and Department for Education and Employment identified creative thinking as a key skill in the National Curriculum (*The National Curriculum Handbook for Primary Teachers in England*, 1999; *The National Curriculum Handbook for Secondary Teachers in England*, 1999). This initiative entailed launching of a number of projects and policies with the focus on introducing creativity to the school curriculum (e.g. *Creativity: Find it, Promote it!*, *Excellence in Cities, Excellence and Enjoyment*) as well as establishing funds encouraging teachers' creativity and thinking (e.g. *Best Practice Research Scholarships* and *Professional Bursaries*, see Craft, 2005, for details). In the same vein, in the communication from the Commission of European Communities (Comission of the European Communities 2008: 3), the role of creative education in the progress of the EU was stressed explicitly:

> The European Council has repeatedly stressed the key role of education and training for the future growth, long-term competitiveness and social cohesion of the Union. To achieve this it is crucial fully to develop the potential for innovation and creativity of European citizens. The education element of the knowledge triangle 'research-innovation-education' should be strengthened, starting early – in schools.

Since Guilford's (1950) seminal presidential address to the American Psychological Association, numerous research works have been aimed at identifying and studying creativity. Creativity was proclaimed as a necessary component of intellectual, economic and social progress (Cropley, 2001). However, society lacks creativity, and this is a problem of education. This unfortunate observation aroused a keen interest in methods and techniques enhancing creativity through formal training. The result of this initiative was a substantial amount of scientific and semiscientific educational programs aimed at fostering creativity as well as popular and commercial publications aimed at organizations and individuals.

It should not come as a surprise that anyone with normal cognitive capacities can reach a level of accomplishment in some domain that results in producing work that some people may consider creative (Amabile, 1983a). This means that everyone has a potential to develop creative abilities. Recently, Kaufman and Beghetto (2009) proposed a model of creativity in which they distinguished between Big-C eminent creativity, Pro-C noneminent but professional creativity, little-c everyday creativity and mini-c interpretive creativity. According to this model, two small-c types of creativity are inherent to any person and can be nurtured by proper development. Research supports this notion by showing that creativity can be enhanced by classroom instruction that has been carefully designed for this purpose (Perkins & Laserna, 1986). Cropley (1992) argues that all students, regardless of their intellectual aptitudes, are capable of thinking both divergently and convergently. However, as a result of experience with traditional educational system they are more likely to think convergently; that is, to look for a single correct answer to a problem without asking 'idle' questions. The reason for this behavior appears to be the nature of an educational process that stifles in many the curiosity inherent to us in childhood: when we approach adulthood, we often learn not to ask questions (Nickerson, 1999). The goal of creative education, therefore, is to change the existing pattern of school behavior and introduce methods and techniques that enhance students' creativity.

The importance of introducing creativity to a school curriculum has long been recognized by the academic community. Vygotsky (2004: 87) believed that 'we should emphasize the particular importance of cultivating creativity in school-age children.' He argued that creativity was the most crucial factor contributing to the future development of the human race. As school prepares children for the future, the 'development and exercise of the imagination should be one of the main forces enlisted for the attainment of this goal' (2004: 88). In his American Psychological Association presidential address, Guilford (1950) expressed particular concerns that the school curriculum discourages school-age children from developing their creative potential. Torrance (1968) validated this concern by providing empirical evidence from longitudinal studies that half the students he studied revealed a 'fourth-grade slump' in divergent thinking. He reported, 'We have seen many indications in our testing of first and second grade children that many with apparently impoverished imagination seemed to have been subjected to concerted efforts to eliminate fantasy from their thinking too early' (Torrance, 1959: 313). Runco (2004) picked up on this debate by arguing that this drop in the creative behavior of young children may reflect the expectations and pressures to conform that characterize many educational settings. In spite of these and many other concerns raised by the academic community, schools seem to express little interest in fostering creativity. Rather, it is quite evident that schools use any opportunity to reduce the creative potential of students and make every possible effort to suppress creative activity in the classroom.

There seem to be two major obstacles standing in the way of introducing creativity to education: teachers' perspectives on creative education and the methods employed by the educational systems. The latter are likely to be instigated by the former, possibly due to the fact that teachers are the ones who often moderate the educational process in the classroom. The first problem with introducing creativity to school curriculum is related to the underestimation of small-c creativity. Recall a distinction between bigger-C and smaller-c creativity mentioned above: the former refers to those endeavors recognized as outstanding creative accomplishment, while the latter addresses mundane cognitive functioning. Many teachers fail to recognize the existence of smaller-c creativity and ascribe the phenomenon of creativity to a small group of highly gifted individuals capable of exceptional achievements. This view is reinforced by what Runco (2005) termed 'product bias': a tendency to recognize creativity only in the presence of an end-product of creative enterprise. In this opinion, only those individuals who 'impressed some qualified audience' (Runco: 616) can be considered creative and therefore present a rare phenomenon. Thus, although some teachers recognize the importance of creative education, they conceptualize creativity and academic learning as two separate curricular goals (Beghetto & Kaufman, 2009). These teachers leave the nurturing of creativity to special gifted education programs and extracurricular activities and do not include the learning of a creative attitude in their academic objectives. In other words, they believe that the schools should develop '*either* academic knowledge *or* creative potential' (Beghetto, 2010: 453) instead of combining both academic goals. Indeed, since the onset of creativity research, the complementary and reciprocal nature of knowledge acquisition and fostering creativity has been emphasized. In this regard, separation of these two goals posits a particular obstacle for efficient education.

This misconception encourages schools to adopt and maintain teaching practices incompatible with fostering creativity. A standard image of a teacher – the one that 200 years of schooling has barely changed (Cuban, 1993) – is an authoritarian figure standing in front of rows of students, conveying factual information to be copied and recited (Sirotnik, 1983). The authority given to a teacher transforms a classroom activity into something 'akin to a game of "intellectual hide-and-seek" [...] in which teachers hold all the answers and student success is contingent on correctly guessing what is held in the minds of teachers' (Beghetto, 2010: 450). There is little place for a classroom discussion, for a response engaging the interpretative capacities of a student. Goodlad's (1984) longitudinal study of more than 1000 elementary and secondary classrooms during the late 1970s and early 1980s in the United States reported an overwhelming passivity among the students in class. The researchers observed that about 70% of the instruction was a one-directional communication from teacher to student. Less than 5% of instruction expected students to provide any form of response, and 'not even 1% required some kind of open response involving reasoning or perhaps an opinion from student' (1984: 229). These convergent thinking practices encourage memorization skills and accurate recall rather than critical thinking or independent decision making. Moreover, any deviation from this method is considered by many teachers as an interruption of schooling process.

Ironically, surveys revealed that in theory teachers enthusiastically support the idea of fostering creativity in the classroom and have respect for students' creativity. For example, Feldhusen and Treffinger (1975) reported that 96% of educators expressed this view. However, in the actual classroom practice, any trait associated with creativity – such as originality, hardiness or venture – is disliked or at least discouraged. As Torrance (1963, 1965) reported in his early work, teachers favor compliant and conforming students demonstrating courteousness, punctuality, obedience and receptiveness to their ideas. More recent research confirmed these tendencies all around the globe. Teachers were found to associate creativity with nonconformity, impulsiveness and disruptive behavior. Scott (1999) showed that US elementary school teachers rated creative students as more disruptive than their less creative counterparts, and Westby and Dawson (1995) found that teachers describe creative children with the characteristics of least favored students. Similarly, Günçer and Oral (1993) reported that children perceived by Turkish teachers as being confrontational and rebellious scored high on creativity tests. In turn, Chan and Chan (1999) demonstrated that primary and secondary school teachers in Hong Kong regarded some characteristics of creative students as socially undesirable. Of course not all teachers were found to view obedient and conformable students as 'ideal' (e.g. Runco et al., 1993; Thomas & Berk, 1981), but they recognized that some of the creativity traits may be undesirable in school environment (Runco & Johnson, 2002). Indeed, on one side it is tempting to foster creative attitudes in the classroom and, on the other side, it is challenging for a teacher to present a curriculum to a class full of fidgety children. As Runco (2007: 178) sarcastically notes, 'No doubt they do respect creativity, in the abstract, but not when faced with a classroom with 30 energetic children!'

Teachers' attitudes and beliefs about creativity in the classroom leave a trace on the teaching methods generally adopted in the school curriculum. When a student is expected to show obedient and compliant behavior, any deviation from this pattern tends to be suppressed. Many teachers stifle the creative expression of students by employing a convergent teaching practice. This practice perceives successful classroom performance as sitting quietly at the desk, listening and thinking about topics chosen by the teacher, and providing an answer expected by the teacher upon his/her request (Runco, 2004). Any unexpected idea or behavior presented in the class is considered as being interruptive to a teaching flow (Beghetto, 2007). Therefore, many teachers habitually dismiss students' unconventional thoughts, thereby 'seriously undermining opportunities for students to share and develop potentially creative ideas' (Beghetto, 2010: 451). A primary reason for convergent teaching styles comes from economic and political considerations, as teachers need to prepare students for taking standardized exams while they have limited resources and time. Teachers are expected to provide students with sufficient factual information to lay a knowledge foundation that facilitates students' performance on these exams. Any deviant thought or behavior in the classroom interrupts or slows down this process. Standard education requires a unified assessment which can be employed to evaluate performance of a large diversity of student population. Despite a vast array of available creativity assessment methods and techniques (see Kaufman *et al.*, 2008; Plucker & Makel, 2010), there is no standard tool that can reliably assess students' creative abilities. Therefore, one should rely on standardized, often externally mandated, fact-based tests. The convergent teaching method aims at preparing students for successful performance on these tests. Most of these tests require convergent thinking skills that rest on the assumption that there is only one correct or conventional answer; they involve primarily memorization of facts that can be obtained from a teacher or a textbook. Consequently, this technique leaves little opportunity for divergent thinking where a student can think about original answers. Moreover, submission of an unpredictable answer may jeopardize student's test results as they could be graded as 'incorrect' response.

Another serious problem may be rooted in the assessment systems employed to grade classroom work. The primary purpose of grades is a conventional reinforcement that motivates students' educational performance. However, grades are imposed on a student externally (by a teacher, institution, etc.) and therefore signify an extrinsic motivation. A line of research on the motivational mechanisms underlying creative behavior (e.g. Amabile, 1996; Collins & Amabile, 1999; Hennessey, 2010) demonstrates that creativity generally prospers under conditions that support intrinsic motivation (stimulated by personal interest and inner potential) and suffocates under conditions accentuating the extrinsic motivation (such as rewards and incentives). The grading system encourages competition and comparison with others, strengthens the pressure of the judgment of teachers, peers and parents and potentially limits future career opportunities. In all, it undermines students' willingness for creative expression (Collins & Amabile, 1999; Runco, 2003a; Tighe *et al.*, 2003). The students realize the importance of a good grade over independent thinking for their present and future standing. What follows is that the students divert their attention from the kind of nonstandard problem-solving strategies that underlie creative endeavors to a search for the sort of conventional solutions that earn them good evaluations. Moreover, students' willingness to take intellectual risks in the classroom was found to relate to their creative self-efficacy – an intrinsic sense of capacity to generate novel and adaptive ideas, solutions and behaviors (Beghetto, 2009). A schooling program that discourages risk taking also dismantles one of the students' most important tool in creative problem solving – their self-efficacy. As Bandura (1997: 239) argues, 'Above all, innovativeness requires an unshakable sense of efficacy to persist in creative endeavors.' While low creative self-efficacy produces individuals willing to collaborate and to perform prescribed and well-defined tasks, it does not produce those who accelerate the creative enterprise.

Thus, teachers' attitudes and methods generally adopted in standard education provide little opportunity for the flourishing of creative potential in the school settings. Students learn conformity instead of innovativeness; they develop habitual behavior to comply with the system rather than to critically evaluate it. Of course, there is a principal difference between unconventional behavior and misbehavior in the classroom. Not all 'troubled' students manifest their creative potential, and the teachers should be able to acknowledge and recognize this difference. They should be able to monitor creative attitudes in their students and provide them with appropriate and supportive feedback to boost their intrinsic motivation and develop healthy self-efficacy beliefs. They should also become a role model for students in their striving for development of creative potential. As Runco (2004: 671) notes, 'The teachers themselves are potential models for children [...] and their expectations may be very influential.' Unfortunately, quite often the government initiatives encouraging creative education are driven by market-related motivations (Craft, 2005) and do not take into account the realities of the classroom. These externally imposed policies encouraging creative education place teachers between two seemingly contradictory demands (Ingersoll, 2003). On one side, they are overwhelmed by initiatives fostering creativity; on the other side, they are restricted by requirements to provide a curriculum that ensures their students' successful performance on standard examinations.

As a result, despite the apparent limitations of standard educational programs and the findings of empirical investigations that reveal these drawbacks, individuals and institutions continue to invest in traditional education skills (such as literacy, math, etc.) rather than in creative skills. Runco (2004: 670) explains this: 'Creativity is a riskier investment, with less-certain payoffs, than literacy and other skills tied to traditional education.' The current education system is reluctant to make radical changes in its philosophy and goals to substitute a standard education with a creative one.

However, the time is ripe for integrating the nurturing of creative skills into the curriculum.

Unfortunately, a growing understanding of the importance of multilingual and creative factors in the educational system has been contaminated with a portion of skepticism. The enthusiasm raised by adding creativity to the school curriculum as well as the optimistic outcomes of bilingual education programs are tempered with caution and taken with a grain of salt by both education professionals and general public. The concerns raised by both forms of education are discussed in the following section.

Concerns about Bilingual and Creative Education Programs

As discussed in Chapter 2, although empirical research provides a growing body of evidence supporting the positive contribution of bilingualism to an individual's linguistic and cognitive development, the opinions of researchers are divided. This tendency is paralleled and even reinforced in bilingual education research. On one side, an increasing number of empirical studies support bilingual education. On the other side, there are sound considerations doubting the results of the studies demonstrating the positive effect of bilingual education. Krashen (1991) argues that research evidence favoring bilingual education is inconclusive due to a considerable number of methodological drawbacks. Esser (2006: 76–77) makes an even more radical claim: 'Up to now no single methodologically adequate empirical study has been carried out which would make it possible to find a reliable response to the question as to the efficacy of bilingual education.' Indeed, there is a substantial controversy in academic writing questioning the efficiency of bilingual education. There is neither convincing evidence advocating bilingual programs nor adequate response to the criticism negating the findings of the studies favoring these programs. Therefore, at present it seems premature to completely rely on scientific support in promoting multilingual programs.

Due to limited empirical support, the existing argument favoring bilingual education is received with caution. A number of fallacies accepted by the general public (e.g. Crawford (1998) also contribute to doubts regarding this educational model. Although these erroneous beliefs were identified regarding the status of bilingual education in the United States, they can be applied to a similar debate in other countries. These fallacies and their inconsistencies are briefly discussed below.

First, there is a misconception that English is losing ground to other languages in the United States, that new generations of immigrants to the

United States are learning English more slowly than in the past. This myth contradicts the real state of affairs because, despite the fact that immigrants to the United States speak a large variety of languages, the only language that has survived was English. Moreover, the data reported by Crawford (1998) demonstrates that new generations of immigrants possess a greater mastery of English than the previous generations, whether it comes at the cost of their native language or in addition to it.

The second myth is concerned with the proportion of English and foreign languages in school instruction. It claims that the best method to acquire English is through the 'total immersion' method. However, there is no credible evidence of the relation between the rate of exposure to English and the rate of English learning. On the same note, there is concern that bilingual education primarily provides instruction in students' native tongues at the cost of learning English. Unfortunately, this concern is premature for it is not feasible to provide instruction in L1 to a linguistically heterogeneous student population. Crawford (1998) delivers evidence that there is a dramatic shortage of instructors who speak their students' native languages. For example, he reports that for immigrants from 136 different countries to California in 1994 there were certified teachers in only 17 languages and that 96% of those teachers were skilled only in Spanish. A majority of bilingual programs deliver a substantial portion of the curriculum in English, and as the students advance through school the amount of English instruction increases.

The third set of fallacies has evolved around the logistics of delivering bilingual programs. There are some alarming signals that schools offering bilingual education retain children too long in the program. This concern seems to be unsubstantiated, for the time children spent in these programs is 'learning time well spent. Knowledge and skills acquired in the native tongue – literacy in particular – are "transferable" to the second language. They do not need to be relearned in English' (Crawford, 1998: 3). Therefore, there is no necessity to prematurely introduce children to mainstream schooling. Likewise, there is a belief that bilingual education is far more costly than regular English as L2 instruction. This misconception also does not hold because although all English learning programs are little more costly than regular programs for native English speakers, there is no budgetary difference between an English-only approach and bilingual programs. Crawford explains this as following:

> The incremental cost was about the same each year ($175–$214) for bilingual and English immersion programs, as compared with $1,198 for English as a second language [...] 'pullout' programs. The reason was

simple: the pullout approach requires supplemental teachers, whereas in-class approaches do not. (Crawford: 5)

In addition, language-minority parents do not support bilingual education because they are more prone to encourage their children to learn English than to maintain their native tongue. This concern reflects the struggle of the parents themselves to assimilate into the mainstream American society. What they overlook is that the goal of bilingual programs is to promote mastery in both languages, and there is convincing evidence that 'students' native language can be maintained and developed at no cost to English' (Crawford: 6).

The empirical research provides no firm ground for the assumption that bilingual education has a clear and undoubtedly positive effect on language development and school performance. However, there is a tendency that programs fostering both languages may have greater benefits for the students than L2-only instruction. Bilingual programs definitely cause no harm, but there is a general understanding that the success of these programs is contingent on many conditions, including the nature of the educational model, teachers' qualification and the quality, consistency and duration of implementation (Esser, 2006).

After discussing apprehensions regarding bilingual education, we shift our attention to the concerns raised due to introducing creativity-fostering programs to a school curriculum. The first concern comes from the assumption mentioned in the first chapter that the capacity for creative thought is limited to a certain class of gifted or especially talented people. This minority, it is thought, are the only ones capable of genuinely creative thinking, a process that comes from cognitive activities radically different from the everyday problem-solving capacities inherent in most individuals. Therefore, it is argued, none of the education programs – no matter how elaborate and sophisticated these are – can systematically cultivate cognitive mechanisms underlying a genuine potential to create. Moreover, this line of thinking holds that if creativity is the special trait of few exceptional people, then promoting creativity may lead to elitism. Creative education program will therefore focus on exceptionally talented children to the exclusion of those not demonstrating high potential. This argument loses its strength if one takes into consideration an opposite view, the creative cognition approach (see Chapter 1), which argues against the notion that extraordinary forms of creativity are the products of a mysterious and unobservable process. In fact, the assumption of a continuity of cognitive functioning between mundane and creative performance justifies the establishment of creative education programs. These programs aim at all students regardless of their penchants or economic, social, ethnic or any other background. The goal of the programs is not to nurture geniuses, but to foster creativity in the general population. As Cropley (2001: 135) suggests:

> The central focus of fostering creativity in the classroom is thus not production of creative geniuses and it is not necessary for teachers interested in fostering creativity to set their sights on achievement scientific, technological, literary, artistic or other revolutions.

The second concern is raised by parents and teachers that some traits of creative behavior are associated with disobedience, recalcitrance, carelessness or ambiguity. Education programs fostering creativity may therefore develop unruly, careless or naughty children who are difficult to control and educate. In the same vein, promoting creative traits such as incompliance and independent thinking may raise children questioning the fundamental principles of right and wrong and undermining the societal structures. This concern can be met by introducing structured education programs that combine methods fostering creativity with the ones teaching children the standards of communal conduct, citizenship, solidarity and democracy. As a result, those children develop both the novelty and the utility functions (see discussion in the previous chapter) which are crucial for successful creative endeavor. They acquire not only the attitudes leading to creative accomplishment but also those that appropriately contextualize their achievements.

The third concern is pertinent to more serious pedagogical consequences of misconception of creative education. An opportunity to promote creativity through education may result in forcing children into creative programs without their consent, which may make them 'victims of creativity fanaticism among teachers and parents' (Cropley, 2001: 134). Research (e.g. Colangelo & Dettmann, 1983) shows that parents force their children to long hours of training in a particular field (e.g. a musical instrument) in the hope that they develop exceptional skills and gain fame in this field. Often, this tendency is observed in parents who use their children to live out their own frustrated ambitions. The results could be a 'loss of childhood' if creative training takes up most of children's time, destruction of their family life if they become the 'slaves' of their creative skills and increasing frustration if the payoff does not come in due time. Creative education that is oriented at general population and rejecting the idea of elitism in creative training may relieve a burden of those children. It may provide them with an opportunity to nurture their creative potential without developing stress or anxiety caused by inflated demands.

Finally, researchers raise concern about the reliability of the empirical findings that provide support for various creative education programs.

Cropley (2001) extrapolates several critical points from Hruby's comments on Jensen's book *Teaching with the Brain in Mind*:

> Among other weaknesses he identified: presenting speculations, conjectures and hypotheses as established facts; confusing correlations with causal relationships; making unjustified sweeping generalizations that are either not unequivocally supported by research or are even contradicted by some findings; drawing unwarranted conclusions about the implications of research findings for practice; failing to understand the factors that inhibit conversion of admirable recommendations into practice. (Cropley: 144)

A successful creative education program should therefore combine both innovative methods of teaching with a solid scientific foundation. In this regard, it is prudent to directly involve creativity researchers in the schooling process, to both raise teachers' awareness of potential obstacles and to help them form strategies to overcome them. Creativity researchers should play a key role in helping teachers to emphasize creativity in the classroom and move it 'from the margins into the mainstream curriculum' (Beghetto, 2010: 459). The BCE program outlined in the next section makes an attempt to fulfill this goal.

Bilingual Creative Education: New Approach to Old Curriculum

So far, we have discussed two types of educational programs: ones fostering foreign language learning and those intended to facilitate students' creative capacities. It is evident that the creativity-fostering programs operate separately from those giving bilingual instruction, and researchers and teachers working on them have mutually exclusive training. They seem to be educated in either creativity or language-related disciplines. Recall from Chapter 3 that the academic community generally disregards the potential relationship between bilingualism and creativity. Similarly, the benefits of merging programs fostering creative potential and multilingual skills seem to escape the attention of the educators. However, the efficacy of the programs combining both efforts can be directly inferred from the research presented in this book. Multingualism was found to facilitate certain cognitive mechanisms underlying an individual's creative performance. Therefore, by combining bilingual and creative trainings, a far greater synergy could be created: a bilingual creative education program would capitalize on the assets of both forms of education to establish an effective and comprehensive curriculum. This section elaborates on this idea and presents future directions for research in bilingual creative education.

The Bilingual Creative Education program constitutes a unified teaching model that introduces both language learning and creativity-fostering instructions to the school curriculum. The rationale is not to establish a special program focusing on children with exceptional abilities, but to suggest modifications to existing curricula and/or the classroom environment to promote multilingualism and creativity in early schooling. The need for this type of program turns out to be immense considering the outcomes of scientific investigation, initiatives advanced by government policies and public opinion. As discussed earlier, an expanding body of empirical research emphasizes the positive role of multilingualism in fostering creative potential. This research confirms a commonsense perspective expressed by laypersons regarding the relationship between multilingualism and creativity. For example, the European Commission has commissioned a study on the contribution of multilingualism to creativity (Marsh & Hill, 2009). This study analyzed the opinions of the citizens of the EU member states, Norway and Turkey about possible links between multilingualism and creativity. Specifically, they were asked whether multilingualism broadens access to information, offers alternative ways of organizing thoughts and perceiving the surrounding world, and whether learning a new language facilitates an individual's creative capacity. The results of the survey revealed that people believe that multilingualism increases the capacity for original and abstract thinking and facilitates flexibility in thinking and thinking outside the box. They also expressed an opinion that multilingualism fosters interpersonal communication skills and stimulates one's ability to learn other languages. The recommendation of Marsh and Hill's study to the EU calls for developing a program that focuses on both multilingual and creative education. In particular, it suggests:

> That a group be formed of Member State stakeholders involved in language teaching and learning to consider the implications of the findings for educational practice, with a view to possible modifications to specific types of methodologies and materials in order to improve their effectiveness. (Marsh & Hill: 24)

This recommendation echoes the goals articulated during the European Year of Creativity and Innovation (2009). These goals highlight the role of creativity, innovation and multilingualism in stimulating educational practices aiming at enhancing personal, social and economic development. More importantly, the conclusion of Marsh and Hill's study emphasizes the role of multilingualism in learning other subjects, which has particular significance for the present discussion. Interpreting this conclusion in terms of the proposed program, introducing BCE to the school curriculum may have an added value, that is, it may provide auxiliary advantages for a wide range of academic endeavors.

To the author's knowledge, there is no existing program that combines language learning and creativity-fostering instruction in a regular school curriculum. The only available evidence of combining bilingual and creative education comes from dual language programs for gifted and talented students. Dual language programs (also known as two-way and two-way immersion programs, Calderón & Minaya-Rowe, 2003) aim at helping children to learn foreign language while maintaining and developing their native tongue. These programs adopt the methods of sheltered programs discussed above and teach languages through content instruction. Although there is a wide diversity in the ratio of language instruction, most programs fall into two main categories. In the 50:50 model, instruction is given half a day in one language and half a day in another throughout the grades. In the 90:10 model, children spend 90% of their kindergarten school days in their native language, and that percentage gradually drops to 50% by fourth or fifth grade. Ideally, the dual language program includes half students speaking one language as their native and another half speaking another language as their native tongue. Thereby, it provides foreign language instruction for all students. One of the apparent advantages of this program is that in case of comparable distribution of native speakers of two languages, the program promotes linguistic and ethnic equity among the children and teaches them cross-cultural awareness. The latter appears to be a valuable attitude in the multicultural context, which emphasizes tolerance to individuals of different linguistic, cultural, ethnic or religious background.

Thus, Bernal (1998) proposed optional two-way bilingual program for academically gifted students. The content of the core subjects in this program was offered in English and other modern languages to students speaking either of these languages as a native tongue. The placement to and within this program was made on the grounds of a language proficiency test given at the onset of the talent pool process and on assessments of academic skills, creativity and critical thinking during the 3-year duration of the program (Bernal, 2007). This program was delivered by qualified bilingual teachers who have been trained to teach gifted and talented students in the early elementary schools. Several school districts now offer this program in their elementary schools, and one program, the *Connecting Worlds/Mundos Unidos Project* of the El Paso Independent School District extends this model to the middle and high schools. The latter program utilizes a 50:50 bilingual immersion language-integrated model (see Bernal, 2007, for description). This is a full-time schooling program that combines native English and Spanish gifted and talented students. The program delivered satisfactory results in terms of both academic and linguistic achievements. Bernal (2007: 488) reports, 'The gifted children have done very well on standardized tests, although native speakers of English still do better on achievement tests in English, whereas native speakers of Spanish have higher average scores on tests in Spanish.'

Furthermore, there is only one empirical study that looked at the interactive effect of bilingualism and creative education (Fleith et al., 2002). Portuguese–English immigrant bilingual and English monolingual third, fourth and fifth grade students from a suburban elementary school in New England (USA) were divided into two groups: one group received special training with The New Directions in Creativity program; the other served as a control group. Researchers specify that 'The theoretical background of the program is based on Guilford's Structure of the Intellect Model (1967) and focuses on the divergent thinking section of the model' (Fleith et al.: 377). The 9-week program implementation period was preceded by 3 weeks of teacher training on how to implement the program in the classroom. The program was designed to help teachers develop students' fluency, flexibility, elaboration and originality. The study revealed that the program had somewhat positive effect on the students' divergent thinking abilities. At the same time, no significant difference was found between bilingual and monolingual students' divergent thinking performance. However, the findings of the study should be taken with caution because the language group placement procedure gives rise to a serious doubt. Fleith and her colleagues report:

Almost half of the sample [...] were bilingual students – Brazilian immigrants who spoke both English and Portuguese (their native language). Brazilian students in this school were placed in bilingual education classrooms. When classroom teachers determined that students' English was adequate, students were placed in monolingual classrooms in which the population is primarily students who speak English only. (Fleith et al.: 376)

In other words, those Brazilian immigrants who revealed adequate English proficiency were placed in the monolingual group. This means that both language groups included English–Portuguese bilinguals with different levels of proficiency in both languages. It is not surprising therefore that there was no difference in language groups' divergent thinking performance, because in line with the earlier discussions the variation in creative performance could be expected between entirely bilingual and monolingual groups.

Essential attributes of the BCE program

The BCE program rests on the four-criterion creativity construct discussed in the previous chapter. In contrast to a traditional view that creativity involves a combination of novelty and utility, this program assumes that successful creative functioning is stipulated by all four aspects of creativity. Therefore, this program fosters aesthetic and authentic aspects in addition to originality and appropriateness. The BCE program is grounded in several conceptual premises. First, in contrast to Bernal's (1998) program, the BCE program disqualifies the elitist view and provides opportunities to enhance linguistic and creative capacities of all students regardless of their intellectual and creative predispositions. This entails the second characteristic of the program, its scope of application: the BCE can be implemented in any school curriculum, depending on the specific details of a given school. The role of the program coordinator would be to modify the core of the program to reflect the specificity of the student body and the economic, sociocultural and political environment of each particular school. Instead of establishing a new school or a special classroom with an entirely new curriculum, this program suggests necessary modifications to convert any curriculum into one fostering foreign language skills and creative potential. Therefore, it reflects the recommendation to the EU member states (Marsh & Hill, 2009) that methodologies should be developed to modify and improve the effectiveness of existing educational programs. Moreover, these modifications can be accomplished at a low cost because they would not require major restructuring of existing school curricula. Third, the goal of the BCE program is to facilitate foreign language learning in a diversity of student populations. This program is designed not only for migrants who speak their native language and who are attempting to acquire the language of the migration country. It is conceived for all children who want, or to be more precise, whose parents want them to acquire a foreign language at the same time as enhancing their native language skills. Fourth, another goal of the program is to foster children's creative potential. The focus of the program is not on bigger-C creativity, but on the smaller-c creative capacities (cf. Kaufman & Beghetto, 2009) that are grounded in mundane cognitive functioning and can be applied to everyday problem solving. The outcomes of this program do not reflect the ambitious aspirations of nurturing eminent individuals (although, this perspective should not be excluded). Rather, the program aims at facilitating the overall linguistic, intellectual and creative competences of young children, thereby meeting the recommendations of certain government policies (e.g. Comission of the European Communities, 2008). Finally, the BCE program in its present state is designed for an elementary school curriculum, for these are the crucial years in a child's linguistic and cognitive development. In the future, this program can be expanded to kindergarten and middle and high schools.

Thus, the purpose of the program is to introduce students to a school curriculum in two languages and to foster the four defining aspects of creativity discussed in the previous chapter, that is, novelty, utility, aesthetics and authenticity. To accomplish this goal, the program utilizes a holistic approach that combines cognitive, personal and environmental factors in education. This approach considers not only educational aspects directly pertinent to the school curriculum but also those reflecting a child's personality and extracurricular settings. The following sections present a sketch of five essential attributes of the BCE that reflect intrapersonal, interpersonal and environmental factors. These attributes (personal, cognitive, administrative, environmental and curricular) were adopted from various studies in bilingual and creative education (August & Hakuta, 1997; Berman, 1996; Cropley, 2001; Feldhusen & Kolloff, 1978; McLeod, 1996; Nickerson & Sternberg, 1994; Thomas & Collier, 2000).

Personal attributes

The program aims at developing personality traits that, on the one side, encourage students to engage in the bilingual creative educational process and, on the other, facilitate their multilingual and creative practices.

First, it is important to instill in students a firm sense of the purpose and intent of this education. The success of the program is directly related to a deep and abiding intent to develop one's linguistic abilities and creative potential. This intent can be secured by fostering a long-term interest in some form of multilingual practice and creative expression. The students need to be convinced that acquired skills entail substantial advantages. Considering that both bilingual and creative educational programs are still received with caution (see discussions above), it might be essential to promote supportable beliefs about the new form of education. On the one side, the empirical research demonstrates that bilingualism promotes cognitive and creative development. On the other side, creativity appears to be not only genetically determined trait but also the one that can be trained assuming that the students express substantial effort and devotion to the program. These considerations should be clearly articulated in the program by emphasizing that acquisition of both linguistic and creative skills is determined to a significant degree by one's effort and motivation.

Second, motivation was shown to play a crucial role in both successful language learning (e.g. Engjn, 2009; Masgoret & Gardner, 2003; Wang, 2008) and prolific creative behavior (e.g. Amabile, 1996; Collins & Amabile, 1999;

Hennessey, 2010). Therefore, the program strives to build motivation, especially intrinsic motivation. As discussed above, external motivation manifested in a school environment in the form of grades, collegial judgment and parental scrutiny may decrease the internal motivation that is stimulated by personal interest and inner potential. In light of this consideration, students' performance might benefit from minimizing their exposure to any form of domination by external rewards such as grading system.

Third, openness to new ideas and experiences has been always regarded as an important creativity trait (e.g. Khosravani & Guilani, 2008; Leung & Chiu, 2008; Silvia *et al.*, 2009). This trait can be fostered by stimulating and rewarding curiosity, exploration and adventurousness. As mentioned earlier, present teaching practices transform children's deep sense of wonder about the world and existence into the 'fourth-grade slump.' The program aims at stimulating child-like attitudes in students by providing more opportunities for curiosity, risk and exploration. This can be accomplished by training students to be more observant, to pay more attention to aspects of their daily experience. Research shows that openness to new experience is related to receptiveness to novel ideas (e.g. Feist, 1998; Feist & Brady, 2004; McCrae & Costa, 1987). This trait can be stimulated by encouraging children to be inquisitive in their search for new ideas and by providing them with exhaustive answers and explanations to any question they ask.

Fourth, in a search for a creative answer, people may face a situation in which they have to simultaneously process several contradictory ideas. An ability to consider several mental sets at the same time appears to be an essential capacity for divergent thinking. This capacity is facilitated by the tolerance for ambiguity, which was found to be an important factor in an individual's creative behavior (e.g. Zenasni *et al.*, 2008). A tolerance for ambiguity may facilitate one's ability to keep a pool of possible solutions open long enough to generate a creative idea. Interestingly, there is a claim that bilingual advantages in divergent thinking (discussed in Chapter 4) may arise from the routine ambiguity inherent to their multilingual practice, in which the same basic idea may have different nuances in different languages (Lubart, 1999). Thus, the tolerance for ambiguity can be fostered by introducing a student to a multilingual context.

Fifth, the program encourages autonomy, positive self-evaluation and high self-esteem. Confidence comes with successful experience. Therefore, it is essential to create an environment that encourages and rewards students' effort per se. What should be rewarded is the effort even when the outcome of this endeavor is not highly successful. Building confidence can be accomplished through careful review of the requirements and expectations, which should be high but not impossible. In this regard, it is important to realize that children with great self-confidence may show disobedience and insubordination, which presents particular challenges to a teacher. The program takes this into account and combines nurturing intellectual independence with appropriate discipline.

Sixth, although competition might be effective under certain circumstances, it often reduces creative tendencies. Competition involves judgment and external evaluation, which per earlier discussion strengthen extrinsic and weaken intrinsic motivation. The program therefore encourages self-improvement and self-comparison rather than 'winning' and outperforming others. It emphasizes mastery orientation rather than outcome orientation, and focuses on self-competence. The students in this program are expected to gain satisfaction from competing with themselves rather than with the others. The focus on self-competence promotes ego strength and acceptance of all (even contradictory) aspects of one's own self. Thereby, it contributes to the development of one of the four creative virtues specified earlier, namely, authenticity. High self-competence, in turn, manifests itself in a willingness to take risks and accept challenges. In response to the challenges presented by this program, students might develop focus, task commitment and a preference for task complexity.

Seventh, special attention is given to the development of an aesthetic sense in students. One of the schooling objectives is to train the students to distinguish between creative solutions of different aesthetic value; using the words of Zuo (1998: 312), they should be able to 'judge good, better, and best answers.' He reported empirical evidence suggesting that the aesthetic sense can be developed by observing mentors modeling the process of aesthetic decision making and disciplined longitudinal practice in the domain of aesthetical judgment. The current program fosters the aesthetic sense of the students by encouraging teachers to become the model of aesthetic judgment and to extensively engage students in aesthetic decision making in different domains. This practice enables students to develop understanding and intuition not only for hard evidence readily available to the beholder but also for more subtle nuances underlying beauty and the truth.

Cognitive attributes

The program aims to foster those cognitive abilities that facilitate students' language acquisition and help develop their creative potential.

First, it builds a fund of general knowledge and basic skills similar to a traditional school curriculum. In contrast to traditional education, curricular material is presented in two languages thereby providing more opportunities for elaborative rehearsal. As empirical research demonstrates, elaborative rehearsal makes long-term memory storage and retrieval more effective (e.g.

Craik & Tulving, 1975; Gabrieli *et al.*, 1996). The rehearsal of the same material in each language may also result in what Ebbinghaus termed 'over-learning' – continued rehearsal even after the material seems to have been mastered (Driskell *et al.*, 1992) – which was found to improve retention of the material (e.g. Bahrick & Hall, 1991). Therefore, by merely receiving curricular material in two languages, students are provided with opportunities to construct a more efficient knowledge base.

Second, the program encourages the acquisition of domain-specific knowledge. Students build specific knowledge base and area-specific skills. Williamson's (2011) finding of no difference in problem-solving skills between arts and science students suggests that the same strategies can be utilized in domain-specific classes. Students in the current program strengthen their languages and learn various structured approaches to creative problem solving through a rich and varied experience in many different settings. Teachers are encouraged to adopt brainstorming techniques (Osborn, 1953). The essential of this creative problem-solving method is to express all the ideas that come to one's mind regardless of how wild or strange they appear. Traditionally, brainstorming takes place in groups so that participants can stimulate each other's idea generation in a relatively uninhibited manner. This last condition is accomplished by prohibiting any form of critique (including self-critique), thereby ensuring an uninterrupted flow of divergent thinking. The same procedure can be used by an individual as long as the process of idea generation is not interrupted by any evaluation procedure. Generally, it is expected that during brainstorming people generate more ideas than during normal problem solving, when each idea needs to be evaluated before being presented. Empirical evidence supports this expectation by demonstrating that groups using brainstorming procedure generated more and better ideas than control groups that used other problem-solving techniques (e.g. Meadow *et al.*, 1959; Parnes, 1963). So, the program encourages teachers to present a problem in question to the class and moderate the discussion emphasizing possible solutions to a problem.

Third, the program teaches the kind of convergent thinking that is manifested in the ability to analyze and synthesize information. Students acquire skills in seeing connections, overlaps, similarities and logical implications.

Fourth, the program teaches the sort of divergent thinking that is manifested in the ability to simultaneously process several pieces of information. Students learn to conceive multiple opposites simultaneously (cf. Janusian thinking, Rothenberg, 1996), to make remote associations (cf. Mednick, 1962), to link apparently separate fields into a new conceptual plane (cf. bisociating, Koestler, 1968) and to form new gestalts. They are encouraged to use their imagination and to acquire speaking and acting skills, which may turn out to be invaluable traits when it comes to presenting one's ideas in public.

Fifth, Piaget (1952) distinguished between two cognitive strategies people use to perceive and adapt to new information: assimilation and accommodation. The former involves the interpretation of new information in terms of existing cognitive structures, whereas the latter refers to changing the existing cognitive structures to reflect new information. The proposed program encourages students to employ accommodation rather than assimilation. This strategy exercises their capacities to construct new conceptual planes rather than to rely on existing knowledge.

Sixth, the program teaches students not only problem solving but also problem finding. In traditional school settings, students typically work on problems provided by instructors. However, people reveal greater intrinsic motivation when they work on the problems of their own choice than on those imposed to them by the others. The empirical research also provides evidence that problem finding trait characterizes inventive individuals in any discipline. Getzels and Csíkszentmihályi (1976) identified problem finding capacity as the most significant variable in determining future success in the art world. Kay (1991) demonstrated that problem finding capacity differentiated between professional and semiprofessional artists. Rostan (1994) revealed that the difference between professionally recognized artists and scientists and their less successful counterparts can be attributed, among other variables, to the amount of time they spent on problem finding. Therefore, it is essential to encourage students to find problems of their own. This can be accomplished by providing them with opportunities for discovery and for making choices. The author's teaching practice provides an illustration of this approach. The students are asked to submit a 'creative assignment,' which has only one restriction: it should be 'creative,' that is, it calls for any form of creative endeavor. The assignments submitted by the students over consequent semesters revealed their general ability to produce work that can be judged by some people as creative. This example illustrates the idea that when students are given a freedom of choice they manage to find and solve problems on their own.

Seventh, metacognitive skills such as self-evaluation and self-management appear to be invaluable capacities in both language learning and creative behavior. One of the crucial issues in both creative and noncreative enterprises appears to be time management. Students' inability to adequately arrange their time often compromises their academic performance. Similarly, students' failure to evaluate their performance may result in an interruption of their educational progress. Both skills can be learned and the proposed program aims at developing the ability to plan one's own learning pace and to evaluate one's own progress. It is also observed that people can be most productive under specific conditions or in specific environments. This consideration is taken into account and the program provides opportunities for students to identify under what conditions they can most effectively employ their metacognitive skills.

Administrative attributes

The program proposes a set of administrative modifications that can be utilized both in BCE and in schools with traditional curriculum.

First, the program requires an innovative leadership. Due to the fact that the goals of the program differ from the ones of the traditional education, it cannot rely on the administrative methods of the latter. The success of the program is contingent on an ability of someone to assume the responsibility for planning, coordinating and administering the program. At least half of 33 studies reviewed by August and Hakuta (1997), name leadership – often that of a school's principal – as an important factor in delivering a program. Therefore, the success of the proposed program depends to a large extent on the innovative approach of the school administration.

Second, the program incorporates an option to customize the learning environment. Because there is no ideal schooling strategy and because there is a great diversity of conditions faced by schools, school staff and community members should be consulted to identify which approaches would be most suitable to each particular environment. Consequently, each individual school can be provided with a specific design of the learning environment that reflects the goals of the students and community as well as the economic, sociocultural and political aspects of the environment.

Third, the school environment is formed by a triad of teachers, students and parents. Attitudes, beliefs, assumptions and expectations of the members of this triad have powerful influence on students' learning opportunities and outcomes (Rutter et al., 1979). The BCE therefore emphasizes the importance of a supportive school-wide climate for effective implementation of the program. The schools reviewed by August and Hakuta (1997) varied in methods of establishing such climate, but overall converged on three aspects: a value placed on linguistic and cultural background of the students, high expectations for their academic achievement and their integral participation in the overall schooling process. The current program adopts these strategies.

Fourth, student involvement in school activity can be achieved by securing a close relationship between teachers and students. The program strives to establish a bond between a group of teachers and a group of students by organizing them in continuous clusters. On the one hand, these clusters or 'families' of students stay together for major part of the school day, thereby establishing more intimate relations within a group. On the other hand, teachers remain with their students for several consequent grades thereby facilitating their awareness and responsiveness to student needs. In addition, the program introduces measures to group students more flexibly to respond to their developmental differences during the entire period of schooling.

Fifth, ongoing professional staff development constitutes an important component of effective program delivery. The high expectations for the students mentioned above can be achieved by providing teachers with skills and knowledge needed to attain greater success with students. Assuming that the teachers are highly qualified in their respective areas, the training focuses on instructional strategies that are specific to the implemented program and to specific student population in each particular school. For example, teachers can learn an additional language spoken by the students or acquire the pedagogical concept of open teaching and learning mentioned below. They can also benefit from the interaction with parents and local community members to incorporate community-based knowledge sources into school curriculum.

Sixth, the program protects and extends instructional time to multiply the opportunities for students to engage in academic learning. It offers supportive computer-based instruction, after-school programs and voluntary Saturday and summer schools. The role of administration here is to motivate full-time teachers and/or to hire external trained tutors to ensure the extension of this learning time.

Seventh, the program assumes articulation between schooling modules and coordination between schools utilizing BCE. The teachers of different subjects collaborate on developing instructions integrating language learning and creativity-fostering techniques into traditional content areas. This method ensures close articulation between program modules, and integrates bilingual and creative components into content area instruction. The effectiveness of this collaboration is facilitated by coordination between different schools. Unique school settings might lead to the development of methodologies specific for this environment, and a fruitful exchange of these methods might enrich each individual school's curriculum.

Environmental attributes

The personal, cognitive and administrative attributes discussed so far do not present a complete picture of the program, because those aspects evolve as a result of the interaction with the environment. The success of the program is largely dependent on what environmental factors are present: discouraging or stimulating and inspiring, inhibiting or nurturing and cultivating. In this regard, the environmental factors can be classified in a threefold way: the individual, micro and macro environments (Cropley, 2001).

The individual environment reflects individual factors and subjective dimensions. First, the program develops a coherent sense of who the students are and what they hope to accomplish. Second, it ensures that the deviant behavior of a student is accepted with tolerance, absence of strict sanctions against minor flaws and approval of creative urges.

The micro environment addresses the family, peer group, school and the local educational system. First, the program provides opportunities for the practice of acquired skills outside the school curriculum. Second, it adapts to mobility and special nonschool needs of students and families. Third, the program involves parents and their community in their children's education. Parents participate in school committees, festivals and celebrations, student field trips and so on. Teachers and program coordinators may interview parents and other community members to identify what knowledge and skills could be beneficial for students inside and outside school and organize the curriculum accordingly. The program may go even further and consider parental involvement as a part of a school contract.

The macro environment embraces the sociocultural, historical, economical and political aspects. First, the program combines the efforts of school staff and social service agencies to modify (if necessary) the schooling context to address students' social and emotional needs. For example, it may transform minority/majority relations to culturally tolerant interactions by integrating a comparable number of migrant and autochthonal students in the same curricular cluster. Second, the program utilizes available resources in highly coordinated ways. For example, it may look for external funding from federal, state/province or local organizations. In addition, it may obtain nonfinancial assistance from local community organizations. One of the major limitations of contemporary education comes from low school budgets. The objective of the program is to allocate additional resources to secure a prolific learning environment.

Curricular attributes

The fifth set of attributes describes the essential characteristics of the curriculum constituting the BCE program. It is important to note that the program intends not to replace the existing school curriculum, but rather to modify it by incorporating new elements pertinent to bilingual and creative education.

First, the program uses current teaching strategies, but presents the academic curriculum through two languages. Calderón and Minaya-Rowe (2003) provide a comprehensive description of the design and implementation of a two-way bilingual program. Their methods are adopted by the BCE program to introduce the dual language curriculum. Their suggestions on planning the program are taken into account. Prior to executing the program, a special committee should gather information on program development and implementation. The information about the program should be shared with all stakeholders: teachers, parents, central administrators, principals, school board members or funders, community and press. Various forms of presentations should be used on several occasions to reach the largest audience: meetings with the target audience, making available printed and online portfolios, distributing flyers and media reports. Consequently, the stakeholders should critically evaluate the program and make decisions on their roles in the program's implementation. When implementing the program, decisions should be made on type of school program (magnet, neighborhood, whole school or strand within school). Furthermore, the dual language model (50:50, 70:30, 80:20 or 90:10) and language distribution (by time, topic or teacher) should be determined. In addition, the onset language combination (L1 first, L2 first or both languages simultaneously) and onset grade (add one grade per year, begin with K-5, or implement from K-12 the first year) should be specified.

Second, the program adapts the existing school curriculum to the diversity of languages and cultures of the students. Traditionally, the content of school curriculum appears to reflect the geographic, cultural and political perspectives of the host country. This one-sided approach may present a potential weakness to the program. For example, in personal communication the author learned that Egyptian students are taught in history class that they belong to the Arabic people. This claim is correct from linguistic perspective, assuming that everyone speaking Arabic as a native language is Arab. At the same time, a genealogical perspective assumes that Arabic people are only those who can trace their ancestry to the tribes of the Arabian Peninsula and the Syrian Desert (Varisco, 1995). Those Egyptians who identify themselves as Arab reject the latter perspective altogether (Jankowski, 1991). In a similar vein, European students are taught the star constellations of the Northern hemisphere in astronomy class and they are unaware of the star map as seen from the Southern hemisphere. These potential glitches can be avoided by the conscious integration of different perspectives in the curriculum. Bernal (2007) presents some examples of the incorporation of a multicultural content in the curriculum, such as introducing the star patterns seen by the Mayans, Babylonians, Chinese or Indians; explanations of the Pythagorean Theorem; and a discussion of racial differences in intelligence from a sociocultural perspective. This process can be facilitated by employing teachers with various linguistic and cultural backgrounds and consultations with parents and local community members.

Third, the program utilizes student-directed instructional strategies enhancing their linguistic and creative abilities. A number of scholars identified the impact of the direction of instruction on divergent thinking and creative problem solving (e.g. Chand & Runco, 1992; Harrington, 1975). Open teaching and learning (Urban, 1995, see also Cropley, 2001) presents an example of pedagogical framework that provides essential conditions for enhancing students' performance. It enables students to initiate self-directed work with a great deal of initiative aimed at producing original ideas without fear of sanctions against undesired behaviors and errors. The BCE program adopts the open teaching and learning strategies. It also considers presenting instruction in a permissive and game-like fashion in order to stimulate free play and the manipulation of objects and ideas. These types of activities are argued to release creativity (Runco, 2004). The program stimulates and appreciates humor, and alternates between periods of concentration on learning material and relaxation, thereby fostering reflection (Cropley & Urban, 2000). Teachers are encouraged to avoid 'suggestive' questions and those requiring a simple 'yes/no' answer, rather they should formulate statements that may stimulate or provoke questions by the students. Instead of directly receiving strategies for solving a problem, students are given hints, leading them step by step to discover solutions on their own. In addition, students are encouraged to develop an interest in the acquisition of new knowledge that consequently might facilitate their ability to consider and elaborate on ideas and problems from a wider range of perspectives.

When it comes to linguistic practice, students are discouraged from code-switching. As discussed in Chapter 5, code-switching refers to concurrent use of more than one language in one's speech. Recall from Chapter 2 that simultaneous activation of both languages makes bilinguals constantly focus on one language, inhibit another language or switch between languages. These processes are controlled by the executive control function that facilitates the focus on the target language and suppresses the interference from another language. Therefore, when students refrain from code-switching, they actively engage in interference suppression, which in turn strengthens their executive control function. The executive control plays an important role in bilingual creative performance and fluid intelligence as was explained in Chapter 4. Moreover, Chapter 2 mentions task-switching studies that also show that the ability to control the switch facilitates cognitive functioning. Therefore, a routine practice of discouraging students from code-switching may facilitate their exercise of executive control, which in turn may increase their cognitive and creative functioning.

Fourth, the program establishes a balanced curriculum that includes both basic and higher order knowledge and skills. A solid background in fundamental ideas appears essential in developing domain-specific ones. Some conceptual models of creativity explicitly recognize that successful acquisition of higher level abilities is related to lower level ones. Feldhusen and Kolloff (1978), for example, proposed a three-level model of creativity development. First-level activities comprise the strengthening of basic language and mathematical skills and encourage the use of imagination. The second and third levels build on basic skills and involve learning various structural approaches with the goal of eventually performing independent, self-directed projects. The BCE program follows a general education paradigm and stresses the acquisition of fundamentals in languages, arts and sciences. Thereby, it provides a solid ground for exploration into domain-specific knowledge. The latter appears to present a necessary condition for the development of creative potential. As research indicates, eminent achievements in both arts and sciences became possible only after substantial amount of training that involved the acquisition of domain-specific knowledge (e.g. Cropley, 1992; Csíkszentmihályi, 1997; Gardner, 1993b). Contemporary scientists need to have sufficient knowledge of their field in order to recognize the significance of their discoveries (Nickerson, 1999). Hayes (1985) presents evidence that contemporary classical composers who have made a significant contribution to music spent at least 10 years composing before they could produce their masterworks. Similarly, to make a substantial contribution in art, poetry or any other creative field, one needs to master critical knowledge and skills in this field. Moreover, there is a valuable argument that people tend to express their greatest creative potential in one particular field (e.g. Amabile, 1983b; Baer, 1993; Gardner, 1983). As Brown (1989: 22) noted, 'Talent and creativity are domain specific whether by dint of "natural" proclivity, extensive training, and/or education.' Runco (1987) found this to be the case with gifted children. Therefore, the current program provides opportunities for children to develop specific knowledge and skills in various domains of arts and sciences. In addition to a traditional general education curriculum, children are placed in special interest groups based on the results of a continuous assessment (see next paragraph). These groups offer in-depth development of domain-specific knowledge and skills (e.g. poetry, visual art, music, design, chemistry, mathematics and physics).

Fifth, to successfully screen students' development, the program incorporates a systematic student assessment. The assessment aims not at the evaluation and judgment of students' accomplishments, but rather at monitoring their performance in order to employ more efficient schooling strategies. This incentive requires more authentic assessment tools and scoring rubrics. The BCE adopts Calderón and Minaya-Rowe's (2003) classification and identifies four groups of assessments that serve the following purposes: screening and identification, placement, progress and achievement. The *screening and identification* assessment is administered in the form of a survey when students register for the program. This assessment intends to collect general information about students' background and attitudes. The *placement* assessment determines one's creative potential and mastery of all languages. This assessment is used for placement in the program and in a specific language class (beginning, intermediate or advanced). In addition, it helps to identify the language dominance and relative language proficiency of the students. The placement assessment is also used to determine the initial creative potential of the students. The *progress* assessment is an ongoing evaluation that intends to monitor students' linguistic, cognitive and creative development as they progress through the education. It guarantees that all students attain expected linguistic and creativity goals and satisfy educational standards. Finally, *achievement* assessment is used to identify whether students' outcomes satisfy linguistic, creative and academic expectations.

These four types of assessment can be implemented using a wide variety of measurements. The screening and identification survey includes questions identifying one's linguistic and cultural background (adopted from the author's MMEQ presented in Chapter 4) and creative attitudes (adopted from Creative Personality Scale, Gough, 1979; the Biographical Inventory of Creative Behaviors, Batey, 2007; and Creative Behavior Inventory, Hocevar, 1980) as well as self-rating scales assessing one's linguistic (similar to self-rating scales in MMEQ) and creative (adopted from Creativity Self-Rating, Batey, 2007) abilities. The other three types of assessment utilize psychometric tools to evaluate students' performance. There is a wide range of standardized tools that can be employed to assess creativity at the level of a person, a process and a product (see Eysenck, 1994; Plucker & Makel, 2010; and Chapter 1 of this book, for an overview). Standardized tests of linguistic skills are also widespread due to the fact that most educational institutions have language exam as an admission criterion for nonnative speakers (e.g. Test of English as a Foreign Language; Cambridge English for Speakers of Other

Languages certificates; *Nederlands als Tweede Taal*; *Deutsch als Fremdsprache*). These tests present a comprehensive assessment of a variety of linguistic skills (e.g. internet-based Test of English as a Foreign Language assesses listening, writing, reading and speaking skills). The European Community sponsored an online diagnostic language assessment system DIALANG, which is based on the Common European Framework of Reference (Council of Europe, 2001). It provides learners with information about their language proficiency in 14 European languages and informs them of their Common European Framework level (Chapelle, 2006). This tool assesses learner's skills in listening, writing, reading, structure and vocabulary. In addition to educational purposes, empirical research in L1 and L2 acquisition and bilingualism delivers several techniques that gained reputation of a reliable language assessment tool. The Cloze procedure (Taylor, 1953) asks participants to complete written texts with various gaps. Extensive empirical investigation presents such tests as the assessment of overall language proficiency (e.g. Dupuis, 1980; Peterson *et al.*, 1972). The Peabody Picture Vocabulary Test (Dunn, 1965) of receptive vocabulary asks participants to indicate which of the four pictures shown corresponds to a name spoken by the experimenter. Clinicians and researchers rely on the test to accurately assess children's and adults' single-word lexical knowledge. A test of productive vocabulary, the Boston Naming Test (Kaplan *et al.*, 1983) is generally used by clinicians to assess word retrieval performance of brain-damaged patients.

Sixth, the program encourages teachers to innovatively organize the classroom environment, for that, it is argued, has an impact on creative thinking (Runco, 2004). The teachers make an additional effort to create student-friendly microclimate in the classroom. The room could have an appearance of a space for informal gathering, which can be accomplished by innovative decoration and/or seating arrangement. Although the chairs and desks are provided, the students are not required to keep a regular seat; rather, they can freely move around the classroom and take any suitable position: sitting, standing or wandering around. This setting establishes the atmosphere in which students feel more comfortable to initiate and engage in game-like activities and discussions without feeling restrained by a more formal classroom setup. Innovative information technology can complement traditional schooling devices (such as whiteboard and overhead projector) to facilitate student learning and creative engagement. Furthermore, as mentioned earlier, the program seeks to establish close relationships between teachers and students by organizing them in clusters. This initiative makes students feel a sense of belonging to the school and encourages them to seek more personal guidance from a sympathetic adult. The advisory period during the last hour of the day develops this sense even further. The advisory class is smaller than regular classes and is devoted to helping students with academic or personal issues. Students report that this relationship with a teacher gives them the opportunity to 'talk to a teacher like a real person' (McLeod, 1996: 20).

Last but not least, teachers are advised to introduce basic meditation practices to establish the spiritual homogeneity of the class, to reduce stress and to increase students' language learning and cognitive and creative functioning. Extensive research demonstrates that meditation has a positive impact on the creative processes (see Krippner & Maliszewski, 1978, for an overview). Ball (1980) found that Maharishi International University students showed an increase in originality after transcendental meditation programs compared to the control group. Gowan (1978) extended this finding by providing empirical evidence that meditation aided in relieving stress and tuning in to minuscule signals, which together facilitated creative performance. Cowger and Torrance (1982) reported a positive effect of transcendental meditation on college undergraduates' expression of emotions, internal visualization and fantasy. They also presented Onda's (1962: 212) argument that 'Zen meditation cultivates creativity by developing such qualities as: seeing reality, making realistic responses, assuming a multiple value viewpoint, spontaneity, pursuing the truth, concentrating, experiencing self, psychological freedom, and discovering potentiality.' Meditation was found to improve other cognitive processes as well. So and Orme-Johnson (2001) demonstrated that the regular practice of transcendental meditation for 15–20 minutes twice a day for 6–12 months improved Taiwanese high school students' performance on a battery of cognitive tests assessing creative thinking, constructive thinking, embedded figures, inspection time and fluid intelligence. In the same fashion, Williams (2010) argued that mindfulness training can affect working memory capacity. Meditation has been also listed among effective strategies lowering anxiety in language learners (e.g. Ehrman & Oxford, 1990; Oxford, 2002; Oxford et al., 1989). Altogether, these studies provide a convincing argument that introducing meditation into a curriculum should have a positive effect on students' language learning, and their academic and creative performance.

Seventh, the program expands the roles and responsibilities of teachers by providing them with more decision-making power when it comes to the choice of curriculum and instructional strategies. Research demonstrates that the teachers themselves might be potential models for children (Graham et al., 1989; Runco, 1993) and their expectations may be highly influential (Runco, 1984). The role model of a teacher in this program stresses the acquisition of both factual knowledge and creative strategies. Teachers present content through a variety of strategies and under different conditions to facilitate their students' acquisition of the material. They take all students' questions seriously and attempt to provide them with comprehensive answers. Teachers strive to establish a classroom climate that permits alternative solutions, tolerates constructive errors and helps students to cope with frustration and failures. They do not threaten those who exhibit deviant behavior and ensure them in systematic and full support. These teachers instill in students courage and a sense of high self-esteem, encourage them to learn independently and to be self-critical. At the same time, they ensure a balance between independence in thinking and adherence to principles. They teach students to recognize and respect rules, bounds and limits without stifling their creativity. This is accomplished by explaining why principles are necessary and why particular rules make sense. Their teaching style assumes a diversity of student's linguistic skills and carefully elaborates on communication of the content when it is presented in a student's nonnative language. These teachers develop a cooperative, socially integrative style of teaching, sensitive to the cultural and linguistic differences of the students. They establish an environment in which students learn these diversities in a constructive manner. It is important to note that the students not only learn the content of the curriculum, they also model the behavior of the teachers. Therefore, teachers should have the same attitudes they try to teach their students. The program provides a sort of a checklist, which indicates the major personal and cognitive attributes teachers should focus on, and behavior patterns they should exhibit when designing and implementing strategies for bilingual creative learning. The goals and expectations of the BCE change and enrich the role of the educator. As Cropley (2001: 151) notes, the teacher is 'no longer just an instructor, evaluator, censor and authority but stimulator, elicitor, moderator, stabilizer, helper, mediator, counselor, friend, participating observer, initiator, partner, instructor, organizer, expert, mentor, and model.'

Summary

The objective of this chapter was to outline a new educational model that combines both multilingual and creative teaching strategies. Both types of educational models were shown to gain increasing credibility in the scientific, educational and legislative communities. A vital necessity of fostering students' creative potentials and multilingual skills has been recognized. However, due to lack of conclusive scientific investigation, these new educational trends are taken with a grain of salt. The author acknowledges this skepticism, but believes that the doubts cast on bilingual and creative education are erroneous in nature.

The analysis of various teaching strategies inherent to both bilingual and creative education programs supplied the author with substantial collection of methods and techniques that formed a theoretical framework of the Bilingual Creative Education program. This program is grounded in several conceptual premises. First, it rests on the four-dimensional creativity construct that includes novelty, utility, aesthetics and authenticity. It assumes that successful creative functioning is stipulated by all four aspects of creativity and therefore fosters all of them. Second, it disqualifies the elitist view and provides the opportunities to enhance linguistic and creative capacities for all students regardless of their intellectual and creative predispositions. Third, the focus of the program is not on bigger-C eminent creativity, but on smaller-c creative capacities that are grounded in mundane cognitive functioning and can be applied in everyday problem solving. The program aims at facilitating the overall linguistic, intellectual and creative competences of young children. Fourth, it is designed to facilitate foreign language learning in a diversity of student population: not only for migrants who speak their native language and attempt to acquire the language of the migration country but also for all children who want to acquire a foreign language simultaneously with their mother tongue. Fifth, it can be implemented in any school curriculum being conditional on specific details of a given school. Finally, although it is designed for elementary school curriculum, it can be expanded to kindergarten and middle and high schools. Thus, the purpose of the program is to introduce students to a school curriculum in two languages and to foster four defining aspects of creativity. To accomplish this goal, the program utilizes the holistic approach, which combines cognitive, personal and environmental factors in education. This approach implicates five essential educational attributes: personal, cognitive, administrative, environmental and curricular.

Notes

(1) The sustainability of the theoretical premises for the programs focusing on development of both languages is challenged by research questioning the reliability of the interdependence hypothesis. The claim is made that this hypothesis has not received sufficient empirical support and therefore cannot be used as a solid foundation for the advantages of bilingual education (see Esser, 2006, for an overview of the controversy around the interdependence hypothesis).

8 Conclusions

I have now completed the task I had set up for myself in the Preface. I have constructed a theoretical framework in which multilingualism is presented as a facilitator of one's creative potential. I have proposed that people's experiences with multiple languages and sociocultural settings have an impact on language-mediated concept activation and selective attention. These cognitive mechanisms, in turn, enhance their generative and innovative capacities of creative thinking. It is important to understand, however, that these practices may encourage creative performance, but they do not guarantee eminent creative accomplishments. Rather, there are many other factors that contribute to one's creative capacity. Note that creativity appears to be a complex and versatile construct, which can be prompted by a large variety of factors such as education, expertise, motivation, personality traits, personal experience and socioeconomic and sociocultural conditions. Multilingualism may play an insignificant role among these factors and its effect can be overridden by them. In other words, multilinguals may have certain advantages due to their practices with several languages and cultural settings, but these advantages can be obtained by those who do not have multilingual experience per se. For example, I have argued that individuals' divergent thinking can be facilitated by their multilingual practice. However, it is entirely possible that this type of creative thinking can be enhanced by aptitudes unrelated to multilingual practice. Recall that divergent thinking refers to an ability to activate a multitude of unrelated concepts simultaneously. The LMCA was argued to trigger shared lexical features of the translation equivalents in two languages. The lexical entries, in turn, activate conceptual representations some of which may represent unrelated concepts. At the same time, a capacity to build metaphors was argued to engage multiple concepts or categories in a simultaneous information processing. Recall from Chapter 1 that a metaphor is defined as an analogy between two instances, conveyed by the use of one instead of another. That is, a metaphor extends a bridge between multiple, often unrelated ideas. An extensive knowledge base might play an important role here as it provides a greater variety of possible ideas engaged in the process of metaphor formation. Poets routinely engage in construction of the metaphors in their creative writing. The richness and colorfulness of metaphorical images might be stipulated by their erudition. Thus, metaphor formation and crystallized intelligence may stimulate divergent thinking. That is, a prolific poet does not need to be multilingual to reveal his or her creative potential. Although, multilingual practice may facilitate this process as I have learned from my personal experience as a poet. The cross-linguistic associations expand a pool of poetic images from which I draw my inspiration.

Similarly, the contribution of selective attention to one's innovative capacity was argued to be encouraged by routine practice with several languages. The ability to focus on one language and inhibit the other may enhance the extraction of innovative and useful ideas by suppressing the interference of the ideas that fail to satisfy task requirements. At the same time, the suppression of irrelevant and/or nonoptimal solutions appears to be our general cognitive capacity. We constantly make choices regarding the stimuli to which we pay attention and the ones we ignore. Thereby, we ensure the focus of our attention on particular informational stimuli, which enhances our ability to manipulate those stimuli for other cognitive processes such as problem solving. For example, we may pay attention to reading a book or to monitoring traffic conditions while ignoring such stimuli as a nearby television or a car radio. In line with creative cognition, people differ in the intensity of application of various cognitive processes, which can be manifested in the variation in their creative performance. The Stroop and other selective attention studies demonstrate variations in this capacity, which entails variations in creative performance. These differences may be caused by general cognition and not by multilingual practices per se. Yet, multilingualism may facilitate these functions.

Thus, multilingualism appears as influential but not sufficient requirement for creative endeavors. This conclusion might explain a contradiction between laboratory research and real-life observations: despite a tendency of multilingual individuals to outperform their monolingual counterparts on creativity tests, the former do not necessarily reveal exceptional creative achievements. However, the mere presence of creativity-fostering factors in multilingual development suggests that a combination of foreign language learning with creativity training might provide fruitful outcomes. I have elaborated on this idea and proposed the Bilingual Creative Education program. It is important to recognize that the essential attributes of the BCE discussed in the previous chapter provide the theoretical framework of the program rather than practical suggestions for the program's design and implementation. Detailed guidelines for administrators, teachers and parents will form the content of a separate monograph. Before this monograph will see the light, the program should pass through the cycles of empirical evaluation. Several critical questions need to be answered in order to provide support for the BCE program.

First, is it feasible to implement this program in regular schools? The objective of the program constitutes modifications to existing curricula aimed at fostering the multilingual and creative practices of the students. The recommendations should be made by a team of BCE experts based on the results of in-depth investigation of the student population, school environment and present curriculum. They will also assist school administrations in implementing the program and provide ongoing support in the initial stages of the program and in later stages, upon request. Considering the innovative nature of this program, it is important to make a conclusive decision as to whether this method is, in principle, realistic. Second, would BCE students demonstrate an increase in their linguistic and creative performances? The answer to this question requires a longitudinal study administering a systematic assessment of students' language skills and creative abilities. It can utilize assessment tools from the pool discussed in the previous chapter. It seems to be feasible to administer the assessments every three months starting from the onset of the program. Substantial improvement in students' performance will signify its success as they progress through the program. Third, would BCE students demonstrate significant differences with their counterparts from schools with traditional education in their academic, linguistic and creative achievements? This question is more intricate as it requires a study of comparable samples from BCE and traditional schools. This study should focus on the relative improvements in academic, linguistic and creative performances in these two groups. It is evident that the anticipated effect of the program will not be revealed before at least 1 year of schooling. Therefore, the comparisons should be made annually starting from the completion of the first year. Another issue pertinent to the implementation of the program is concerned with special training for the school staff. As indicated in the previous chapter, the BCE program requires innovative teaching approaches in both delivering the curriculum and establishing a stimulating and facilitating educational climate. Although many teachers may favor these approaches in principle, they might not have sufficient knowledge and skills to implement these ideas in practice. Therefore, in addition to recommendations and modifications, the BCE expert team should provide special training for administrators, teachers and parents. Various training methods can be utilized such as printed and online guidelines, seminars and intensive courses. As the program disseminates, a special qualification procedure can be implemented to award the BCE certificate upon the completion of the training.

Another consideration arises from an objective of the BCE to target both migrant and local student populations, which may produce fruitful outcomes for both parties. Note that the goal of bilingual education for migrants is to both facilitate their autochthonal language learning and improve their cultural adaptation. At the same time, the goal for autochthonal students is to improve their foreign language skills and multicultural awareness. The combination of these two goals in the BCE program will provide a rich linguistic context in which foreign language learners interact with the native speakers. A dual language program discussed in the previous chapter seems to be the most suitable model in the regions with multilingual population such as the EU. The combination of languages could be either intra-European (e.g. Swedish–Italian, English–Spanish and German–French) or inter-European (e.g. German–Turkish, Spanish–Arabic and English–Chinese). A large migrant population in Europe ensures sufficient number of native speakers of the respective languages both at student and instructor level. Thereby, this resolves several issues inherent to bilingual education. First, there will be no need to accommodate students with a variety of linguistic backgrounds in one class, because each program will have only two languages: one native to one group of students and the other native to another group of students. Second, the problem of finding certified foreign language teachers will be solved due to a large migrant population: the teachers speaking respective languages and having appropriate education could be found among the migrants. Third, ethnic/racial segregation will be avoided by accommodating an equal number of students with different native languages and cultural perspectives. In this respect, the BCE may facilitate building intercultural skills and thereby closing a sociocultural gap between migrant children and their peers. Note that the latter goals were deliberately emphasized by the Commission of the European Communities (2009) in *Results of the Consultation on the Education of Children from a Migrant Background*. The BCE program may encourage the training of both native and migrant individuals in citizenship and solidarity and help motivate them to participate in open and democratic societies from a young age.

On the final note, investing in the BCE is a riskier enterprise than supporting literacy and other skills tied to traditional education. Despite the less certain payoffs, this new form of education promises to have important ramifications for students' learning and their future employment. It is important for educators to recognize the positive effect of bilingual creative education and to start transforming schools into educational enterprises that value linguistic and cultural diversity and creative potential. Bringing students from different linguistic and cultural backgrounds into the same classroom provides a rich source of learning opportunities that can potentially stimulate the acquisition of a range of competencies, including initiative taking, entrepreneurship, creative problem solving and idea generation and cultural awareness and expression. Eventually, this form of education supplies more skilled, committed and innovation-oriented individuals.

I hope that the reader understands that the objective of this book was to breach for multilingual creative cognition and to provide a theoretical framework in which long awaited scientific inquiries can be posited. The reviewed studies merely outlined the directions for the future studies rather than providing an exhaustive inventory of possible investigations in this area. So, what else does the empirical exploration of the relationship between multilingualism and creativity have to offer to the academic community? One direction of scientific research stems from the four-criterion construct of creativity presented in Chapter 6. What creativity traits may benefit the most from the multilingual practice? So far, we found a positive effect of cross-linguistic and cross-cultural experiences on the LMCA and selective attention. These cognitive mechanisms facilitate generative and innovative capacities and therefore hint at the benefits of multilingualism for novelty and, possibly, for utility in creative thinking. That is, generation of original solutions satisfies criteria of novelty, and extracting these solutions from a pool of related ones ensures placing it in the appropriate context. The question that future research may explore is whether multilingual experience enhances aesthetic and authentic characteristics of creative process. The answer to this question can be obtained from a longitudinal study conducted within a network of the BCE program. Would the students, as they progress through this program, reveal particular authentic involvement and aesthetic maxims?

Another cluster of scientific studies might tap into questions widely discussed in multilingualism research, but in this case, from the perspective of multilingual creative cognition. As the reader might have noticed, most studies reviewed in this book have been conducted with bilingual individuals, those speaking two languages. What about those speaking more than two languages? Although the book made predictions about multilingual creative cognition, I have to acknowledge that there is very little research on creativity that involves participants speaking more than two languages. At the same time, there is a growing body of empirical evidence hinting to potential cognitive differences between individuals speaking two and three languages. Similar to bilinguals' languages, trilinguals' languages were found to be interconnected (Lemhöfer et al., 2004) and to influence each other during lexical access (Goral et al., 2006). In addition, a number of languages spoken by trilingual individuals contributed to the prediction of alleviation of cognitive decline with aging (Kavé et al., 2008). Moreover, trilinguals were found to show greater performance on creativity tests compared to their bi- and monolingual counterparts (Srivastava, 1991). Although these findings are highly scattered, one can see a tendency for three languages to enhance human cognition more than two languages do. Would this linguistic arithmetic sustain for human creativity?

Furthermore, in the past two decades, the relationship between language, emotions and cognition has come to the vanguard in the study of cognitive and cultural psychology, cognitive linguistics, neurolinguistics and linguistic anthropology. Increasing number of studies demonstrated cross-linguistic and cross-cultural variability in emotion words, categories and scripts. The interest in emotions has infiltrated into the camp of multilingualism where several authors have begun examining the role of affect in multilingual cognitive performance. At the same time, in the past three decades, empirical research has examined the impact of emotional states on creative cognition. Specifically, the effects of positive or negative states or mood on creative performance attracted attention of the researchers. These considerations make it evident that emotions should not be avoided from the scientific inquiries in multilingual creativity. My colleague and I have already planted the seeds for this inquiry by looking at the interactive effect of bilingualism and emotions on an individual's creativity (Kharkhurin & Altarriba, 2011). We induced Arabic–English bilingual college students to positive and negative emotional states in their respective L1 or L2. Participants revealed significantly greater innovative capacity when they were induced to positive emotions in their L2 or to negative emotions in their L1, compared to when they were induced to positive emotions in their L1 or negative emotions in their L2.

Another line of research might be extracted from an argument presented in the previous chapter that code-switching practice could be detrimental to the development of an individual's creative potential. This claim stems from an assumption that the unintentional switch between languages entails poor development of each of them as well as less developed inhibition mechanism of selective attention. However, there is another side to this argument that claims that code-switching might actually be advantageous to creative thinking. This claim is based on the observation that people can intentionally switch to another language to reflect a particular emotional state, to convey a message with more precision, to achieve special communicative effect or to say something unusual. In this case, the practice of switching between languages can be beneficial for creativity for it provides a tool for creative expression. This controversy has been addressed in the study, which my colleague and I have conducted with bilingual college students in the United Arab Emirates and which is still pending the formal report.

Last but not least, there is an apparent controversy concerning the inability of empirical studies to disentangle the cognitive and creative ramifications of multilingualism from the ones of multiculturalism. I have addressed this issue on several occasions throughout the book. The problem arises from the fact that most studies in the field were conducted with individuals who had exposure to multiple cultural settings in addition to the virtue of speaking multiple languages. To distinguish between the cross-linguistic and cross-cultural effects, one can conduct a longitudinal study with nonmigrant foreign language learners residing within a single sociocultural environment. This allows us to measure the effect of multilingualism while controlling for the effect of multiculturalism. This study should regularly assess students' creative performance as they progress through the language program and develop their L2. Their gradual increase in creative performance would suggest a positive effect of cross-linguistic experience on an individual's creative potential. However, we need to be aware of confounding factors such as intelligence that could mask this effect. Another approach to this problem constitutes a cross-regional study, which manipulates both bilingualism and biculturalism factors. The ideal study should consider at least four groups: (1) a bilingual/bicultural group that includes individuals who lived in one country and migrated to another country where they acquired L2; (2) a bilingual/monocultural group that includes individuals who lived only in one bilingual country; (3) a monolingual/bicultural group that includes individuals who lived in a monolingual country, never acquired L2 and immigrated to another country where they speak the same language; and (4) a monolingual/ monocultural group that includes individuals who lived in a monolingual country and never lived in any other one. Note that this design is possible only with the individuals who lived in two different countries that share the same language. Moreover, the target courtiers need to be sufficiently diverse culturally to reveal a significant effect of the cross-cultural experience, if any. Belgium (with Dutch and French as two official languages) and French Guiana (with French as official language) could present a possible combination of two countries that share the same official language (French) and yet sufficiently differ in the cultural standards and norms (one is European country, whereas the other one is South American).

I have presented here only few directions for future research in the immense realm of scientific opportunities in multilingual creative enterprise. I have strong belief that despite the fact the academic community has abandoned this area of research for many years, there is a vital necessity to explore the effect of multilingual practice on one's creativity. This book will help researchers to reestablish the trust in significance of the multilingual creative cognition and will encourage them to pursue this endeavor.

Bibliography

Aguirre, N. (2003) ESL students in gifted education. In J.A. Castellano (ed.) *Special Populations in Gifted Education: Working with Diverse Gifted Learners* (pp. 17–28). Boston, MA: Allyn & Bacon.

Albert, R.S. (1980) Genius. In R.H. Woody (ed.) *Encyclopedia of Clinical Assessment* (Vol. 2). San Francisco: Jossey-Bass.

Allopenna, P.D. Magnuson, J.S. and Tanenhaus, M.K. (1998) Tracking the time course of spoken word recognition using eye movements: Evidence for continuous mapping models. *Journal of Memory and Language* 38(4), 419–439.

Altarriba, J. and Mathis, K.M. (1997) Conceptual and lexical development in second language acquisition. *Journal of Memory and Language* 36(4), 550–568.

Am Ende, J. (1987) *Joseph Beuys und die Fettecke: Eine Dokumentation zur Zerstörung der Fettecke in der Kunstakademie Düsseldorf*. Heidelberg, DE: Edition Staeck.

Amabile, T.M. (1982) Social psychology of creativity: A consensual assessment technique. *Journal of Personality and Social Psychology* 43(5), 997–1013.

Amabile, T.M. (1983a) *The Social Psychology of Creativity*. New York: Springer-Verlag.

Amabile, T.M. (1983b) The social psychology of creativity: A componential conceptualization. *Journal of Personality and Social Psychology* 45(2), 357–376.

Amabile, T.M. (1996) *Creativity in Context: Update to "The Social Psychology of Creativity. "* Boulder, CO: Westview Press.

Appel, R. (2000) Language, concepts and culture: Old wine in new bottles? *Bilingualism: Language and Cognition* 3(1), 5–6.

Aragno, A. and Schlachet, P. J. (1996) Accessibility of early experience through the language of origin: A theoretical integration. *Psychoanalytic Psychology* 13(1), 23–34.

Aristotle (1998) *The Metaphysics* (H. Lawson-Tancred, Trans.). London: Penguin Books.

Arnheim, R. (1957) *Film as Art*. Berkeley, CA: University of California Press.

Arnheim, R. (1971) *Entropy and Art: An Essay on Disorder and Order*. Berkeley, CA: University of California Press.

Arnheim, R. (1974) *Art and Visual Perception* (2nd edn). Berkeley, CA: University of California Press.

Arnheim, R. (1977) *The Dynamics of Architectural Form*. Berkeley, CA: University of California Press.

Arnheim, R. (1992) *To the Rescue of Art: Twenty-Six Essays*.

August, D. and Hakuta, K. (1997) *Improving Schooling for Language-Minority Children: A Research Agenda*. Washington, DC: National Academy Press.

August, D. and Shanahan, T. (eds) (2006) *Developing Literacy in Second-Language Learners: Report of the National Literacy Panel on Language Minority Children and Youth*. Mahwah, NJ: Lawrence Erlbaum.

Averill, J.R., Chon, K.K. and Hahn, D.W. (2001) Emotions and creativity, East and West. *Asian Journal of Social Psychology* 4(3), 165–183.

Aviram, A. and Milgram, R. M. (1977) Dogmatism, locus of control and creativity in children educated in the Soviet Union, the United States, and Israel. *Psychological Reports* 40(1), 27–34.

Baer, J. (1993) *Divergent Thinking and Creativity: A Task-Specific Approach*. Hillsdale, NJ: Erlbaum.

Baer, J. (1994) Why you still shouldn't trust creativity tests. *Educational Leadership* 52(2), 72–73.

Baer, J. (1998) The case for domain specificity of creativity. *Creativity Research Journal* 11(2), 173–177.

Baer, J. (2003) Evaluative thinking, creativity, and task specificity: Separating wheat from chaff is not the same as finding needles in haystacks. In M.A. Runco (ed.) *Critical Creative Processes* (pp. 129–151). Cresskill, NJ: Hampton Press.

Bahador, D. and Somerville, A.W. (1969) Youth at the crossroads: A comparison of American and Iranian adolescence. *Adolescence* 4(13), 1–18.

Bahrick, H.P. and Hall, L.K. (1991) Lifetime maintenance of high school mathematics content. *Journal of Experimental Psychology: General* 120(1), 20–33.

Ball, O.E. (1980) The effects of Transcendental Meditation (TM) and the TM Sidhis Program on verbal and figural creativity (TTCT), auditory creativity (S&I), and hemispheric dominance (SOLAT). Unpublished dissertation thesis, University of Georgia.

Ball, O.E. and Torrance, E.P. (1978) Culture and tendencies to draw objects in internal visual perspective. *Perceptual and Motor Skills* 47(3), 1071–1075.

Bandura, A. (1997) *Self-Efficacy: The Exercise of Control*. New York, NY: Freeman.

Barron, F. and Harrington, D.M. (1981) Creativity, intelligence, and personality. *Annual Review of Psychology* 32, 439–476.

Barron, F. and Welsh, G. S. (1952) Artistic perception as a possible factor in personality style: Its measurement by a figure preference test. *Journal of Psychology* 33, 199–203.

Bartlett, M.M. and Davis, G.A. (1974) Do the Wallach and Kogan tests predict real creative behavior? *Perceptual & Motor Skills* 39(2), 730.

Batey, M. (2007) A psychometric investigation of everyday creativity. Unpublished doctoral thesis, University College, London.

Beghetto, R.A. (2007) Does creativity have a place in classroom discussions? Prospective teachers' response preferences. *Thinking Skills and Creativity* 2(1), 1–9.

Beghetto, R.A. (2009) Correlates of intellectual risk taking in elementary school science. *Journal of Research in Science Teaching* 46(2), 210–223.

Beghetto, R.A. (2010) Creativity in the classroom. In J.C. Kaufman and R.J. Sternberg (eds) *The Cambridge Handbook of Creativity* (pp. 447–463). New York, NY: Cambridge University Press.

Beghetto, R.A. and Kaufman, J.C. (2009) Intellectual estuaries: Connecting learning and creativity in programs of advanced academics. *Journal of Advanced Academics* 20(2), 296–324.

Ben-Zeev, S. (1977) The influence of bilingualism on cognitive strategy and cognitive development. *Child Development* 48(3), 1009–1018.

Benn, G. (1912) *Morgue und andere Gedichte*. Berlin-Wilmersdorf: Meyer.

Berger, R.M. and Guilford, J.P. (1969) *Pilot Titles*. Beverly Hills, CA: Sheridan Psychological Services.

Berman, P. (1996) High performance learning communities: Proposal to the US Department of Education.

Bernal, E.M. (1998) Could gifted English-language learners save gifted and talented programs in the age of reform and inclusion. *TAGT Tempo* 18(1), 11–14.

Bernal, E.M. (2007) Educating culturally and linguistically diverse gifted and talented students through a dual-language, multicultural curriculum. In G.B. Esquivel,

E.C. Lopez and S.G. Nahari (eds) *Handbook of Multicultural School Psychology: An Interdisciplinary Perspective* (pp. 479–495). Mahwah, NJ: Lawrence Erlbaum Associates Publishers.

Besemer, S.P. and O'Quin, K. (1987) Creative product analysis: Testing a model by developing a judging instrument. In S.G. Isaksen (ed.) *Frontiers of Creativity Research: Beyond the Basics* (pp. 367–389) Buffalo, NY: Bearly.

Bialystok, E. (1988) Levels of bilingualism and levels of linguistic awareness. *Developmental Psychology* 24(4), 560–567.

Bialystok, E. (2001) *Bilingualism in Development: Language, Literacy, and Cognition*. New York: Cambridge University Press.

Bialystok, E. (2005) Consequences of bilingualism for cognitive development. In J.F. Kroll and A.M.B. de Groot (eds) *Handbook of Bilingualism: Psycholinguistic Approaches* (pp. 417–432) New York: Oxford University Press.

Bialystok, E. (2009) Bilingualism: The good, the bad, and the indifferent. *Bilingualism: Language and Cognition* 12(01), 3–11.

Bialystok, E., Craik, F.I.M., Grady, C., Chau, W., Ishii, R., Gunji, A., *et al.* (2005) Effect of bilingualism on cognitive control in the Simon task: Evidence from MEG. *NeuroImage* 24(1), 40–49.

Bialystok, E., Craik, F. I. M., Klein, R. and Viswanathan, M. (2004) Bilingualism, aging, and cognitive control: Evidence from the Simon task. *Psychology and Aging* 19(2), 290–303.

Bialystok, E., Craik, F.I.M. and Luk, G. (2008a) Cognitive control and lexical access in younger and older bilinguals. *Journal of Experimental Psychology: Learning, Memory, & Cognition* 34(4), 859–873.

Bialystok, E., Craik, F.I.M. and Luk, G. (2008b) Lexical access in bilinguals: Effects of vocabulary size and executive control. *Journal of Neurolinguistics* 21(6), 522–538.

Bialystok, E. and DePape, A-M. (2009) Musical expertise, bilingualism, and executive functioning. *Journal of Experimental Psychology: Human Perception and Performance* 35(2), 565–574.

Bialystok, E. and Feng, X. (2009) Language proficiency and executive control in proactive interference: Evidence from monolingual and bilingual children and adults. *Brain and Language* 109(2–3), 93–100.

Bialystok, E. and Martin, M.M. (2004) Attention and inhibition in bilingual children: Evidence from the dimensional change card sort task. *Developmental Science* 7(3), 325–339.

Bialystok, E. and Shapero, D. (2005) Ambiguous benefits: The effect of bilingualism on reversing ambiguous figures. *Developmental Science* 8(6), 595–604.

Bijeljac-Babic, R., Biardeau, A. and Grainger, J. (1997) Masked orthographic priming in bilingual word recognition. *Memory & Cognition,* 25(4), 447–457.

Birman, D. and Trickett, E.J. (2001) Cultural transitions in first-generation immigrants: Acculturation of Soviet Jewish refugee adolescents and parents. *Journal of Cross-Cultural Psychology* 32(4), 456–477.

Birman, D., Trickett, E.J. and Vinokurov, A. (2002) Acculturation and adaptation of Soviet Jewish refugee adolescents: Predictors of adjustment across life domains. *American Journal of Community Psychology* 30(5), 585–607.

Birman, D. and Tyler, F.B. (1994) Acculturation and alienation of Soviet Jewish refugees in the United States. *Genetic, Social, & General Psychology Monographs,* 120(1), 101–115.

Birnbaum, D. (2009) Ein Kunstwerk ist mehr als ein Objekt: Ein Gespräch mit dem Leiter der 53. Kunstbiennale von Venedig. *Neue Zürcher Zeitung Online*. Retrieved from http://www.nzz.ch/nachrichten/kultur/aktuell/ein_kunstwerk_ist_mehr_als_ein_objekt_1.2662826.html.

Bloom, B. S. (1985) *Developing Talent in Young People*. New York: Ballantine.

Boden, M. A. (1999) Computer models of creativity. In R.J. Sternberg (ed.) *Handbook of Creativity* (pp. 351–372). New York, NY: Cambridge University Press.

Borrell Fontelles, J. and Enestam, J-E. (2006) Recommendation of the European Parliament and of the Council of 18 December 2006 on key competences for lifelong learning. *Official Journal of the European Union* 49(10), 10–18.

Bourdon, D. (1995) *Warhol*. New York, NY: Abrams.

Breton, A. (2002) *Surrealism and Painting* (S.W.Taylor, Trans.). Boston, MA: MFA Publications.

Brown, R.T. (1989) Creativity: What are we to measure? In J.A. Glover and R.R. Ronning (eds) *Handbook of Creativity* (pp. 3–32). New York: Plenum Press.

Bruce, D.J. (1964) The analysis of word sounds by young children. *British Journal of Educational Psychology* 34(2), 158–170.

Brysbaert, M. and New, B. (2009) Moving beyond Kučera and Francis: A critical evaluation of current word frequency norms and the introduction of a new and improved word frequency measure for American English. *Behavior Research Methods* 41(4).

Brysbaert, M., Wijnendaele, I.V. and Deyne, S.D. (2000) Age-of-acquisition effects in semantic processing tasks. *Acta Psychologica* 104(2), 215–226.

Bunge, M. (1980) *The Mind-Body problem*. Oxford: Pergamon.

Bunge, S.A., Dudukovic, N.M., Thomason, M.E., Vaidya, C.J. and Gabrieli, J.D. (2002) Immature frontal lobe contributions to cognitive control in children: Evidence from fMRI. *Neuron* 33, 301–311.

Burck, C. (2004) Living in several languages: Implications for therapy. *Journal of Family Therapy* 26(4), 314–339.

Calderón, M. E. and Minaya-Rowe, L. (2003) *Designing and Implementing Two-Way Bilingual Programs: A Step-By-Step Guide for Administrators, Teachers, And Parents*. Thousand Oaks, CA: Corwin Press.

Calwelti, S., Rappaport, A. and Wood, B. (1992) Modeling artistic creativity: An empirical study. *Journal of Creative Behavior* 26, 83–94.

Campbell, D.T. (1960) Blind variation and selective retentions in creative thought as in other knowledge processes. *Psychological Review* 67(6), 380–400.

Campbell, D.T. and Stanley, J.C. (1963) *Experimental and Quasi-Experimental Designs for Research*. Boston, MA: Houghton, Mifflin and Company.

Carringer, D.C. (1974) Creative thinking abilities of Mexican youth: The relationship of bilingualism. *Journal of Cross-Cultural Psychology* 5(4), 492–504.

Cattell, R.B. (1963) Theory of fluid and crystallized intelligence: A critical experiment. *Journal of Educational Psychology* 54(1), 1–22.

Cattell, R.B. (1973) *Manual for the Cattell Culture Fair Intelligence Test*. Champaign, IL: Institute for Personality and Ability Testing.

Chan, D.W. and Chan, L-k. (1999) Implicit theories of creativity: Teachers' perception of student characteristics in Hong Kong. *Creativity Research Journal* 12(3), 185–195.

Chan, W. (1967) *Chinese Philosophy, 1949–1963: An Annotated Bibliography of Mainland China Publications*. Honolulu, HI: East-West Center Press.

Chand, I. and Runco, M.A. (1992) Problem finding skills as components in the creative process. *Personality and Individual Differences* 14, 155–162.

Chapelle, C.A. (2006) DIALANG: A diagnostic language test in 14 European languages. *Language Testing* 23(4), 544–550.

Chavez, L. (1992) *Out of the Barrio: Toward a New Politics of Hispanic Assimilation*. New York, NY: Basic Books.

Chen, H-C. and Leung, Y-S. (1989) Patterns of lexical processing in a nonnative language. *Journal of Experimental Psychology: Learning, Memory, & Cognition*, 15(2), 316–325.

Cheung, H., Chung, K.K.H., Wong, S.W.L., McBride-Chang, C., Penney, T.B. and Ho, C.S-H. (2010) Speech perception, metalinguistic awareness, reading, and vocabulary in Chinese–English bilingual children. *Journal of Educational Psychology* 102(2), 367–380.

Chomsky, N. (1972) *Language and Mind*. New York: Harcourt, Brace, Jovanovich.

Chorney, M. (1978) The Relationship of Bilingualism and Creativity. Unpublished honors thesis, University of Adulate.

Chou, C-T.E. (2008) *Factors Affecting Language Proficiency of English Language Learners at Language Institutes in the United States*. ProQuest Information & Learning, US.

Christensen, P.R., Guilford, J.P., Merrifield, P.R. and Wilson, R.C. (1960) *Alternative Uses*. Beverly Hills, CA: Sheridan Psychological Services.

Christensen, P.R., Merrifield, P.R. and Guilford, J.P. (1953) *Consequences*. Beverly Hills, CA: Sheridan Psychological Services.

Colangelo, N. and Dettmann, D.F. (1983) A review of research on parents and families of gifted children. *Exceptional Children* 50(1), 20–27.

Collins, M.A. and Amabile, T.M. (1999) Motivation and creativity. In R.J. Sternberg (ed.) *Handbook of Creativity* (pp. 297–312). New York, NY: Cambridge University Press.

Cook, V.J. (1997) The consequences of bilingualism for cognitive processing. In A.M.B. de Groot and J.F. Kroll (eds) *Tutorials in Bilingualism: Psycholinguistic Perspectives* (pp. 279–299). Hillsdale, NJ: Erlbaum.

Comission of the European Communities (2008) Improving competences for the 21st century: An agenda for European cooperation on schools. Brussels: Comission of the European Communities. (Report No. COM(2008) 425 final.) Retrieved from http://eur-lex.europa.eu/LexUriServ/LexUriServ.do?uri=COM:2008:0425:FIN:EN:PDF.

Commission of the European Communities (2009) Results of the consultation on the education of children from a migrant background. Brussels: Commission of the European Communities (Report No. SEC(2009) 1115 final). Retrieved from http://ec.europa.eu/education/news/doc/sec1115_en.pdf. Costa, A., Albareda, B. and Santesteban, M. (2008) Assessing the presence of lexical competition across languages: Evidence from the Stroop task. *Bilingualism: Language and Cognition* 11(1), 121–131.

Costa, A. (2005) Lexical access in bilingual production. In J.F. Kroll and A.M.B. de Groot (eds) *Handbook of Bilingualism: Psycholinguistic Approaches* (pp. 289–307). New York: Oxford University Press.

Costa, A., Hernandez, M. and Sebastián-Gallés, N. (2008) Bilingualism aids conflict resolution: Evidence from the ANT task. *Cognition* 106(1), 59–86.

Council of the European Communities (2009) Council conclusions on the education of children with a migrant background. Brussels: Council of the European Communities. Retrieved from http://www.consilium.europa.eu/uedocs/cms_data/docs/pressdata/en/educ/111482.pdf.

Cowger, E.L. and Torrance, E.P. (1982) Further examination of the quality of changes in creative functioning resulting from meditation (Zazen) training. *Creative Child & Adult Quarterly* 7(4), 211–217.

Craft, A. (2005) *Creativity in Schools: Tensions and Dilemmas*. London, Routledge.

Craft, A. (2007) Possibility thinking in the early years and primary classroom. In A-G. Tan (ed.) *Creativity: A Handbook for Teachers* (pp. 231–249). Singapore: World Scientific.

Craik, F. I. and Tulving, E. (1975) Depth of processing and the retention of words in episodic memory. *Journal of Experimental Psychology: General* 104(3), 268–294.

Craik, F.I.M. and Bialystok, E. (2010) Bilingualism and aging: Costs and benefits. *Memory, Aging and the Brain: A Festschrift in Honour of Lars-Göran Nilsson* (pp. 115–131). New York, NY: Psychology Press.

Craik, F.I.M. and Jennings, J.M. (1992) Human memory. In F.I.M. Craik and T.A. Salthouse (eds) *Handbook of Aging and Cognition* (pp. 51–110). Hillsdale, NJ: Erlbaum.

Cramond, B. (1994) The Torrance tests of creative thinking: From design through establishment of predictive validity. In R.F. Subotnik and K.D. Arnold (eds) *Beyond Terman: Contemporary Longitudinal Studies of Giftedness and Talent* (pp. 229–254). Westport, CT: Ablex Publishing.

Crawford, J. (1998) Ten common fallacies about bilingual education. Washington, DC: Digest for the ERIC Clearinghouse on Languages and Linguistics (Report No. EDO-FL-98-10). Retrieved from http://www.eric.ed.gov/PDFS/ED424792.pdf.

Cropley, A. (2006) In praise of convergent thinking. *Creativity Research Journal* 18(3), 391–404.

Cropley, A.J. (1992) *More Ways than One: Fostering Creativity*. Westport, CT: Ablex Publishing.

Cropley, A.J. (2001) *Creativity in Education & Learning: A Guide for Teachers and Educators*. London, UK: Kogan Page.

Cropley, A.J. and Urban, K.K. (2000) Programs and strategies for nurturing creativity. In K.A. Heller, F.J. Mönks, R.J. Sternberg and R.F. Subotnik (eds) *International Handbook of Giftedness and Talent* (2nd edn, pp. 485–498). New York, NY: Pergamon.

Cropley, D. and Cropley, A. (2008) Elements of a universal aesthetic of creativity. *Psychology of Aesthetics, Creativity, and the Arts* 2(3), 155–161.

Csíkszentmihályi, M. (1988) Society, culture, and person: A systems view of creativity. In R.J. Sternberg (ed.) *The Nature of Creativity: Contemporary Psychological Perspectives* (pp. 325–339). New York, NY: Cambridge University Press.

Csíkszentmihályi, M. (1990) The domain of creativity. In M.A. Runco and R.S. Albert (eds) *Theories of Creativity* (pp. 190–212). Thousand Oaks, CA: Sage Publications, Inc.

Csíkszentmihályi, M. (1997) *Creativity: Flow and the Psychology of Discovery and Invention*. New York, NY: HarperCollins Publishers.

Cuban, L. (1993) *How Teachers Taught: Constancy and Change in American Classrooms, 1890–1990*. New York, NY: Teachers College Press.

Cummins, J. (1976) The influence of bilingualism on cognitive growth: A synthesis of research findings and explanatory hypothesis. *Working Papers on Bilingualism* 9, 1–43.

Cummins, J. (1978a) Bilingualism and the development of metalinguistic awareness. *Journal of Cross-Cultural Psychology* 9(2), 131–149.

Cummins, J. (1978b) Educational implications of mother tongue maintenance in minority language groups.

Cummins, J. (1979) Linguistic interdependence and the educational development of bilingual children. *Review of Educational Research* 49, 222–251.

Cummins, J. (1984) The role of primary language development in promoting educational success for language minority students. In *Schooling and Language Minority Students: A Theoretical Framework* (pp. 3–49). Los Angeles, CA: Evaluation, Dissemination and Assessment Center, California State University.

Cummins, J. and Gulutsan, M. (1974) Some effects of bilingualism on cognitive functioning. In S.T. Carey (ed.) *Bilingualism, Biculturalism and Education: Proceeding from the Conference at College Universitaire Saint-Jean* (pp. 129–136). Edmonton: University of Alberta.

Curran, T. (1997) Effects of aging on implicit sequence learning: Accounting for sequence structure and explicit knowledge. *Psychological Research/Psychologische Forschung,* 60(1), 24–41.

Cushen, P.J. and Wiley, J. (2011) Aha! Voila! Eureka! Bilingualism and insightful problem solving. *Learning and Individual Differences* 21(4), 458–462.

Davis, G. and Belcher, T.L. (1971) How shall creativity be measured? Torrance tests, RAT, Alpha Biographical and IQ. *Journal of Creative Behavior* 5, 153–161.

Davis, G.A. (1991) Identifying creative students and measuring creativity. In N. Colangelo and G.A. Davis (eds) *Handbook of Gifted Education* (pp. 269–281). Boston, MA: Allyn and Bacon.

de Groot, A.M.B. (2000) On the source and nature of semantic and conceptual knowledge. *Bilingualism: Language and Cognition* 3(1), 7–9.

Dehaene, S., Dupoux, E., Mehler, J., Cohen, L., Paulesu, E., Perani, D., *et al.* (1997) Anatomical variability in the cortical representation of first and second language. *Neuroreport: An International Journal for the Rapid Communication of Research in Neuroscience* 8(17), 3809–3815.

Diaz, R.M. (1985) Bilingual cognitive development: Addressing three gaps in current research. *Child Development* 56(6), 1376–1388.

Dijkstra, T. (2005) Bilingual visual word recognition and lexical access. In J.F. Kroll and A.M.B. de Groot (eds) *Handbook of Bilingualism: Psycholinguistic Approaches* (pp. 179–201). New York: Oxford University Press.

Doyle, C.L. (1998) The writer tells: The creative process in the writing of literary fiction. *Creativity Research Journal* 11(1), 29–37.

Driskell, J.E., Willis, R.P. and Copper, C. (1992) Effect of overlearning on retention. *Journal of Applied Psychology* 77(5), 615–622.

Duncan, J., Emslie, H., Williams, P., Johnson, R. and Freer, C. (1996) Intelligence and the frontal lobe: The organization of goal-directed behavior. *Cognitive Psychology* 30(3), 257–303.

Duncker, K. (1945) On problem solving. *Psychological Monographs,* 58:5 (Whole No. 270)

Dunn, L.M. (1965) *Peabody Picture Vocabulary Test.* Circle Pines, MN: American Guidance Service.

Dunn, L.M. and Dunn, D.M. (2007) *Peabody Picture Vocabulary Test-IV.* Circle Pines, MN: American Guidance Service.

Dupuis, M.M. (1980) The cloze procedure as a predictor of comprehension in literature. *Journal of Educational Research* 74(1), 27–33.

Echevarria, J.L., Vogt, M.E.J. and Short, D.J. (2000) *Making Content Comprehensible for English Language Learners: The SIOP Model.* Boston, MA: Allyn and Bacon.

Eco, U. (2007) *On Ugliness.* New York: Rizzoli.

Ehrman, M. and Oxford, R.L. (1990) Adult language learning styles and strategies in an intensive training setting. *The Modern Language Journal* 74(3), 311–327.

Eindhoven, J.E. and Vinacke, W.E. (1952) Creative processes in painting. *Journal of General Psychology* 47, 139–164.

Einstein, A. (1920) *Relativity: the Special and General Theory* (R. W. Lawson, Trans.). New York, NY: H. Holt and Company.

Ellis, N. (1992) Linguistic relativity revisited: The bilingual word-length effect in working memory during counting, remembering numbers, and mental calculation. In R.J. Harris (ed.) *Cognitive Processing in Bilinguals* (pp. 137–155). Oxford, England: North-Holland.

Ellison, B.A. (1973) Creativity in black artists: A comparison of selected creativity measures using judged creativity as a criterion. *Journal of Non-White Concerns in Personnel & Guidance* 1(3), 150–157.

Elman, J.L. (1993) Learning and development in neural networks: The importance of starting small. *Cognition* 48(1), 71–99.

Engjn, A.O. (2009) Second language learning success and motivation. *Social Behavior and Personality* 37(8), 1035–1042.

Ervin-Tripp, S. (2000) Bilingual minds. *Bilingualism: Language and Cognition* 3(1), 10–12.

Esser, H. (2006) *Migration, language and integration. AKI Research Review 4.* Berlin: Wissenschaftszentrum. Retrieved from http://www.wzb.eu/alt/aki/files/aki_research_review_4.pdf.

Council of Europe (2001) *Common European Framework of Reference for Languages: Learning, Teaching, Assessment.* Cambridge, MA: Cambridge University Press.

Department for Education and Employment/Qualifications and Curriculum Authority (1999) *The National Curriculum Handbook for Primary Teachers in England.* London: Department for Education and Employment/Qualifications and Curriculum Authority.

Department for Education and Employment/Qualifications and Curriculum Authority (1999) *The National Curriculum handbook for secondary teachers in England.* London: Department for Education and Employment/Qualifications and Curriculum Authority.

European Commission (2006) Europeans and their languages. Brussels: European Commission. Retrieved from http://ec.europa.eu/public_opinion/archives/ebs/ebs_243_en.pdf.

Eysenck, H.J. (1994) The measurement of creativity. In M.A. Boden (ed.) *Dimensions of Creativity* (pp. 199–242). Cambridge, MA: The MIT Press.

Eysenck, H.J. (1995) *Genius: The Natural History of Creativity.* New York: Cambridge University Press.

Fainsilber, L. and Ortony, A. (1987) Metaphorical uses of language in the expression of emotions. *Metaphor & Symbolic Activity* 2(4), 239–250.

Feist, G.J. (1998) A meta-analysis of personality in scientific and artistic creativity. *Personality and Social Psychology Review* 2(4), 290–309.

Feist, G.J. (1999) The influence of personality on artistic and scientific creativity. In R.J. Sternberg (ed.) *Handbook of Creativity* (pp. 273–296). New York, NY: Cambridge University Press.

Feist, G.J. and Brady, T.R. (2004) Openness to experience, non-conformity, and the preference for abstract art. *Empirical Studies of the Arts* 22(1), 77–89.

Feldhusen, J.F. and Kolloff, M.B. (1978) A three-stage model for gifted education. *Gifted Child Today* 1(4), 3–5, 53–57.

Feldhusen, J.F. and Treffinger, D.J. (1975) Teachers' attitudes and practices in teaching creativity and problem-solving to economically disadvantaged and minority children. *Psychological Reports* 37(3/2), 1161–1162.

Fischman, N. (2005) Implicit Learning and Aging. Unpublished dissertation, City University of New York, New York.

Fleith, D.d.S. (1999) *Effects of a Creativity Training Program on Creative Abilities and Self-Concept in Monolingual and Bilingual Elementary Classrooms.* ProQuest Information & Learning, US.

Fleith, D.d.S., Renzulli, J.S. and Westberg, K.L. (2002) Effects of a creativity training program on divergent thinking abilities and self-concept in monolingual and bilingual classrooms. *Creativity Research Journal* 14(3–4), 373–386.

Fox, B. and Routh, D.K. (1975) Analysing spoken language into words, syllables, and phonemes: A developmental study. *Journal of Psycholinguistic Research* 4(4), 331–342.

Francis, N. (2002) Literacy, second language learning, and the development of metalinguistic awareness: A study of bilingual children's perceptions of focus on form. *Linguistics and Education* 13(3), 373–404.

Francis, W.S. (2000) Clarifying the cognitive experimental approach to bilingual research. *Bilingualism: Language and Cognition* 3(1), 13–15.

Francis, W.S. (2005) Bilingual semantic and conceptual representation. In J.F. Kroll and A.M.B. de Groot (eds) *Handbook of Bilingualism: Psycholinguistic Approaches* (pp. 251–267). New York: Oxford University Press.

Frenck-Mestre, C. and Vaid, J. (1993) Activation of number facts in bilinguals. *Memory and Cognition* 21(6), 809–818.

Gabrieli, J.D.E., Desmond, J.E., Demb, J.B. and Wagner, A.D. (1996) Functional magnetic resonance imaging of semantic memory processes in the frontal lobes. *Psychological Science* 7(5), 278–283.

Garcia, E.E. (2008) Bilingual education in the United States. In J. Altarriba and R.R. Heredia (eds) *An Introduction to Bilingualism: Principles and Processes* (pp. 321–343). Mahwah, NJ US: Lawrence Erlbaum Associates Publishers.

Garcia, J.H. (1996) *The Influences of Oral Language Proficiency and Acculturation on the Creative Thinking of Second Grade Children.* ProQuest Information & Learning, US.

Garcia, J.H. (2003) Nurturing creativity in Chicano populations: Integrating history, culture, family, and self. *Inquiry: Critical Thinking Across the Disciplines* 22(3), 19–24.

Gardner, H. (1983) *Frames of Mind: The Theory of Multiple Intelligences.* New York: Basic Books.

Gardner, H. (1993a) *Creating Minds.* New York: Basic Books.

Gardner, H. (1993b) *Creating Minds: An Anatomy of Creativity Seen Through the Lives of Freud, Einstein, Picasso, Stravinsky, Eliot, Graham, and Gandhi.* New York, NY: Basic Books.

Genesee, F. (1978) Language processing in bilinguals. *Brain & Language* 5(1), 1–12.

Gerard, L.D. and Scarborough, D.L. (1989) Language-specific lexical access of homographs by bilinguals. *Journal of Experimental Psychology: Learning, Memory, & Cognition* 15(2), 305–315.

Getzels, J.W. and Csikszentmihályi, M. (1964) Creative thinking in art students: An exploratory study. Office of Education, U.S. Department of Health, Education and Welfare, University of Chicago (Report No. Cooperative Research Project No. E-008).

Getzels, J.W. and Csikszentmihályi, M. (1976) *The Creative Vision: A Longitudinal Study of Problem Finding in Art.* New York, NY: Wiley.

Getzels, J.W. and Jackson, P.W. (1962) *Creativity and Intelligence: Explorations with Gifted Students.* New York, NY: Wiley.

Goertzel, M.G., Goertzel, V. and Goertzel, T.G. (1978) *300 Eminent Personalities: A Psychological Analysis of the Famous.* San Francisco: Jossey-Bass.

Goff, K. and Torrance, E.P. (2002) *Abbreviated Torrance Test for Adults.* Bensenville, IL: Scholastic Testing Service.

Goldschmidt, G. (1991) The dialectics of sketching. *Creativity Research Journal* 4(2), 123–143.

Gollan, T. H. and Acenas, L-A. R. (2004) What is a TOT? Cognate and translation effects on tip-of-the-tongue states in Spanish–English and Tagalog–English Bilinguals. *Journal of Experimental Psychology: Learning, Memory, & Cognition* 30(1), 246–269.

Gollan, T.H., Montoya, R.I. and Bonanni, M.P. (2005) Proper names get stuck on bilingual and monolingual speakers' tip of the tongue equally often. *Neuropsychology* 19(3), 278–287.

Gollan, T.H., Montoya, R.I., Fennema-Notestine, C. and Morris, S.K. (2005) Bilingualism affects picture naming but not picture classification. *Memory & Cognition* 33(7), 1220–1234.

Gollan, T.H., Montoya, R.I. and Werner, G.A. (2002) Semantic and letter fluency in Spanish–English bilinguals. *Neuropsychology* 16(4), 562–576.

Gollan, T.H. and Silverberg, N.B. (2001) Tip-of-the-tongue states in Hebrew–English bilinguals. *Bilingualism: Language and Cognition* 4(1), 63–83.

Goodlad, J.I. (1984) *A Place Called School: Prospects for the Future*. New York, NY: McGraw-Hill.

Goral, M., Levy, E.S., Obler, L.K. and Cohen, E. (2006) Cross-language lexical connections in the mental lexicon: Evidence from a case of trilingual aphasia. *Brain and Language* 98(2), 235–247.

Gordon, M.M. (1964) *Assimilation in American Life: The Role of Race, Religion, and National Origins*. New York: Oxford University Press.

Gough, H.G. (1979) A creative personality scale for the Adjective Check List. *Journal of Personality and Social Psychology* 37(8), 1398–1405.

Gowan, J.C. (1978) The facilitation of creativity through meditational procedures. *Journal of Creative Behavior* 12(3), 156–160.

Gowan, J.C. and Torrance, E.P. (1965) An intercultural study of non-verbal ideational fluency. *The Gifted Child Quarterly* 9(13–15).

Graham, B.C., Sawyers, J.K. and DeBord, K.B. (1989). Teachers' creativity, playfulness, and style of interaction with children. *Creativity Research Journal* 2(1), 41–50.

Granada, J. (2003) Casting a wider net: Linking bilingual and gifted education. In J.A. Castellano (ed.) *Special Populations in Gifted education: Working with Diverse Gifted Learners* (pp. 1–16). Boston, MA: Allyn & Bacon.

Green, D. W. (1998) Mental control of the bilingual lexico-semantic system. *Bilingualism: Language and Cognition* 1(2), 67–81.

Grosjean, F. (1998) Studying bilinguals: Methodological and conceptual issues. *Bilingualism: Language and Cognition* 1(2), 131–149.

Gruber, H.E. and Wallace, D.B. (1999) The case study method and evolving systems approach for understanding unique creative people at work. In R.J. Sternberg (ed.) *Handbook of Creativity* (pp. 93–115). New York, NY: Cambridge University Press.

Gruber, S.A. and Yurgelun-Todd, D.A. (2005) Neuroimaging of marijuana smokers during inhibitory processing: A pilot investigation. *Cognitive Brain Research* 23(1), 107–118.

Guilford, J.P. (1950) Creativity. *American Psychologist* 5, 444–454.

Guilford, J.P. (1967) *The Nature of Human Intelligence*. New York: McGraw-Hill.

Guilford, J.P. and Christensen, P.R. (1973) The one-way relation between creative potential and IQ. *Journal of Creative Behavior* 7(4), 247–252.

Guimerà , R., Uzzi, B., Spiro, J. and Amaral, L.A.N. (2005) Team assembly mechanisms determine collaboration network structure and team performance. *Science* 308(5722), 697–702.

Günçer, B. and Oral, G. (1993) Relationship between creativity and nonconformity to school discipline as perceived by teachers of Turkish elementary school children, by controlling for their grade and sex. *Journal of Instructional Psychology* 20(3), 208–214.

Hakuta, K. (1984) The causal relationship between the development of bilingualism, cognitive flexibility, and social-cognitive skills in Hispanic elementary school children [Final report]. New Haven, CT: Yale University, Department of Psychology (Report No. ERIC Document Reproduction Service No. ED 264 3 14).

Hakuta, K. and Diaz, R.M. (1985) The relationship between degree of bilingualism and cognitive ability: A critical discussion and some new longitudinal data. In K.E. Nelson (ed.) *Children's Language* (Vol. 5, pp. 319–344). Hillsdale, NJ: Erlbaum.

Hardy, G.H. (1940) *A Mathematician's Apology*. Cambridge, MA: Cambridge University Press.

Harley, B. and Wang, W. (1997) The critical period hypothesis: Where are we now? In A.M.B. de Groot and J.F. Kroll (eds) *Tutorials in Bilingualism: Psycholinguistic Perspectives* (pp. 19–51). Hillsdale, NJ: Erlbaum.

Harrington, D.M. (1975) Effects of explicit instructions to "be creative" on the psychological meaning of divergent thinking test scores. *Journal of Personality,* 43, 434–454.

Harris, J.G., Cullum, C.M. and Puente, A.E. (1995) Effects of bilingualism on verbal learning and memory in Hispanic adults. *Journal of the International Neuropsychological Society* 1(1), 10–16.

Hattie, J. (1980) Should creativity tests be administered under testlike conditions? An empirical study of three alternative conditions. *Journal of Educational Psychology,* 72(1), 87–98.

Hayes, J. R. (1985) Three problems in teaching general skills. In J.W. Segal, S.F. Chipman and R. Glaser (eds) *Thinking and Learning Skills: Research and Open Questions* (pp. 391–405). Hillsdale, NJ: Erlbaum.

Heinzen, T.E., Mills, C. and Cameron, P. (1993) Scientific innovation potential. *Creativity Research Journal* 6(3), 261–269.

Hennessey, B.A. (2010) The creativity-motivation connection. In J.C. Kaufman and R.J. Sternberg (eds) *The Cambridge Handbook of Creativity* (pp. 342–365). New York, NY: Cambridge University Press.

Hocevar, D. (1980) Intelligence, divergent thinking, and creativity. *Intelligence* 4(1), 25–40.

Hocevar, D. (1981) Measurement of creativity: Review and critique. *Journal of Personality Assessment* 45(5), 450–464.

Hofstede, G. (2001) *Culture's Consequences: Comparing Values, Behaviors, Institutions, and Organizations Across Nations* (2 ed). Thousand Oaks, CA: Sage.

Holtzman, W.H. (1980) Divergent thinking as a function of the degree of bilingualism of Mexican-American and Anglo fourth-grade students. Unpublished dissertation, University of Texas.

Hommel, B., Colzato, L.S., Fischer, R. and Christoffels, I. (2011) Bilingualism and creativity: Benefits in convergent thinking come with losses in divergent thinking. [Original Research]. *Frontiers in Psychology* 2.

Horng, R-Y. (1981) Imagery abilities, sex, and intelligence as predictors of creative thinking. Unpublished dissertation, University of Georgia.

Howard, D.V. and Howard, J.H., Jr. (2001) When it does hurt to try: Adult age differences in the effects of instructions on implicit pattern learning. *Psychonomic Bulletin & Review* 8(4), 798–805.

Hudson, H.D. and Hoffman, A.J. (1993) Educational reform in Russia and the USA: Where are the troops? *Educational Studies* 19(3), 255–265.

Hudson, L. (1969) *Frames of Mind: Ability, Perception and Self-Perception in the Arts and Sciences*. London, UK: Methuen.

Hultsch, D.F. and Dixon, R.A. (1990) Learning and memory in aging. In J.E. Birren and K.W. Schaie (eds) *Handbook of the Psychology of Aging* (3rd edn, pp. 258–274). San Diego, CA: Academic Press, Inc.

Ianco-Worrall, A.D. (1972) Bilingualism and cognitive development. *Child Development* 43(4), 1390–1400.

Ingersoll, R.M. (2003) *Who Controls Teachers' Work? Power and Accountability in America's Schools*. Cambridge, MA: Harvard University Press.

Israeli, N. (1962) Creative processes in painting. *Journal of General Psychology* 67(2), 251–263.

Israeli, N. (1981) Decision in painting and sculpture. *Academic Psychology Bulletin* 3(1), 61–74.

Ivanova, I. and Costa, A. (2008) Does bilingualism hamper lexical access in speech production. *Acta Psychologica* 127(2), 277–288.

Jacobs, J.F. and Pierce, M.L. (1966) Bilingualism and creativity. *Elementary English* 40, 499–503.

Jankowski, J. (1991) Egypt and early Arab nationalism. In R. Khalidi, L. Anderson, M. Muslih and R. Simon (eds) *The Origins of Arab Nationalism*. New York, NY: Columbia University Press.

Jaquish, G.A. and Ripple, R.E. (1985) A life-span developmental cross-cultural study of divergent thinking abilities. *International Journal of Aging & Human Development* 20(1), 1–11.

Jessner, U. (2008) A DST model of multilingualism and the role of metalinguistic awareness. *Modern Language Journal* 92(2), 270–283.

Johnson, J.S. and Newport, E.L. (1989) Critical period effects in second language learning: The influence of maturational state on the acquisition of English as a second language. *Cognitive Psychology* 21(1), 60–99.

Kandinsky, W. (1912/1994) On the spiritual in art (P. Vergo, Trans.). In K.C. Lindsay and P. Vergo (eds) *Kandinsky, Complete Writings on Art* (pp. 114–220). New York: Da Capo Press.

Kant, I. (1790/2007) *Critique of Judgement* (J.H. Bernard, Trans.). New York, NY: Cosmo Classics.

Kaplan, E., Goodglass, H. and Weintraub, S. (1983) *The Boston Naming Test*. Philadelphia, PA: Lea & Febiger.

Karapetsas, A. and Andreou, G. (1999) Cognitive development of fluent and nonfluent bilingual speakers assessed with tachistoscopic techniques. *Psychological Reports* 84(2), 697–700.

Kaufman, J.C. and Beghetto, R.A. (2009) Beyond big and little: The four c model of creativity. *Review of General Psychology* 13(1), 1–12.

Kaufman, J.C., Plucker, J.A. and Baer, J. (2008) *Essentials of Creativity Assessment*. Hoboken, NJ: John Wiley & Sons, Inc.

Kaufman, J.C. and Sternberg, R.J. (2006) *The International Handbook of Creativity*. New York, NY: Cambridge University Press.

Kaufmann, G. (2003) What to measure? A new look at the concept of creativity. *Scandinavian Journal of Educational Research* 47(3), 235–251.

Kaufmann, W.A. (1965) *Hegel: Reinterpretation, Texts, and Commentary*. Garden City, NY: Doubleday.

Kavé, G., Eyal, N., Shorek, A. and Cohen-Mansfield, J. (2008) Multilingualism and cognitive state in the oldest old. *Psychology and Aging* 23(1), 70–78.

Kay, S. (1991) The figural problem solving and problem finding of professional and semiprofessional artists and nonartists. *Creativity Research Journal* 4(3), 233–252.

Kay, S. (1996) The development of a personal aesthetic in creative accomplishments. *Journal of Aesthetic Education* 30(1), 111–114.

Keats, J. (1819/2000) *Ode on a Grecian Urn and Other Poems*. Whitefish, MT: Kessinger Publishing.

Kecskes, I. and Papp, T. (2003) How to demonstrate the conceptual effect of L2 on L1? Methods and techniques. In V.J. Cook (ed.) *Effects of the Second Language on the First* (pp. 247–265). Clevedon: Multilingual Matters.

Kemper, S. (1992) Language and aging. In F.I.M. Craik and T.A. Salthouse (eds) *Handbook of Aging and Cognition* (pp. 213–270). Hillsdale, NJ: Erlbaum.

Kharkhurin, A.V. (2005) On the possible relationships between bilingualism, biculturalism and creativity: A cognitive perspective. Unpublished dissertation, City University of New York, New York, NY.

Kharkhurin, A.V. (2007) The role of cross-linguistic and cross-cultural experiences in bilinguals' divergent thinking. In I. Kecskes and L. Albertazzi (eds) *Cognitive Aspects of Bilingualism* (pp. 175–210). Dordrecht, The Netherlands: Springer.

Kharkhurin, A.V. (2008) The effect of linguistic proficiency, age of second language acquisition, and length of exposure to a new cultural environment on bilinguals' divergent thinking. *Bilingualism: Language and Cognition* 11(2), 225–243.

Kharkhurin, A.V. (2009) The role of bilingualism in creative performance on divergent thinking and Invented Alien Creatures tests. *Journal of Creative Behavior* 43(1), 59–71.

Kharkhurin, A.V. (2010a) Bilingual verbal and nonverbal creative behavior. *International Journal of Bilingualism* 14(2), 1–16.

Kharkhurin, A.V. (2010b) Sociocultural differences in the relationship between bilingualism and creative potential. *Journal of Cross-Cultural Psychology* 41(5–6), 776–783.

Kharkhurin, A.V. (2011) The role of selective attention in bilingual creativity. *Creativity Research Journal* 23(3), 239–254.

Kharkhurin, A.V. (2012) A preliminary version of an internet-based Picture Naming Test. *Open Journal of Modern Linguistics* 2(1), 34–41.

Kharkhurin, A.V. and Altarriba, J. (2011) The influence of bilinguals' emotions on their creative performance. Paper presented at the 8th International Symposium on Bilingualism, Oslo, Norway.

Kharkhurin, A.V., Kempe, V. and Brooks, P. (2001) How can vocabulary learning mediate working memory effects on grammatical category learning? Paper presented at the 42nd Annual Meeting of The Psychonomic Society.

Kharkhurin, A.V. and Samadpour Motalleebi, S.N. (2008) The impact of culture on the creative potential of American, Russian, and Iranian college students. *Creativity Research Journal,* 20(4) 404–411.

Khosravani, S. and Guilani, B. (2008) Creativity and five factors of personality. *Psychological Research* 10(3–4), 30–45.

Kiesel, A., Steinhauser, M., Wendt, M., Falkenstein, M., Jost, K., Philipp, A.M., *et al.* (2010) Control and interference in task switching: A review. *Psychological Bulletin* 136(5), 849–874.

Kim, K.H. (2006) Can we trust creativity tests?: A review of the Torrance Tests of Creative Thinking (TTCT). *Creativity Research Journal* 18, 3–14.

Kim, K.H. (2008) Meta-analyses of the relationship of creative achievement to both IQ and divergent thinking test scores. *Journal of Creative Behavior* 42(2), 106–130.

Kim, K.H.S., Relkin, N.R., Lee, K.-M. and Hirsch, J. (1997) Distinct cortical areas associated with native and second languages. *Nature* 388(6638), 171–174.

Kirsner, K., Smith, M.C., Lockhart, R.S., King, M.L. and Jain, M. (1984) The bilingual lexicon: Language-specific units in an integrated network. *Journal of Verbal Learning and Verbal Behavior* 23(4), 519–539.

Koestler, A. (1964) *The Act of Creation.* Lewiston, NY: Macmillan.

Koestler, A. (1968) *The Ghost in the Machine.* Lewiston, NY: Macmillan.

Kohnert, K.J., Hernandez, A.E. and Bates, E. (1998) Bilingual performance on the Boston Naming Test: Preliminary norms in Spanish and English. *Brain and Language* 65(3), 422–440.

Kolmogorov, A. (1965) Three approaches to the quantitative definition of information. *Problems in Information Transmission* 1, 1–7.

Konaka, K. (1997) The relationship between degree of bilingualism and gender to divergent thinking ability among native Japanese-speaking children in the New York area. Unpublished dissertation, New York University.

Kozbelt, A. and Durmysheva, Y. (2007) Understanding creativity judgments of invented alien creatures: The roles of invariants and other predictors. *Journal of Creative Behavior* 41(4), 223–248.

Krashen, S. (1973) Lateralization, language learning, and the critical period. *Language Learning* 23, 63–74.

Krashen, S. (1991) The input hypothesis: An update. In J.E. Alatis (ed.) *Georgetown Unniversity Round Table on Languages and Linguistics* (pp. 409–431). Washington, DC: Georgetown University Press.

Krippner, S. and Maliszewski, M. (1978) Meditation and the creative process. *Journal of Indian Psychology* 1(1), 40–58.

Kroll, J. F. and Curley, J. (1988) Lexical memory in novice bilinguals: The role of concepts in retrieving second language words. In M. Gruneberg, P. Morris and R. Sykes (eds) *Practical Aspects of Memory* (Vol. 2, pp. 389–395). London: Wiley.

Kroll, J.F. and de Groot, A.M.B. (1997) Lexical and conceptual memory in the bilingual: Mapping form to meaning in two languages. In A.M.B. de Groot and J.F. Kroll (eds) *Tutorials in Bilingualism: Psycholinguistic Perspectives* (pp. 169–199). Hillsdale, NJ: Erlbaum.

Kroll, J.F. and Stewart, E. (1994) Category interference in translation and picture naming: Evidence for asymmetric connection between bilingual memory representations. *Journal of Memory & Language* 33(2), 149–174.

Kroll, J.F. and Tokowicz, N. (2005) Models of bilingual representation and processing: Looking back and to the future. In J.F. Kroll and A.M.B. de Groot (eds) *Handbook of Bilingualism: Psycholinguistic Approaches* (pp. 531–533). New York: Oxford University Press.

Kučera, H. and Francis, W.N. (1967) *Computational Analysis of Presentday American English.* Providence, RI: Brown University Press.

Kuhn, T.S. (1993) Metaphor in science. In A. Ortony (ed.) *Metaphor and Thought* (2nd edn, pp. 137–163). New York: Cambridge University Press.

Lamb, S. (1999) *Pathways of the Brain.* Amsterdam: John Benjamins.

Lambert, W.E. (1955) Measurement of the linguistic dominance of bilinguals. *Journal of Abnormal & Social Psychology* 50, 197–200.

Lambert, W.E. (1975) Culture and language as factors in learning and education. In A. Wolfgang (ed.) *Education of Immigrant Students* (pp. 55–83). Toronto, ON: Institute for Studies in Education.

Lambert, W.E. (1977) The effect of bilingualism on the individual: Cognitive and social consequences. In P.A. Hornby (ed.) *Bilingualism: Psychological, Social and Educational Implications*. New York: Academic Press.

Lambert, W.E., Tucker, G.R. and d'Anglejan, A. (1973) Cognitive and attitudinal consequences of bilingual schooling. *Journal of Educational Psychology* 65(2), 141–159.

Landry, R.G. (1974) A comparison of second language learners and monolinguals on divergent thinking tasks at the elementary school level. *Modern Language Journal* 58(1), 10–15.

Lao-tzu (1992) *Te-Tao Ching; A New Translation Based on the Recently Discovered Ma-Wang-Tui Texts* (R.G. Henricks, Trans.). New York, NY: Random House Publishing Group.

Lao, D.C. (1983) *Confucius: The Analects*. London: Penguin.

Lee, H. and Kim, K.H. (2011) Can speaking more languages enhance your creativity? Relationship between bilingualism and creative potential among Korean American students with multicultural link. *Personality and Individual Differences* 50(8), 1186–1190.

Lehman, J.D., Kahle, J.B. and Nordland, F. (1981) Cognitive development and creativity: A study in two high schools. *Science Education* 65(2), 197–206.

Leikin, M. (in print). The effect of bilingualism on creativity: Developmental and educational perspectives. *International Journal of Bilingualism*.

Lemhöfer, K., Dijkstra, T. and Michel, M.C. (2004) Three languages, one ECHO: Cognate effects in trilingual word recognition. *Language and Cognitive Processes* 19(5), 585–611.

Lemmon, C.R. and Goggin, J.P. (1989) The measurement of bilingualism and its relationship to cognitive ability. *Applied Psycholinguistics* 10(2), 133–155.

Lenneberg, E.H. (1967) *Biological Foundations of Language*. Oxford, England: Wiley.

Leung, A.K-y. and Chiu, C-y. (2008) Interactive effects of multicultural experiences and openness to experience on creative potential. *Creativity Research Journal* 20(4), 376–382.

Leung, A.K-y. and Chiu, C-y. (2010) Multicultural experience, idea receptiveness, and creativity. *Journal of Cross-Cultural Psychology*.

Leung, A.K-y., Maddux, W.W., Galinsky, A.D. and Chiu, C-y. (2008) Multicultural experience enhances creativity: The when and how. *American Psychologist* 63(3), 169–181.

Levine, S.K. (2002) Chaos and order: Rudolph Arnheim's gestalt psychology of art. *Gestalt Theory* 24(4), 266–282.

Li, J. (1997) Creativity in horizontal and vertical domains. *Creativity Research Journal* 10(2–3), 107–132.

Lissitz, R.W. and Willhoft, J.L. (1985) A methodological study of the Torrance Tests of Creativity. *Journal of Educational Measurement* 22, 1–111.

List of Nobel laureates by country per capita (n.d.). Retrieved 6 July, 2010, from http://en.wikipedia.org/wiki/List_of_Nobel_laureates_by_country_per_capita

Livingstone, M. and Cameron, D. (1992) *Pop Art: An International Perspective*. New York, NY: Rizzoli.

Long, M.H. (1990) Maturational constraints on language development. *Studies in Second Language Acquisition,* 12, 251–285.

Lopez, E.C. (2003) Creativity issues concerning linguistically and culturally diverse children. In J. Houtz (ed.) *Educational Psychology of Creativity* (pp. 107–127). Cresskill, NJ: Hampton Press, Inc.

Lubart, T.I. (1999) Creativity across cultures. In R.J. Sternberg (ed.) *Handbook of Creativity* (pp. 339–350). New York, NY: Cambridge University Press.

Lubart, T.I. (2000) Models of the creative process: Past, present and future. *Creativity Research Journal* 13(3–4), 295–308.

Lubart, T.I. and Getz, I. (1997) Emotion, metaphor and the creative process. *Creativity Research Journal* 10(4), 285–301.

Lumsden, C.J. (1999) Evolving creative minds: Stories and mechanisms. In R.J. Sternberg (ed.) *Handbook of Creativity* (pp. 153–168). New York, NY: Cambridge University Press.

MacCormac, E.R. (1986) Creative metaphors. *Metaphor & Symbolic Activity* 1(3), 171–184.

MacKinnon, D.W. (1962) The nature and nurture of creative talent. *American Psychologist* 17(7), 484–495.

MacNab, G.L. (1979) Cognition and bilingualism: A reanalysis of studies. *Linguistics* 17, 231–255.

Macniven, J.A.B., Davis, C., Ho, M.Y., Bradshaw, C.M., Szabadi, E. and Constantinescu, C.S. (2008) Stroop performance in multiple sclerosis: Information processing, selective attention, or executive functioning? *Journal of the International Neuropsychological Society* 14(5), 805–814.

Maddux, W.W. and Galinsky, A.D. (2007, September) Cultural borders and mental barriers: Living in and adapting to foreign cultures facilitates creativity. Paper presented at INSEAD, Fontainebleau, France.

Mägiste, E. (1992) Leaning to the right: Hemispheric involvement in bilinguals. In R.J. Harris (ed.) *Cognitive Processing in Bilinguals* (pp. 549–560). Oxford, England: North-Holland.

Malevich, K.S. (1926/2003) *The Non-Objective World: The Manifesto of Suprematism* (H. Dearstyne, Trans.). Mineola, NY: Dover Publications.

Marchman, V.A. (1993) Constraints on plasticity in a connectionist model of the English past tense. *Journal of Cognitive Neuroscience* 5(2), 215–234.

Marian, V. and Neisser, U. (2000) Language-dependent recall of autobiographical memories. *Journal of Experimental Psychology: General* 129(3), 361–368.

Marian, V. and Spivey, M. (2003) Competing activation in bilingual language processing: Within- and between-language competition. *Bilingualism: Language and Cognition* 6(2), 97–115.

Marin, G., Sabogal, F., Marin, B.V. and Otero-Sabogal, R. (1987) Development of a short acculturation scale for Hispanics. *Hispanic Journal of Behavioral Sciences* 9(2), 183–205.

Markus, H.R. and Kitayama, S. (1991) Culture and the self: Implications for cognition, emotion, and motivation. *Psychological Review* 98(2), 224–253.

Marsh, D. and Hill, R. (2009) Study on the contribution of multilingualism to creativity. Final report. Brussels: European Commission (Report No. EACEA/2007/3995/2). Retrieved from http://eacea.ec.europa.eu/llp/studies/documents/study_on_the_contribution_of_multilingualism_to_creativity/final_report_en.pdf.

Marsh, L.G. and Maki, R.H. (1978) Efficiency of arithmetic operations in bilinguals as a function of language. *Memory & Cognition* 4, 459–464.

Martin-Rhee, M.M. and Bialystok, E. (2008) The development of two types of inhibitory control in monolingual and bilingual children. *Bilingualism: Language and Cognition* 11(1), 81–93.

Martindale, C. (1989) Personality, situation, and creativity. In J.A. Glover and R.R. Ronning (eds), *Handbook of Creativity* (pp. 211–232). New York: Plenum Press.

Martindale, C. (1999) Biological bases of creativity. In R.J. Sternberg (ed.) *Handbook of Creativity* (pp. 137–152). New York, NY: Cambridge University Press.

Martorell, M.F. (1992) *Language Proficiency, Creativity, and Locus-of-Control Among Hispanic Bilingual Gifted Children.* ProQuest Information & Learning, US.

Masgoret, A.M. and Gardner, R.C. (2003) Attitudes, motivation, and second language learning: A meta-analysis of studies conducted by gardner and associates. *Language Learning,* 53(S1), 167–210.

Maslow, A.H. (1943) A theory of human motivation. *Psychological Review* 50(4), 370–396.

Masson, M.E.J. (1991) A distributed memory model of context effects in word identification. In D. Besner and G. W. Humphreys (eds) *Basic Processes In Reading: Visual Word Recognition* (pp. 233–263). Hillsdale, NJ: Erlbaum.

Mayer, R.E. (1999a) Fifty years of creativity research. In R.J. Sternberg (ed.) *Handbook of Creativity* (pp. 449–460). New York: Cambridge University Press.

Mayer, R.E. (1999b) Problem solving. In M.A. Runco and S.R. Pritzker (eds) *Encyclopedia of Creativity* (Vol. 2, pp. 437–447). San Diego, CA: Academic Press.

McClelland, J.L. and Rumelhart, D.E. (1985) Distributed memory and the representation of general and specific information. *Journal of Experimental Psychology: General* 114(2), 159–188.

McCrae, R.R. and Costa, P.T. (1987) Validation of the five-factor model of personality across instruments and observers. *Journal of Personality and Social Psychology* 52(1), 81–90.

McLaughlin, B. (1984) *Second-Language Acquisition in Childhood, Vol. 1: Preschool Children* (2nd edn). Hillsdale, NJ: Erlbaum.

McLeod, B. (1996) *School Reform and Student Diversity: Exemplary Schooling for Language Minority Students.* Washington, DC: George Washington University: Institute for the Study of Language and Education.

Meadow, A., Parnes, S.J. and Reese, H. (1959) Influence of brainstorming instructions and problem sequence on a creative problem solving test. *Journal of Applied Psychology* 43(6), 413–416.

Mednick, S.A. (1962) The associative basis of the creative process. *Psychological Review* 69(3), 220–232.

Mednick, S.A. and Mednick, M.T. (1967) *Examiner's Manual: Remote Associates Test.* Boston: Houghton Mifflin.

Metcalfe, A.R.J. (1978) Divergent thinking "threshold effect": IQ, age, or skill? *Journal of Experimental Education* 47(1), 4–8.

Meyer, D.E. and Schvaneveldt, R.W. (1971) Facilitation in recognizing pairs of words: Evidence of a dependence between retrieval operations. *Journal of Experimental Psychology* 90(2), 227–234.

Miall, D.S. (1987) Metaphor and affect: The problem of creative thought. *Metaphor & Symbolic Activity* 2(2), 81–96.

Millar, G.W. (2002) *The Torrance Kids at Midlife*. Westport: Ablex Pub.

Miller, N.A. and Kroll, J.F. (2002) Stroop effects in bilingual translation. *Memory & Cognition* 30(4), 614–628.

Mitchell, R.L.C. (2005) The BOLD response during Stroop task-like inhibition paradigms: Effects of task difficulty and task-relevant modality. *Brain and Cognition* 59(1), 23–37.

Moaddel, M. (2004) The future of Islam after 9/11. *Futures* 36(9), 961–977.

Morales, R.V., Shute, V.J. and Pellegrino, J.W. (1985) Developmental differences in understanding and solving simple mathematics word problems. *Cognition and Instruction* 2(1), 41–57.

Moreno, E.M. and Kutas, M. (2005) Processing semantic anomalies in two languages: An electrophysiological exploration in both languages of Spanish–English bilinguals. *Cognitive Brain Research* 22(2), 205–220.

Mumford, M.D. (2000) Something old, something new: Revising Guilford's conception of creative problem solving. *Creativity Research Journal* 13(3–4), 267–276.

Mumford, M.D., Marks, M.A., Connelly, M.S., Zaccaro, S.J. and Johnson, J.F. (1998) Domain-based scoring of divergent-thinking tests: Validation evidence in an occupational sample. *Creativity Research Journal* 11(2), 151–163.

Mumford, M.D., Mobley, M.I., Uhlman, C.E., Reiter-Palmon, R. and Doares, L.M. (1991) Process analytic models of creative capacities. *Creativity Research Journal* 4(2), 91–122.

Mumford, M.D., Peterson, N.G. and Childs, R.A. (1999) Basic and cross-functional skills. In N.G. Peterson and M.D. Mumford (eds) *An Occupational Information System for the 21st Century: The Development of O*NET* (pp. 49–69). Washington, D.C.: American Psychological Association.

Naumov, A.I. and Puffer, S.M. (2000) Measuring Russian culture using Hofstede's dimensions. *Applied Psychology: An International Review* 49(4), 709–718.

Newport, E.L. (1990) Maturational constraints on language learning. *Cognitive Science* 14(1), 11–28.

Nickerson, R.S. (1999) Enhancing creativity. In R.J. Sternberg (ed.) *Handbook of Creativity* (pp. 392–430). New York, NY: Cambridge University Press.

Nickerson, R.S. and Sternberg, R.J. (1994) The teaching of thinking and problem solving *Thinking and Problem Solving* (pp. 409–449). San Diego, CA: Academic Press.

Nicoladis, E. (2008) Bilingualism and language cognitive development. In J. Altarriba and R.R. Heredia (eds) *An Introduction to Bilingualism: Principles and Processes.* (pp. 167–181). Mahwah, NJ: Lawrence Erlbaum Associates Publishers.

Nisbett, R.E. (2003) *The Geography of Thought: How Asians and Westerners Think Differently … and Why*. New York: Free Press.

Niu, W. and Sternberg, R. (2002) Contemporary studies on the concept of creativity: The East and the West. *Journal of Creative Behavior* 36(4), 269–288.

Niu, W. and Sternberg, R.J. (2001) Cultural influences on artistic creativity and its evaluation. *International Journal of Psychology* 36(4), 225–241.

Niu, W. and Sternberg, R.J. (2006) The philosophical roots of Western and Eastern conceptions of creativity. *Journal of Theoretical and Philosophical Psychology* 26(1–2), 18–38.

Okoh, N. (1980) Bilingualism and divergent thinking among Nigerian and Welsh school children. *Journal of Social Psychology* 110(2), 163–170.

Oller, D.K. and Eilers, R.E. (eds) (2002) *Language and Literacy in Bilingual Children*. Clevedon: Multilingual Matters.

Onda, A. (1962) Zen and creativity. *Psychologia: An International Journal of Psychology in the Orient* 5(1), 13–20.

Osborn, A. (1953) *Applied Imagination*. New York: Scribners.

Ovando, C.J., Combs, M.C. and Collier, V.P. (2006) *Bilingual and ESL Classrooms: Teaching in Multicultural Contexts* (4th edn). Boston, MA: McGraw Hill.

Oxford, R.L. (2002) Language learning strategies in a nutshell: Update and ESL suggestions. In J.C. Richards and W.A. Renandya (eds) *Methodology in Language Teaching: An Anthology of Current Practice* (pp. 124–132). Cambridge, MA: Cambridge University Press.

Oxford, R.L., Lavine, R.Z. and Crookall, D. (1989) Language learning strategies, the communicative approach, and their classroom implications. *Foreign Language Annals* 22(1), 29–39.

Padilla, A.M. and Ruiz, R.A. (1973) *Latino Mental Health: A Review of Literature*. Washington, D.C.: U.S. Government Printing Office, Dh.

Paduch, I. (2005) Musik als Erfahrungs und Gestaltungsraum. Bericht über ein Musikprojekt 'Der Seelenvogel' mit Kindergartenkindern. *Musiktherapeutische Umschau* 26(2), 156–195.

Palaniappan, A.K. (1994) Preliminary study of the bilingual version of Creative Motivation Inventory. *Perceptual and Motor Skills* 79(1/2), 393–394.

Palmer, M.B. (1972) Effects of categorization, degree of bilingualism and language upon recall of select monolinguals and bilinguals. *Journal of Educational Psychology* 63(2), 160–164.

Paradis, M. (1997) The cognitive neuropsychology of bilingualism. In A.M.B. de Groot and J.F. Kroll (eds) *Tutorials in Bilingualism: Psycholinguistic Perspectives* (pp. 331–354). Hillsdale, NJ: Erlbaum.

Paradis, M. (2000) Cerebral representation of bilingual concepts. *Bilingualism: Language and Cognition* 3(1), 22–24.

Paradis, M. (2004) *A Neurolinguistic Theory of Bilingualism* (Vol. 18). Amsterdam: John Benjamins.

Paradis, M. (2007) The neurofunctional components of the bilingual cognitive system. In I. Kecskes and L. Albertazzi (eds) *Cognitive Aspects of Bilingualism* (pp. 3–28). Dordrecht, The Netherlands: Springer.

Park, R.E. (1928) Human migrations and the marginal man. *American Journal of Sociology* 33, 881–893.

Parnes, S.J. (1963) Development of individual creative talent. In C.W. Taylor and F. Barron (eds) *Scientific Creativity: Its Recognition and Development* (pp. 311–320). Oxford, UK: John Wiley & Sons.

Pavlenko, A. (1997) Bilingualism and cognition. Unpublished dissertation, Cornell University.

Pavlenko, A. (1999) New approaches to concepts in bilingual memory. *Bilingualism: Language and Cognition* 2(3), 209–230.

Pavlenko, A. (2000) New approaches to concepts in bilingual memory. *Bilingualism: Language and Cognition* 3(1), 1–4.

Pavlenko, A. (2005) Bilingualism and thought. In J.F. Kroll and A.M.B. de Groot (eds) *Handbook of Bilingualism: Psycholinguistic Approaches* (pp. 433–453). New York: Oxford University Press.

Peal, E. and Lambert, W.E. (1962) The relation of bilingualism to intelligence. *Psychological Monographs* 76(27), 23.

Perani, D., Dehaene, S., Grassi, F., Cohen, L., Cappa, S.F., Dupoux, E., *et al.* (1996) Brain processing of native and foreign languages. *NeuroReport* 7(15–17), 2439–2444.

Perani, D., Paulesu, E., Galles, N.S., Dupoux, E., Dehaene, S., Bettinardi, V., *et al.* (1998) The bilingual brain: Proficiency and age of acquisition of the second language. *Brain* 121(10), 1841–1852.

Perkins, D. N. (1988) The possibility of invention. In R.J. Sternberg (ed.) *The Nature of Creativity: Contemporary Psychological Perspectives* (pp. 362–385). New York, NY: Cambridge University Press.

Perkins, D. N. and Laserna, C. (1986) Inventive thinking. In M.J. Adams (ed.) *Odyssey: A Curriculum for Thinking*. Watertown, MA: Mastery Education Corporation.

Peterson, J., Peters, N. and Paradis, E. (1972) Validation of the Cloze procedure as a measure of readability with high school, trade school, and college populations. In F.B. Greene (ed.) *Investigations Relating to Mature Readers, Twenty-First Yearbook of the National Reading Conference* (pp. 45–50). Milwaukee: The National Reading Conference, Inc.

Piaget, J. (1952) *The Origins of Intelligence in Children*. New York, NY: International University Press.

Pinker, S. (1994) *The Language Instinct*. New York: William Morrow & Co, Inc.

Plato (1991) *The Republic: The Complete And Unabridged Jowett Translation* (B. Jowett, Trans.). New York: Vintage Books.

Plucker, J.A. (1999) Is the proof in the pudding? Reanalyses of Torrance's (1958 to present) longitudinal data. *Creativity Research Journal* 12(2), 103–114.

Plucker, J.A. and Makel, M.C. (2010) Assessment of creativity. In J.C. Kaufman and R.J. Sternberg (eds) *The Cambridge Handbook of Creativity* (pp. 48–73). New York, NY: Cambridge University Press.

Plucker, J.A. and Renzulli, J.S. (1999) Psychometric approaches to the study of human creativity. In R.J. Sternberg (ed.) *Handbook of Creativity* (pp. 35–61). New York: Cambridge University Press.

Poplack, S. (2004) Code-switching. In U. Ammon, N. Dittmar, K.J. Mattheier and P. Trudgill (eds) *Soziolinguistik: An International Handbook of the Science of Language* (2nd edn). Berlin: Walter de Gruyter.

Potter, M.C., So, K-f., von Eckardt, B. and Feldman, L.B. (1984) Lexical and conceptual representation in beginning and proficient bilinguals. *Journal of Verbal Learning & Verbal Behavior* 23(1), 23–38.

European Council (2002) Presidency conclusions. Barcelona: European Council (Report No. 100/1/02 REV 1). Retrieved from http://www.consilium.europa.eu/uedocs/cms_data/docs/pressdata/en/ec/71025.pdf.

Price-Williams, D.R. and Ramirez, M. (1977) Divergent thinking, cultural differences, and bilingualism. *Journal of Social Psychology* 103(1), 3–11.

Rabinowitz, J.C., Craik, F.I. and Ackerman, B.P. (1982) A processing resource account of age differences in recall. *Canadian Journal of Psychology* 36(2), 325–344.

Reber, R., Brun, M. and Mitterndorfer, K. (2008) The use of heuristics in intuitive mathematical judgment. *Psychonomic Bulletin & Review* 15(6), 1174–1178.

Reber, R., Schwarz, N. and Winkielman, P. (2004) Processing fluency and aesthetic pleasure: Is beauty in the perceiver's processing experience? *Personality and Social Psychology Review* 8(4), 364–382.

Reynolds, A.G. (1991) *Bilingualism, Multiculturalism, and Second Language Learning: The McGill Conference in Honour of Wallace E. Lambert.* Hillsdale, NJ: Erlbaum.

Ricciardelli, L.A. (1992a) Bilingualism and cognitive development in relation to threshold theory. *Journal of Psycholinguistic Research* 21(4), 301–316.

Ricciardelli, L.A. (1992b) Creativity and bilingualism. *Journal of Creative Behavior* 26(4), 242–254.

Richards, A., French, C.C., Nash, G., Hadwin, J.A. and Donnelly, N. (2007) A comparison of selective attention and facial processing biases in typically developing children who are high and low in self-reported trait anxiety. *Development and Psychopathology* 19(2), 481–495.

Richards, R., Kinney, D.K., Benet, M. and Merzel, A.P. (1988) Assessing everyday creativity: Characteristics of the Lifetime Creativity Scales and validation with three large samples. *Journal of Personality and Social Psychology* 54(3), 476–485.

Richter, H. (1965) *Dada: Art and Anti-Art.* Oxford: Oxford University Press.

Roberts, P.M., Garcia, L.J., Desrochers, A. and Hernandez, D. (2002) English performance of proficient bilingual adults on the Boston Naming Test. *Aphasiology* 16(4–6), 635–645.

Rodriguez-Fornells, A., Rotte, M., Heinze, H-J., Noesselt, T. and Muente, T.F. (2002) Brain potential and functional MRI evidence for how to handle two languages with one brain. *Nature* 415(6875), 1026–1029.

Rodriguez, R. (1985) *Hunger of Memory: The Education of Richard Rodriguez.* New York, NY: Bantam Books.

Rogers, C. R. (1961) *On Becoming a Person.* Boston, MA: Houghton Mifflin.

Rosenblum, T. and Pinker, S.A. (1983) Word magic revisited: Monolingual and bilingual children's understanding of the word–object relationship. *Child Development* 54(3), 773–780.

Rosenkranz, K. (1853) *Aesthetik des Hässlichen.* Königsberg: Gebrüder Bornträger.

Rosselli, M., Ardila, A., Araujo, K., Weekes, V.A., Caracciolo, V., Padilla, M., *et al.* (2000) Verbal fluency and repetition skills in healthy older Spanish–English bilinguals. *Applied Neuropsychology* 7(1), 17–24.

Rossion, B. and Pourtois, G. (2001) Revisiting Snodgrass and Vanderwart's object database: Color and texture improve object recognition. Paper presented at Vision Science Conference, Sarasota, FL.

Rostan, S.M. (1994) Problem finding, problem solving, and cognitive controls: An empirical investigation of critically acclaimed productivity. *Creativity Research Journal* 7(2), 97–110.

Rothenberg, A. (1979) *The Emerging Goddess: The Creative Process in Art, Science and Other Fields.* Chicago, IL: University of Chicago Press.

Rothenberg, A. (1996) The Janusian process in scientific creativity. *Creativity Research Journal* 9(2), 207–231.

Runco, M.A. (1984) Teachers' judgments of creativity and social validation of divergent thinking tests. *Perceptual Motor Skills* 59, 711–717.

Runco, M.A. (1986) Divergent thinking and creative performance in gifted and nongifted children. *Educational and Psychological Measurement* 46(2), 375–384.

Runco, M.A. (1987) The generality of creative performance in gifted and nongifted children. *Gifted Child Quarterly* 31(3), 121–125.

Runco, M.A. (1989) The creativity of children's art. *Child Study Journal* 19(3), 177–189.

Runco, M.A. (1991) *Divergent Thinking.* Westport, CT: Ablex Publishing.

Runco, M.A. (1993) *Creativity as an Educational Objective for Disadvantaged Students*. Storrs, CT: National Research Center on the Gifted and Talented.

Runco, M.A. (2003a) Creativity, cognition, and their educational implications. In J. Houtz (ed.) *The Educational Psychology of Creativity* (pp. 25–56). Cresskill, NJ: Hampton Press.

Runco, M.A. (2003b) Idea evaluation, divergent thinking, and creativity. In M.A. Runco (ed.) *Critical Creative Processes* (pp. 69–94). Cresskill, NJ: Hampton Press.

Runco, M.A. (2004) Creativity. *Annual Review of Psychology* 55, 657–687.

Runco, M.A. (2005) Motivation, competence, and creativity. In A.J. Elliot and C.S. Dweck (eds) *Handbook of Competence and Motivation* (pp. 609–623). New York, NY: Guilford Publications.

Runco, M.A. (2007) *Creativity: Theories and Themes: Research, Development, and Practice*. San Diego, CA: Elsevier Academic Press.

Runco, M.A., Dow, G. and Smith, W.R. (2006) Information, experience, and divergent thinking: An empirical test. *Creativity Research Journal* 18(3), 269–277.

Runco, M.A. and Johnson, D.J. (2002) Parents' and teachers' implicit theories of children's creativity: A cross-cultural perspective. *Creativity Research Journal* 14(3–4), 427–438.

Runco, M.A., Johnson, D.J. and Bear, P.K. (1993) Parents' and teachers' implicit theories of children's creativity. *Child Study Journal* 23(2), 91–113.

Runco, M.A. and Mraz, W. (1992) Scoring divergent thinking tests using total ideational output and a creativity index. *Educational and Psychological Measurement* 52(1), 213–221.

Rutter, M., Maughan, B., Mortimore, P. and Ouston, J. (1979) *Fifteen Thousand Hours: Secondary Schools and Their Effects on Children*. Cambridge, MA: Harvard University Press.

Salthouse, T.A. (1992) *Mechanisms of Age-Cognition Relations in Adulthood*. Hillsdale, NJ: Erlbaum.

Sartre, J-P. (1943/1992) *Being and Nothingness: A Phenomenological Essay on Ontology*. New York, NY: Washington Square Press.

Schärer, M.R. (2009) Hat das Kunstwerk einen besonderen status? Oder: Sind alle objekte museologisch gleich? *kunsttexte.de Journal für Kunst- und Bildgeschichte* 3. Retrieved from http://edoc.hu-berlin.de/kunsttexte/2009-3/schaerer-martin-r.-7/PDF/schaerer.pdf.

Schmidhuber, J. (1997) Low-complexity art. *Leonardo* 30(2), 97–103.

Scholem, G. (1974) *Kabbalah*. Jerusalem: Keter.

Schumann, J.H. (1978) *The Pidginization Process: A model for Second Language Acquisition*. Rowley, MA: Newbury House.

Scott, C.L. (1999) Teachers' biases toward creative children. *Creativity Research Journal* 12(4), 321–337.

Silverberg, S. and Samuel, A.G. (2004) The effect of age of second language acquisition on the representation and processing of second language words. *Journal of Memory and Language* 51(3), 381–398.

Silvia, P.J., Nusbaum, E.C., Berg, C., Martin, C. and O'Connor, A. (2009) Openness to experience, plasticity, and creativity: Exploring lower-order, high-order, and interactive effects. *Journal of Research in Personality* 43(6), 1087–1090.

Simonton, D.K. (1988) *Scientific Genius: A Psychology of Science*. New York: Cambridge University Press.

Simonton, D.K. (1997) Foreign influence and national achievement: The impact of open milieus on Japanese civilization. *Journal of Personality and Social Psychology* 72(1), 86–94.

Simonton, D.K. (1999) *Origins of Genius: Darwinian Perspectives on Creativity*. New York, NY: Oxford University Press.

Simonton, D.K. (2003) Creative cultures, nations, and civilizations: Strategies and results. In P.B. Paulus and B.A. Nijstad (eds) *Group Creativity: Innovation through Collaboration*. (pp. 304–325). New York, NY: Oxford University Press.

Simonton, D.K. (2008) Bilingualism and creativity. In J. Altarriba and R.R. Heredia (eds) *An Introduction to Bilingualism: Principles and Processes* (pp. 147–166). NJ: Erlbaum.

Simos, P.G., Castillo, E.M., Fletcher, J.M., Francis, D.J., Maestu, F., Breier, J.I., *et al.* (2001) Mapping of receptive language cortex in bilingual volunteers by using magnetic source imaging. *Journal of Neurosurgery* 95(1), 76–81.

Sirotnik, K.A. (1983) What you see is what you get: Consistency, persistency, and mediocrity in classrooms. *Harvard Educational Review* 53(1), 16–31.

Snodgrass, J.G. and Vanderwart, M. (1980) A standardized set of 260 pictures: Norms for name agreement, image agreement, familiarity, and visual complexity. *Journal of Experimental Psychology: Human Learning & Memory* 6(2), 174–215.

So, K-T. and Orme-Johnson, D.W. (2001) Three randomized experiments on the longitudinal effects of the Transcendental Meditation technique on cognition. *Intelligence* 29(5), 419–440.

Soares, C. and Grosjean, F. (1984) Bilinguals in a monolingual and a bilingual speech mode: The effect on lexical access. *Memory & Cognition* 12(4), 380–386.

Spivey, M.J. and Marian, V. (1999) Cross talk between native and second languages: Partial activation of an irrelevant lexicon. *Psychological Science* 10(3), 281–284.

Srivastava, A.L. and Khatoon, R. (1980) Effect of difference between mother tongue and another tongue as medium of instruction on achievement, mental ability and creativity of the VII standard children. In E. Annamalai (ed.) *Bilingualism and Achievement in Schools*. Mysore: CIIL.

Srivastava, B. (1991) Creativity and linguistic proficiency. *Psycho-Lingua* 21(2), 105–109.

Stephens, M.A. (1997) *Bilingualism, Creativity, and Social Problem-Solving*. ProQuest Information & Learning, US.

Sternberg, R.J. (1999) *Handbook of Creativity*. New York: Cambridge University Press.

Sternberg, R.J., Kaufman, J.C. and Pretz, J.E. (2001) The propulsion model of creative contributions applied to the arts and letters. *Journal of Creative Behavior* 35(2), 75–101.

Sternberg, R.J. and Lubart, T.I. (1991) An investment theory of creativity and its development. *Human Development* 34(1), 1–31.

Sternberg, R.J. and Lubart, T.I. (1995) *Defying the Crowd: Cultivating Creativity in a Culture of Conformity*. New York: Free Press.

Sternberg, R.J. and O'Hara, L.A. (1999) Creativity and intelligence. In R.J. Sternberg (ed.) *Handbook of Creativity* (pp. 251–272). New York: Cambridge University Press.

Stewart, I. (2007) *Why Beauty is Truth: A History of Symmetry*. New York: Basic Books.

Stokes, P. (2000) Variations on Guilford's creative abilities. *Creativity Research Journal* 13, 196–207.

Stone, S. (1993) *Divergent Thinking: Nontraditional or Creative Talents of Monolingual, Bilingual, and Special Education Students in an Elementary School*. ProQuest Information & Learning, US.

Stroop, J.R. (1935) Studies of interference in serial verbal reactions. *Journal of Experimental Psychology* 18(6), 643–662.

Sutton, T.M., Altarriba, J., Gianico, J.L. and Basnight-Brown, D.M. (2007) The automatic access of emotion: Emotional stroop effects in Spanish–English bilingual speakers. *Cognition & Emotion* 21(5), 1077–1090.

Swain, M. and Lapkin, S. (1982) *Evaluating Bilingual Education: A Canadian Case Study.* Clevedon: Multilingual Matters.

Szapocznik, J., Scopetta, M.A., Kurtines, W. and Aranalde, M.D. (1978) Theory and measurement of acculturation. *Revista Interamericana de Psicología* 12(2), 113–130.

Taylor, W.L. (1953) Cloze procedure: A new tool for measuring readability. *Journalism Quarterly* 30, 415–433.

Thomas, N.G. and Berk, L.E. (1981) Effects of school environments on the development of young children's creativity. *Child Development* 52(4), 1153–1162.

Thomas, V.C. (1998) Authenticity and creativity: An existentialist perspective. In A-T. Tymieniecka (ed.) *Analecta Husserliana. Phenomenology of Life and the Human Creative Condition* (Vol. LII, pp. 317–332). Dordrecht, the Netherlands: Kluwer Academic Publishers.

Thomas, W. and Collier, V. (2000) A national study of school effectiveness for language minority students' long-term academic achievement. Final Report. Berkeley, CA: Center for Research on Education, Diversity & Excellence, University of California. Retrieved from http://escholarship.org/uc/item/65j213pt.

Tighe, E., Picariello, M.L. and Amabile, T.M. (2003) Environmental influences on motivation and creativity in the classroom. In J. Houtz (ed.) *The Educational Psychology of Creativity* (pp. 199–222). Cresskill, NJ: Hampton Press.

Tisdall, C. (1979) *Joseph Beuys*. New York, NY: Solomon R. Guggenheim Museum.

Tomkins, C. (1998) *Duchamp: A Biography*. New York, NY: H. Holt.

Torrance, E.P. (1959) Current research on the nature of creative talent. *Journal of Counseling Psychology* 6(4), 309–316.

Torrance, E.P. (1962) Explorations in creative thinking in the early school years. In S.J. Parnes and H.F. Harding (eds) *A Source Book for Creative Thinking* (pp. 363–364). New York: Scribners.

Torrance, E.P. (1963) The creative personality and the ideal pupil. *Teachers College Record* 65(3), 220–226.

Torrance, E.P. (1965) *The Minnesota Studies of Creative Thinking: Widening Horizons in Creativity*. New York, NY: John Wiley.

Torrance, E.P. (1966) *Torrance Test of Creative Thinking*. Princeton, NJ: Personnel Press.

Torrance, E.P. (1968) A longitudinal examination of the fourth grade slump in creativity. *Gifted Child Quarterly* 12, 195–199.

Torrance, E.P. (1988) The nature of creativity as manifest in its testing. In R.J. Sternberg (ed.) *The Nature of Creativity: Contemporary Psychological Perspectives* (pp. 43–75). New York: Cambridge University Press.

Torrance, E.P. (2000) *Research Review for the Torrance Tests of Creative Thinking: Figural and Verbal Forms a and b*. Bensenville, IL: Scholastic Testing Service, Inc.

Torrance, E.P., Gowan, J.C., Wu, J-J. and Aliotti, N.C. (1970) Creative functioning of monolingual and bilingual children in Singapore. *Journal of Educational Psychology* 61(1), 72–75.

Torrance, E.P. and Safter, H.T. (1999) *Making the Creative Leap Beyond...* Buffalo, NY: Creative Education Foundation Press.

Torrance, E.P. and Sato, S. (1979) Differences in Japanese and United States styles of thinking. *Creative Child & Adult Quarterly* 4(3), 145–151.

Torrance, E.P., Wu, T.H. and Ando, T. (1980) *Preliminary Norms-Technical Manual: Demonstrator Torrance Tests of Creative Thinking*. Athens, GA: Georgia Studies of Creative Behavior.

Townsend, J.W., Torrance, E.P. and Wu, T.H. (1981) Role of creative ability and style in the production of humor among adults. *Journal of Creative Behavior* 15, 280.

Triandis, H.C. (1975) Social psychology and culture analysis. *Journal for the Theory of Social Behaviour* 5, 81–106.

Triandis, H.C. (1977) Theoretical framework for evaluation of cross-cultural training effectiveness. *International Journal of Intercultural Relations* 1, 19–45.

Triandis, H.C. (1995) *Individualism & Collectivism*. Boulder, CO: Westview Press.

Triandis, H.C., Leung, K., Villareal, M.J. and Clack, F.L. (1985) Allocentric versus idiocentric tendencies: Convergent and discriminant validation. *Journal of Research in Personality* 19(4), 395–415.

Tropp, L.R., Erkut, S., Coll, C.G., Alarcon, O. and Garcia, H.A.V. (1999) Psychological acculturation development of a new measure for Puerto Ricans on the U.S. mainland. *Educational and Psychological Measurement* 59(2), 351–367.

Tsai, J.L., Ying, Y-W. and Lee, P.A. (2000) The meaning of "being Chinese" and "being American": Variation among Chinese American young adults. *Journal of Cross-Cultural Psychology* 31(3), 302–332.

Tu, W.M. (1985) *Confucian Thought: Selfhood as Creative Transformation*. Albany, NY: State University of New York Press.

Urban, K.K. (1995) Openness: A "magic formula" for an adequate development and promotion of giftedness and talents?! *Gifted and Talented International* 10, 15–19.

Vaid, J. (2000) New approaches to conceptual representations in bilingual memory: The case for studying humor interpretation. *Bilingualism: Language and Cognition* 3(1), 28–30.

Vaid, J. and Genesee, F. (1980) Neuropsychological approaches to bilingualism: A critical review. *Canadian Journal of Psychology* 34(4), 417–445.

Varisco, D.M. (1995) Metaphors and sacred history: The genealogy of Muhammad and the Arab "tribe". *Anthropological Quarterly* 68(3), 139–156.

Vernon, P.E. (1964) Creativity and intelligence. *Educational Research* 6(3), 163–196.

Vincent, A.S., Decker, B.P. and Mumford, M.D. (2002) Divergent thinking, intelligence, and expertise: A test of alternative models. *Creativity Research Journal* 14(2), 163–178.

Vygotsky, L.S. (1971) *Psychology of Art*. Cambridge, MA: MIT Press.

Vygotsky, L.S. (2004) Imagination and creativity in childhood. *Journal of Russian and East European Psychology* 42(1), 7–97.

Wallach, M.A. (1976) Tests tell us little about talent. *American Scientist* 64(1), 57–63.

Wallach, M.A. and Kogan, N. (1965) *Modes of Thinking in Young Children: A Study of the Creativity–Intelligence Distinction*. New York: Holt, Rinehart & Winston.

Wallas, G. (1926) *The Art of Thought*. London: J. Cape.

Wallbrown, F.H. and Huelsman, C.B. (1975) The validity of the Wallace–Kogan creativity operations for inner-city children in two areas of visual art. *Journal of Personality* 43(1), 109–126.

Wang, F. (2008) Motivation and English achievement: An exploratory and confirmatory factor analysis of a new measure for Chinese students of English learning. *North American Journal of Psychology* 10(3), 633–646.

Ward, T.B. (1994) Structured imagination: The role of category structure in exemplar generation. *Cognitive Psychology* 27(1), 1–40.

Ward, T.B. (2007) Creative cognition as a window on creativity. *Methods* 42(1), 28–37.

Ward, T.B., Patterson, M.J., Sifonis, C.M., Dodds, R.A. and Saunders, K.N. (2002) The role of graded category structure in imaginative thought. *Memory & Cognition* 30(2), 199–216.

Ward, T.B., Smith, S.M. and Finke, R.A. (1999) Creative cognition. In R.J. Sternberg (ed.) *Handbook of Creativity* (pp. 189–212). New York: Cambridge University Press.

Ward, T.B., Smith, S.M. and Vaid, J. (1997) *Creative Thought: An Investigation of Conceptual Structures and Processes*. Washington, D.C.: American Psychological Association.

Westby, E.L. and Dawson, V.L. (1995) Creativity: Asset or burden in the classroom? *Creativity Research Journal* 8(1), 1–10.

Whitney, C. (1974) The relationship of bilingualism and biculturalism to divergent thinking. Unpublished honors thesis, University of Adulate.

Williams-Whitney, D., Mio, J.S. and Whitney, P. (1992) Metaphor production in creative writing. *Journal of Psycholinguistic Research* 21(6), 497–509.

Williams, J. M. G. (2010) Mindfulness and psychological process. *Emotion* 10(1), 1–7.

Williamson, P.K. (2011) The creative problem solving skills of arts and science students: The two cultures debate revisited. *Thinking Skills and Creativity* 6(1), 31–43.

Yeni-Komshian, G.H., Flege, J.E. and Liu, S. (2000) Pronunciation proficiency in the first and second languages of Korean–English bilinguals. *Bilingualism: Language and Cognition* 3(2), 131–149.

Zandpour, F. and Sadri, G. (1996) Communication in personal relationships in Iran: A comparative analysis. In W.B. Gudykunst, S. Ting-Toomey and T. Nishida (eds) *Communication in Personal Relationships Across Cultures.* (pp. 174–196). Thousand Oaks, CA: Sage Publications, Inc.

Zeelenberg, R. and Pecher, D. (2003) Evidence for long-term cross-language repetition priming in conceptual implicit memory tasks. *Journal of Memory and Language* 49(1), 80–94.

Zenasni, F., Besançon, M. and Lubart, T. (2008) Creativity and tolerance of ambiguity: An empirical study. *Journal of Creative Behavior* 42(1), 61–73.

Zha, P., Walczyk, J.J., Griffith-Ross, D.A., Tobacyk, J.J. and Walczyk, D.F. (2006) The impact of culture and individualism collectivism on the creative potential and achievement of American and Chinese adults. *Creativity Research Journal* 18(3), 355–366.

Zhurova, L.E. (1971) The development of sound analysis or words in pre-school children. *Early Child Development and Care* 1(1), 53 66.

Zied, K.M., Phillipe, A., Karine, P., Valerie, H-T., Ghislaine, A., Arnaud, R., et al. (2004) Bilingualism and adult differences in inhibitory mechanisms: Evidence from a bilingual stroop task. *Brain and Cognition* 54(3), 254–256.

Zuo, L. (1998) Creativity and aesthetic sense. *Creativity Research Journal* 11(4), 309–313.

Appendix A: Internet-Based Multilingual and Multicultural Experience Questionnaire

Demographics

(1)   Subject #
(2)   Name
(3)   Phone
(4)   E-mail
(5)   Age
(6)   Sex
(7)   Are you right- or left-handed? | right | left | both
(8)   If you are right-handed, were you forced to use your right hand? For example, when trying to do something with your left hand you were told to use the right one. | Yes | No
(9)   What is your socioeconomic status? | upper | middle | lower
(10)   Are you a student? | Yes | No
(11)   If you are a student, what is your current college/school level? If you are not a student, what is your highest level of education? | PhD/MD | MA/MS/MBA | BA/BS | High School | Secondary School | Elementary/Primary School

First language (L1)

Please provide the information about your first language.

(12)   What language would you consider to be your first language? This is a language that you have acquired first.
(13)   How did you learn this language up to this point? | Mainly through interacting with family members at home | Mainly through interacting with other people | Mainly through formal classroom instructions | Other
(14)   Rate your ability in this language on the following aspects: speaking proficiency; listening proficiency; reading proficiency; writing proficiency. | Very poor | Poor | Fair | Functional | Good | Very good | Native-like

(15)   Provide the age at which you were first exposed to this language in terms of speaking, reading and writing.

(16)   Provide the number of years you have spent on learning this language.

(17)   Do you have foreign accent in this language? | Yes | No

(18)   If Yes, rate the strength of your accent on a scale from 1 (very strong accent) to 7 (not much of an accent).

(19)   If you have taken a standardized test of proficiency for this language (e.g. TOEFL, SAT), indicate the name of the test and the score you received.

Second language (L2)

(20)   Do you speak a second language? | Yes | No

If Yes, [Repeat questions 12 through 14 for L2.]

(21)   Specify the age at which you started learning this language in the following situations (If you started learning this language at birth, put 0): At Home | In school | After arriving in the country where this language is spoken

[Repeat questions 15 through 19 for L2.]

Bilingual balance scale

Check the radio button that reflects your degree of bilingualism among your L1 and L2. Ignore any other language(s) you may speak. If you speak only L1 you would check the most left radio button. If you speak only L2 you would check the most right radio button. If you speak both languages equally, you check the one in the middle. The more you go to the left, the stronger is your L1 in comparison with your L2. The more you go to the right, the stronger is your L2 in comparison with your L1.

Third language (L3)

(22)   Do you speak a third language? | Yes | No

If Yes, [Repeat questions 12 through 19 and 21 for L3.]

Fourth language (L4)

(23)   Do you speak a fourth language? | Yes | No

If Yes, [Repeat questions 12 through 19 and 21 for L4.]

(24)   Do you speak more than four languages? |Yes|No
(25)   What language would you consider to be your fifth language (L5)?
(26)   What language would you consider to be your sixth language (L6)?
(27)   What language would you consider to be your seventh language (L7)?
(28)   Rate your ability in each of these languages. |Very poor|Poor|Fair |Functional|Good|Very good|Native-like
(29)   Indicate your degree of multilingualism by providing your proportional proficiency (in percentage) in each language you have indicated earlier.

Parental languages

(30)   What language(s) do you usually speak with your mother at home?
(31)   What language(s) do you usually speak with your father at home?
(32)   What language(s) can your mother speak fluently?
(33)   What language(s) can your father speak fluently?
(34)   What language(s) do your parents usually speak to each other at home?

Language use

When you answer each of the following questions, consider all languages you have indicated earlier.

(35)   What language(s) could you speak in your childhood before school?
(36)   Which language(s) did you receive instructions in |Primary/ Elementary School|Secondary/Middle School|High School|College/ University?
(37)   Estimate, in terms of percentages, how often you use your languages per day (in all daily activities combined).
(38)   List the percentage of a typical day during which you |SPEAK|READ|WRITE in your languages.
(39)   Estimate how often you watch TV or listen to radio in your languages per day.
(40)   Estimate how often you use your languages per day for work- or study-related activities. (e.g. going to classes or work, writing papers, talking to colleagues, classmates or peers).
(41)   Estimate how often you use your languages per day for leisure related activities (e.g. going out, chatting on the phone or in the internet chat room).

(42)   Estimate how often you read newspapers, magazines and other general reading materials in your languages per day.

(43)   In which language(s) do you usually add, multiply and do simple arithmetic?

(44)   In which language(s) do you usually dream?

(45)   In which language(s) do you usually express anger or affection?

(46)   When at home, which language(s) do you feel you usually do better in based on the following aspects? Reading|Writing|Speaking| Understanding

(47)   When at work or school, which language(s) do you feel you usually do better in based on the following aspect? |Reading|Writing| Speaking|Understanding

(48)   Which language is the one that you would prefer to use in these situations? |At home|At work/In school|At a party|In general

(49)   When you are speaking, do you ever mix words or sentences from the two or more languages you know? |Yes|No

(50)   Check the languages that you mix and rate on a scale from 1 (mixing is very rare) to 5 (mixing is very frequent) the frequency of mixing in normal conversation with |your spouse/partner/family members |your friends|your coworkers/classmates.

(51)   Rate your ability to learn foreign languages, on a scale from 1 (can't learn at all) to 5 (very easy).

(52)   At what age did your usage of second language begin to exceed the usage of your first language (i.e., the age at which you started to use second language more than 50% of the time)? Leave blank if it never happened.

(53)   If there is anything else that you feel is interesting or important about your language background or language use, please comment below.

Language preference scale

Please rate your language preference on the following scales: |always L1|mostly L1|more often L1|both equally|more often L2|mostly L2|always L2. Note that some situations may not be directly applied to you. In this case, to answer the question you will have to imagine yourself in this situation. Also note that in most questions, you have to assume that you deal with bilingual interlocutors who share both languages with you and are equally competent in L1 and L2.

(54)   In what language do you prefer writing a letter?

(55)   In what language do you prefer watching TV?

(56)   What language do you prefer to use in a heated argument?
(57)   What language do you dream in?
(58)   In what language do you prefer to communicate by means of mobile phone, text messaging and/or internet chat room?
(59)   In what language do you prefer to listen to music (songs)?
(60)   What language do you prefer to speak with your bilingual family members?
(61)   What language would you use to communicate with God (for example, supplication)?
(62)   In what language do you conduct mental arithmetic operations (for example, balancing a check book)?
(63)   What language do you prefer to express and receive positive affect (e.g. love, affection, intimacy, pleasure, praise)?
(64)   What language do you prefer to speak with your bilingual friends?
(65)   What language do you think in?
(66)   What language do you use to address animals?
(67)   What language would you prefer for writing/reading poetry?
(68)   Do you prefer to hang out with L1- or L2-speaking friends?
(69)   In what language do you prefer reading for pleasure?
(70)   What language do you prefer to express and receive negative affect (e.g. anger, irritation, frustration, sadness)?
(71)   If you kept a diary, which language would you write it in?
(72)   In what language do you prefer to write quick notes in your calendar/shopping list?
(73)   In what language do you understand jokes better?
(74)   If you do curse, what language do you prefer for curse and taboo words? Explain WHY.

Country of origin (C1)

(75)   What is your country of origin?
(76)   How long have you lived in this country?
(77)   What language(s) did you acquire in this country?
(78)   How many years did you spend at each of the following levels of education in this country? (Put 0 for none). |PhD/MD|MA/MS/MBA|BA/BS|High School|Secondary School|Elementary/Primary School
(79)   Check the radio button that reflects your agreement with the following statements: |strongly disagree|disagree|somewhat disagree|neutral|somewhat agree|agree|strongly agree

(80)   I am aware of and knowledgeable about the history, institutions, rituals and everyday practices of this country.
(81)   I hold positive attitudes about people from this country and their rituals and everyday practices.
(82)   I behave in the manner that is expected from me in this country.
(83)   I am able to effectively communicate my ideas and feelings to individuals from this country.
(84)   Establishing social networks with individuals from this country eases my immersion in a new cultural environment.

Country of current residence (C2)

(85)   Did/do you live in a country different from the one you were born in? |Yes|No
(86)   If Yes, what is the country of your current residence?
(87)   At what age did you arrive in this country?
(88)   How long have you lived in this country?
[Repeat questions 77 through 84 for C2.]

Country of past residence (C3, C4)

(89)   Were you a resident to a country other than your country of origin and the country of your current residence? |Yes|No
If Yes, [Repeat questions 86 through 88 and 77 through 84 for C3.]
(90)   What is the country of your past residence (different from the ones mentioned above)?
If Yes, [Repeat questions 86 through 88 and 77 through 84 for C4.]
(91)   Were you a resident to more countries other than the previously mentioned ones? |Yes|No
(92)   If Yes, please indicate the name(s) of the country or countries, your length of residence (in years) and the language(s) you learned or attempted to learn. Separate the country name, length of residence and languages by ;.

Country of parents

(93)   Do your parents originate from different countries? |Yes|No
(94)   If Yes, what is the country of origin of your mother/father?
(95)   Estimate the extent (in percentage) to which you identify with the culture of your mother/father.

Multicultural exposure

(96)   Estimate the extent (in percentage) to which each of the following contexts has contributed to your exposure to the culture of C1|C2|C3|C4|country of the father|country of the mother. Family|Peers|School|Work|Media.

Multicultural competence

When you answer each of the following questions, think about countries you have indicated earlier as the ones of your origin, your present and past residence and your parents.

(97)   Estimate the extent (in percentage) to which you are involved in the festivity-related events of each of the following countries.

(98)   Estimate how much time (in percentage) you spend with people from each of the following countries.

(99)   Estimate the extent (in percentage) to which the culture of each of the following countries influences your personal belief/value system.

(100) Estimate the extent (in percentage) to which you affiliate with the culture of each of the following countries. Hint: Think about a situation in which people ask you 'where are you from?' What is the likelihood that you say that you are from this country?

Check the radio button that reflects your agreement with the following statements:

(101) I feel conflicted by the values and beliefs of my identified cultures.

(102) I feel I can live effectively within two or more cultural groups without compromising my own sense of cultural identity.

Psychological acculturation scale

Indicate the percentage that reflects your cultural preferences for each question. When you answer each of these questions, think about people and/or culture of the countries you have indicated earlier as the ones of your origin, your present and past residence, and your parents.

(103) With which group(s) of people do you feel you share most of your beliefs and values?

(104) With which group(s) of people do you feel you have the most in common?

(105) With which group(s) of people do you feel the most comfortable?

(106) In your opinion, which group(s) of people best understands your ideas (your way of thinking)?

(107) Which culture(s) do you feel proud to be a part of?

(108)   In which culture(s) do you know how things are done and feel that you can do them easily?

(109)   In which culture(s) do you feel confident that you know how to act?

(110)   In your opinion, which group(s) of people do you understand best?

(111)   In which culture(s) do you know what is expected of a person in various situations?

(112)   Which culture(s) do you know the most about the history, traditions and customs, and so forth?

(113)   Do you feel a strong affinity with any other culture(s)? |Yes|No

(114)   If YES, specify

Appendix B: Internet-Based Picture Naming Test

	Page 1		Page 2		Page 3		Page 4
1.	anchor	1.	cow	1.	iron	1.	screw
2.	apple	2.	cup	2.	kangaroo	2.	screwdriver
3.	arrow	3.	desk	3.	key	3.	shirt
4.	ashtray	4.	dog	4.	kite	4.	shoe
5.	ball	5.	door	5.	ladder	5.	skirt
6.	balloon	6.	doorknob	6.	lips	6.	skunk
7.	banana	7.	dress	7.	lobster	7.	sled
8.	barrel	8.	drum	8.	monkey	8.	snake
9.	bed	9.	duck	9.	motorcycle	9.	snowman

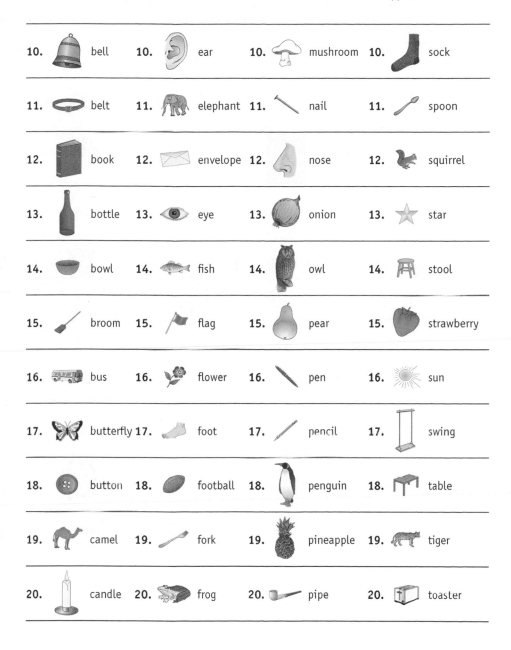

10.	bell	10.	ear	10.	mushroom	10.	sock
11.	belt	11.	elephant	11.	nail	11.	spoon
12.	book	12.	envelope	12.	nose	12.	squirrel
13.	bottle	13.	eye	13.	onion	13.	star
14.	bowl	14.	fish	14.	owl	14.	stool
15.	broom	15.	flag	15.	pear	15.	strawberry
16.	bus	16.	flower	16.	pen	16.	sun
17.	butterfly	17.	foot	17.	pencil	17.	swing
18.	button	18.	football	18.	penguin	18.	table
19.	camel	19.	fork	19.	pineapple	19.	tiger
20.	candle	20.	frog	20.	pipe	20.	toaster

21.	canon	21.	giraffe	21.	potato	21.	toothbrush
22.	carrot	22.	glass	22.	pumpkin	22.	tree
23.	cat	23.	glove	23.	rabbit	23.	umbrella
24.	chain	24.	grapes	24.	refrigerator	24.	vase
25.	chair	25.	hand	25.	ring	25.	vest
26.	church	26.	harp	26.	ruler	26.	watch
27.	cigarette	27.	hat	27.	sailboat	27.	wheel
28.	clock	28.	heart	28.	sandwich	28.	windmill
29.	cloud	29.	horse	29.	saw	29.	window
30.	comb	30.	house	30.	scissors	30.	zebra

Index

Note: Bold indicates the page on which the definition of a term can be found.